THE
TRANSFORMATIVE
WORK*PLACE*

GROWING PEOPLE, PURPOSE, PROSPERITY AND PEACE

THE
TRANSFORMATIVE
WORK*PLACE*

GROWING PEOPLE, PURPOSE, PROSPERITY AND PEACE

CAROLE AND DAVID SCHWINN

CREATORS OF THE TRANSFORMATION OF
AMERICAN INDUSTRY

TRANSFORMATIONS PRESS UNLTD.

ISBN-13: 978-0-9863298-0-7
LCCN: 2015905533

Distributed by Itasca Books

Printed in the United States of America

DEDICATION

This book is dedicated to Dr. Michael J. Cleary

Friend

Teacher

Mentor

Exemplar

ACKNOWLEDGMENTS

We have been married for nearly thirty years and worked together even longer than that. Our work has always been driven by noticing a problem to be solved or a question to be answered, followed by a desire to find a solution, and then a search for some theory to take to practice in a way that would be accessible to people trying to make a real difference in their lives, their organizations, their communities or their societies. None of that work or this book would have been possible without the rare opportunities we have had to learn from and with some of the most notable teachers in the world.

Those teachers include Dr. Russell Ackoff, Thomas Berry, Rita Cleary, Dr. W. Edwards Deming, Jamshid Gharjedaghi, Dr. Lee Howser, Lorri Johnson, John Kesler, Dr. Susan Leddick, Dr. Clyde LeTarte, Dr. John McKnight, Dr. Gerald Nadler, Mark Nepo, Dr. Peter Norlin, Dr. Myron Tribus, Dr. Peter Senge, and Dr. Ira Shor. Angeles Arrien, Meg Wheatley and Peter Block hold special places in our hearts for the role each played in encouraging us to make our voices heard through this book.

Enormous gratitude is due those forty-one individuals who took the time to tell us their stories during our travels around the world. They are among the most generous, wise and courageous people we have ever met. Each is listed here by country in which our interview took place, and with the role and affiliation they held at the time.

Cambodia
Mor Lean, Associate, VBNK
Seoung Sothearwat, Associate, VBNK
Graeme Storer, Director, VBNK

Canada

Paul Born, President, Tamarack - An Institute for Community
Engagement

Wayne Cadwallader, Managing Partner, Elkhorn Partners Limited
Partnership

Joe Mancini, President, The Working Centre

Costa Rica

Dr. Amr Abdalla, Vice Rector, University for Peace

José Miguel Aguilar Berrocal, Executive Director, Fundación Acción
Joven

Rita Marie Johnson, Founder, Rasur International Foundation

Robert Kopper, COO, NatureAir

Alex E. Khajavi, Founder-CEO, NatureAir

Max Loria, Vice Minister of Peace

Erika Acuna Ordonez, teacher

Nika Salvetti, Coordinator, RMSED, University for Peace

Nic Marks, New Economics Foundation (nef)

Denmark

Kit Lykketoft, Deputy Director, MindLab

England

Neville Hodgkinson, Brahma Kumaris World Spiritual University

Sister Jayanti (Alka Patel), Director, Brahma Kumaris World
Spiritual University

Germany

Bruno Brunetti, Cluster Manager, Software-Cluster

Hungary

Dr. Imre Lovey, Managing Partner, Concordia

India

Prakash Apte, Chairman, Syngenta/India

Rear Admiral (REetd) SVS Chary, Mazagon Dock Limited

Johny Joseph, Director, Creative Handicrafts

Ravi Kant, Vice Chairman, Tata Motors Limited
Pooja Warier, UnLtd India

Norway
Kolbjorn Valestrand and Signe Aarhus, Owners, Oleana

South Africa
Maryse Barak, Barak Learning and Development Consultant
Heidi Holland, The Melville House, South Africa
Colleen Magner, Reos Social Innovation
Mabule Mokhine, The GreenHouse Project
Zelda, Chaeli and Erin Mycroft, The Chaeli Campaign
Dr. Chené Swart, Transformations
Diane, Tarryn, Justine, and Chelsea Terry, The Chaeli Campaign
Nomfundo Walaza, Executive Director, Desmond Tutu Peace Center

United States
Dr. Tom Inui, Regenstrief Institute, Indiana University Medical School

Acknowledging our six adult children and their loving partners as our most profound teachers is much more than the casual and obligatory nod to family often encountered in book dedications. The lives they lead, the paths they have chosen, the values they exhibit, the purposes they serve, and the learning they share with us enrich our lives every day. Their passion, each in their own way, to in some way make the world a better place is inspiring to us and to others who know of their work. There is no greater comfort at this point in our lives and careers to know that they, along with our six precious grandchildren, are always at our backs, encouraging us to do what we want to do, and to speak out about what we think is important.

The opportunity to put it all together in *The Transformative Workplace: Growing People, Purpose, Prosperity and Peace* comes from the remarkable sabbatical opportunity offered David as a Professor of Management and Leadership at Lansing Community College in Lansing, Michigan. Neither of us could ever have dreamed before it became real that we would actually embark upon a trip around the world to discover transformative management and leadership practices. And, neither of us could ever express the gratitude we feel to those forty-one extraordinary individuals who allowed us to interview them, except, perhaps by sharing their stories in this book.

Our work together has always been a kind of praxis, which Paulo Freire defined as "reflection and action upon the world in order to transform it."[1] Political theorist, Hannah Arendt, said of praxis that it is "the highest and most important level of the active life," and "the true realization of human freedom."[2] What we know now that we didn't recognize earlier in our careers is that our work has continually transformed the way we think, act and interact in the world. Just as we have been blessed to find in our work together the space for our own growth and development, we wish for all others that same opportunity.

CONTENTS

The larger purpose of business—or sports, or any competitive activity, for that matter—is not to succeed, but to serve as a theater for self-knowledge, self-actualization, and self-transcendence. We discover who we are and what we really stand for when we respond to (business) situations. We establish our values through our behavior and our dealings with other people and the world. We transcend ourselves as we expand our circle of care and concern to include colleagues, customers, and others.[1]

— FRED KOFMAN

As we progress through each of these levels of consciousness, we feel an increasing sense of connectedness to the world that shows up as an expanded sense of identity. We feel a sense of oneness with ourselves, with our family, with our community, with the organization we work for, with our nation, with humanity and the planet, and eventually with the whole of creation.[2]

—RICHARD BARRETT

INTRODUCTION
Work that Transforms

The question addressed in this book is, "How might the places where we work—in addition to being places where we accomplish the goals and purposes of the enterprise—also be the places where we become more and more of who we are meant to be as human beings?" We address that question in three ways, explaining what we mean by transformative work,

1) by highlighting examples of where it is occurring around the world;

2) by offering ideas about how workplaces can benefit from equally valuing and focusing on the purposes of their work, the purposes of the people who work there, and the purposes of their communities and the larger society; and

3) by making suggestions about how people can create transformative work in their own lives.

The theme of the book is that a commitment to expanding the consciousness of *people* enlarges the *purpose* of the organization, leads to its *prosperity* and, ultimately, creates greater possibilities of a more *peaceful* world for all.

Our interest in this topic stems from David's sabbatical leave from his position as a professor of management and leadership at Lansing Community College in Lansing, Michigan. To meet the requirements of his sabbatical, we traveled to thirteen countries on four continents, and interviewed forty-one managers and leaders. We visited places and landmarks around the world that serve to inspire both reflection and positive action. David's purpose in requesting a leave was to search for a higher and more conscious practice of management and leadership. What we found was not only more conscious managers and leaders, but places where the people they touch are able to become more fully who they are meant to be in the world. The term we decided to use for these places is the *trans-formative workplace*:

> *The transformative workplace, as a part of its essential purpose, creates the context in which people can grow and develop to their highest potential as fully aware and conscious participants in the evolution of life on our planet.*

In applying for his sabbatical, David articulated the importance of his search for more conscious managers and leaders. He pointed to his own beliefs and assumptions about the times we live in, the challenges we face as human beings, the nature of the transformation required, the role of enterprise, and the management and leadership practices that might help bring about a global transformation to a higher level of consciousness. Part of what he said was:

> *In 1982, the physicist Fritjof Capra noted in* The Turning Point *that humanity was in the midst of the kind of breakpoint described by Land and Jarman in* Breakpoint and Beyond: Mastering the Future. *At this point—the edge of chaos—breakthrough and break down become equally possible. As people observe terrorism, financial collapse, hunger, disease, global warming, and despotic leadership, many believe that humanity is at that point and that mankind's future is significantly dependent on our ability to shift our level of consciousness and behave in different ways.*

We choose to believe that a breakthrough is possible, and that there are already significant strides being made by many people all over the world, providing evidence that a future that works for all is possible. We also believe that in order for humanity to break through to another way of being together in the world, a breakthrough to a higher level of consciousness is required. We must become more

> Since periods of great change, such as the present one, come so rarely in human history, it is up to each of us to make the best use of our time to help create a happier world.[3]
>
> — THE DALAI LAMA

aware of who we are as a part of the larger world, to recognize that we are all in this together, and to understand that all of us must work together across difference to move beyond the current state of affairs.

David's premise is that the places where we work, and the people who manage and lead us, can influence a shift in how we address the challenges we face. Surely, he thought, there must be leaders and managers around the world whose practices, if emulated, have the potential for transforming organizations, communities, societies, and the people who inhabit them. If he could find those leaders and managers and tell their stories, he might be able to inspire his students and others to shift the way they lead and manage in their own workplaces. He might be able to encourage his students and others to find their own work, rather than trying to land a job. He might be able to shine a light on places that offer a different model for getting work done, in a way that honors both people and the planet. It was important to him to find stories around the world and across disciplines so that people could identify with them, and resist the temptation to dismiss them as being possible only in some cultures and in some sectors.

The places we work can be crucibles of change in our lives. Our belief is that we are living in challenging times and that the future of life depends on expanding our level of consciousness. We need places that allow encounters through which we are able to individually and collectively transform ourselves.

Other authors have written about more enlightened or conscious organizations. They have eloquently spoken to what leaders in these organizations must do, how their policies and procedures are different, how their visions and values contribute to their character, and how these differences impact their performance in the marketplace. *The Transformative Workplace* stands out because it shows how people themselves can be different, and how these differences positively affect their own lives, the lives of their families, their workplaces, their communities, and the wider society.

We wrote this book for managers and leaders whose role is to help make their organizations and communities prosperous and successful. The very definition of management and leadership is the ability to get work done through others. Who would not want employees who are continually learning, improving themselves, and increasing their capacity to thrive in an ever more demanding and complex work environment? Who would not want to create a workplace where people can meet their basic needs, increase their competence, and challenge their assumptions? Such a workplace allows people to attend to their well-being and connect their passion to their productivity. It allows workers to make and fulfill commitments, express their creativity, collaborate across differences, embrace great work, work peacefully with others, become happier, and give back to others.

We also wrote this book for the increasing number of people who are suffering at work. Individuals in the workplace are feeling more and more stressed and oppressed. They have less and less time to spend with their families and friends, and have practically no time to focus on their own happiness and well-being. *The Transformative Workplace* is for those who have lost sight of their desires or aspirations in their own lives, and for those who are unable to find any work at all, satisfying or otherwise.

In this book, we suggest that somewhere between "living to work" or "working to live," there is room for work that transforms us as we transform it, where we can grow lives of purpose and passion, where all people may prosper, and where we can contribute to a better and more peaceful world. Given how much time and energy most of us expend in work, let us hope that work of this kind one day becomes the standard by which we all measure our labor.

A Word about the Book's Organization

Each chapter of *The Transformative Workplace* focuses on a developmental challenge, or a way of being in the world, that would allow us to live purposeful, prosperous, and peaceful lives, and to help create a better world for all. The chapters are organized around three themes: Selfness, Otherness, and Wholeness. We chose these simple themes, rather than complicating the narrative by using one of many already existing theoretical frameworks for psychological or spiritual development.

The Selfness theme includes those early developmental challenges where we begin to realize a sense of our own individuality and who we are in relationship to our families and those closest to us. At this stage of our development we are most concerned about biological, safety, and survival issues, as well as seeing to our need for recognition and self-esteem.

The Otherness theme includes development of a sense of who we are beyond our immediate relationships and surroundings. It includes an increased valuing of other people, groups, and communities in our lives. Otherness also includes a concern for meeting the needs and expectations of others, as well as our own.

The Wholeness theme refers to an expansion of consciousness that includes an awareness and concern for all living things. A wider embrace of all life leads to decisions and actions that lead to a more sustainable and peaceful way of living.

Around these three themes, in every chapter of the book, we tell the story of at least one organization we encountered in our travels. In "Meeting Basic Needs," an early chapter on the Selfness theme, you will meet Johny Joseph, the Director of Creative Handicrafts. Creative Handicrafts is a Mumbai-based nonprofit that trains women from the slums to sew and embroider clothing and other items suitable for a global market. In "Challenging Assumptions," Graeme Storer shares the story of how VBNK, a Phnom Penh organization, works with emerging leaders to help them overcome the deeply held beliefs and assumptions that limit their ability to function in the world of cultural and economic development. "Attending to Well-Being" and "Practicing Inner Reflection" are chapters that speak to the importance of nurturing our physical, emotional, psychological, and spiritual lives, and how wise managers and leaders make this possible in our workplaces.

It is not our intention to say that the organizations whose stories we tell represent the ideal, or that their managers and leaders are models of perfection. In fact, each of them would likely be the first to point out their own flaws and shortcomings, and admit to the work yet to be done. Similarly, none of the organizations we focus on employ all the practices it would take to create an ideal environment for human growth and development. Only an organization that employed many or all of the practices highlighted here could truly be a crucible for becoming what each and every one of us could be in the world. It is our intention, however, to point out the practices employed by each of the leaders and managers we interviewed—practices that make their organizations places where their clients, employees, and other stakeholders integrate their personal work of becoming with the work of the enterprise.

We hope that *The Transformative Workplace* will serve as an invitation to further exploration about what transformative workspaces are like now, and what they might be in the future. We have created a website and a blog at www.transformunltd.com, where we will continue to bring forth other ideas as they emerge, and to highlight the work of others who have explored these same ideas through their books, articles, videos, and blogs. We invite you to visit the website, add your thoughts and experiences, and join in this conversation.

SELFNESS

If it falls to your lot to be a street sweeper, sweep streets like Michelangelo painted pictures, sweep streets like Beethoven composed music, sweep streets like Leontyne Price sings before the Metropolitan Opera. Sweep streets like Shakespeare wrote poetry. Sweep streets so well that all the hosts of heaven and earth will have to pause and say: Here lived a great street sweeper who swept his job well. If you can't be a pine at the top of the hill, be a shrub in the valley. Be the best little shrub on the side of the hill. Be a bush if you can't be a tree. If you can't be a highway, just be a trail. If you can't be a sun, be a star. For it isn't by size that you win or fail. Be the best of whatever you are.[1]

— DR. MARTIN LUTHER KING, JR.

He who would learn to fly one day must first learn to stand and walk and run and climb and dance; one cannot fly into flying.[2]

— FREIDRICH NIETZSCHE

ONE

MEETING BASIC NEEDS

The Story of Creative Handicrafts

Johny Joseph leads an organization in Mumbai that is a model for creating work in which people can meet their basic needs. Now named Creative Handicrafts, the work of the organization was initiated in 1984 by Sister Isabel Martin, a Spanish missionary of the congregation of the Missionaries of Christ Jesus. A tribute to Sister Martin upon her passing in 2013 told of her early work with women in the slums.

> *She felt the suffering of the women, uneducated and unemployed. She said that she heard a strong inner voice telling her, 'you cannot leave them unattended, do something for them.' She dreamed of offering a means of livelihood to these women so that they would become self reliant.*[3]

In the early days, Sister Isabel and her congregation reached out to children who were frequently absent from school because they were working to bring in money for their families. Providing educational activities for these children led to the development of relationships with the women, who soon formed their first Women's Self Employed Cooperative (WSEC) under the auspices of a local nonprofit. A small production center was started where women could learn to sew simple items for sale, including toys, simple clothing items, and other handicrafts. By 1994, Creative Handicrafts became an independent, nonprofit social business.

More than a dozen years ago, Johny Joseph left a position of leadership in Nepal's College of Social Work and moved back to his native India, taking over as Director of Creative Handicrafts from Sister Isabel. Johny took this challenging position—despite his complete lack of background in management or marketing—during a period when the organization was struggling with a limited market and lagging sales, along with increased demand from women to get jobs and produce more. Determined to make the business sustainable and to explore its potential for growth, he set out to totally reengineer the organization. Designers were brought in from abroad, in-house designers were hired, and a new apparel line expanded the organization's offerings. Johny says that things just began to click: they were able to bring in and train more women, the quality of their products improved dramatically, and the organization was able to develop a global market for their goods.

These developments resulted in a remarkable change in the lives of women who were involved in this productive work. These are women for whom life has been extremely difficult. Many migrated with their families from rural areas, where their station in life did not allow them to own property or homes. Just being able to survive life in the slums of Mumbai is unimaginable to most in the Western world, especially when these women are trying to care for their children. A great many of the men are alcoholics, deserters of their families, abusers, or worse. As Johny told us, "They [the women] have no means of earning a living because they have no skill."[4]

For the women of Creative Handicrafts, developing a skill and earning a living is the beginning of economic freedom.

Creative Handicrafts now employs 300 women, organized into 12 cooperatives of 25–30 women. Some of them work from a new headquarters building donated by the Spanish government, and others work from their homes in the slums. Women who learn about the organization, or who are referred by others, are screened before entering the four- to twelve-month training program. The length of a program is determined by the individual woman's pace in mastering sewing and embroidery skills. Once they complete training, they join a cooperative—or form a new cooperative—composed of both experienced and beginning workers.

The organization then provides sewing machines, space, and work, which is delivered to those working off-site. A CNN report on Creative Handicrafts' noted that

> *quality control is strictly enforced by the women themselves.*
> *The collective is divided into groups that elect their own*
> *leaders. They work with professional designers and carefully*
> *inspect each finished product. And because the focus is on true*
> *empowerment, each group sets its own production goals. So*
> *they're accountable to each other and not some profiteering*
> *overlord. The more they produce, the more they earn. But*
> *vacation time, childcare and a base salary are guaranteed.*[5]

When the work is completed, it is returned to Creative Handicrafts headquarters. The cooperative is paid 75–80% of the retail value of the goods. The cooperative pays for the fabric and the salaries of the women, and retains any additional earnings for a shared distribution once or twice a year, usually during festival season. In addition, 40% of revenues above the organization's administrative expenses are distributed to the cooperatives through the profit-sharing plan.

We visited and observed the women's training spaces and workplaces, and found that their strength, determination, skill, courage, and joy in their work were obvious. In the slum workshops where we walked with Johny, the women knew that their children were safe in the provided crèches, and they were able to work productively and cooperatively with other women in their own environment. Along the way, we encountered women who are a part of Creative Handicrafts' newest enterprise, Asli Foods, a "dabba" service through which women who have been unable to master sewing skills are preparing and delivering box lunches to office buildings in the area.

Few women leave Creative Handicrafts for employment elsewhere, as the profit-driven environment of textile factories are far more stressful, and their wages would be roughly the same. Some women stay in the organization's employment for as long as fifteen or twenty years, leaving only when their children are able to become wage earners. Johny describes the success of the business:

> *Ten years ago, we felt that the women would not be able to produce a product that could sell on the global market based on its merit, rather than its story. And today we are able to do that. The women have risen to the challenge. We put the challenge to them, we trained them, and now we are able to do that. If you know that your purchase contributes to the development of women, it does add value. The story adds value, but you will buy a sweater if it meets your needs.*[6]

Johny is rightfully proud of the business model Creative Handicrafts has developed. Seventy percent of Creative Handicrafts' products are sold in department stores in the UK, Sweden, Spain, and Italy, while another 30% are sold globally through Fair Trade buyers. While he notes that the majority of non-governmental organizations "survive on charity," they have learned that "you can convert business into a human development story. Businesses can help people. You need a productive community if change is to happen." He adds, "The answer to poverty is a movement from mass production to production by the masses."[7]

Still, Creative Handicrafts does more than reduce poverty among the women of Mumbai's slums. As Johny notes,

> *Skill training and production is only the economic aspect. Simultaneously, every Saturday, we hold a training program and organize discussion groups. We help them look at the culture that is oppressive. We help them look at religion that is oppressive. We help them to understand how important it is to educate their children. This opportunity is extended to other women in the community also.*[8]

The empowerment and development of these women are dramatic. As the CNN report mentioned above observed:

*The result? Women like Sheela Patel can know—for sure—that
her kids will have a better life than the one she has led. When
her husband grumbles that dinner isn't ready on time, she
no longer cowers. "I have to work, so what if dinner's a little
late?" Lalita Kamble, whose husband now attends an alcohol
counseling program, says, "I know now that I can take care of
my two children. That I am strong. My husband no longer beats
me because he knows that I will leave him, and I am not afraid.
Dil mein abhi himmat hai. There's courage in my heart now."[9]*

The women of Creative Handicrafts are well on their way to adequately and safely feeding, housing, and educating their children, as
well as developing their own self esteem, sense of belonging, and the
capacity for managing their own lives and relationships in a healthy
way. They are on a path toward lifelong development as fully-func-
tioning, productive members of their community and society.

Meeting Basic Needs and Transformation

Meeting basic needs is the ground upon which we begin to travel
a lifelong development pathway. This concept is probably most associated with the work of American psychologist Abraham Maslow.
Maslow's famous theory proposed that all humans develop through
meeting a progression of needs, arranged in a hierarchy, beginning
with the physiological and moving through needs for safety, love and
belonging, esteem, and self-actualization (although his later work also
included a higher level called self-transcendence). The lower four levels were termed deficiency needs by Maslow, suggesting that only
through meeting these needs are we able to attend to our innate desire for growth and happiness.

Maslow's work has had its fair share of critics over the years, but
in the recent past it has also experienced a revival of interest among
psychologists, theorists, and researchers. Quite recently, for example,
Ed Diener and Louis Tay of the University of Illinois led a study based
on the Gallup World Poll, which conducted surveys in 155 countries.

Their research largely supported the idea that the needs identified by Maslow are, indeed, universal. "Maslow's theory is largely correct," they write. "In cultures all over the world the fulfillment of his proposed needs correlates with happiness."[10]

Another pair of researchers, Edward Deci and Richard Ryan—developers of what is called Self-Determination Theory (SDT)—confirm Maslow's theory of universal motivation toward development by "embracing the assumption that all individuals have natural, innate, and constructive tendencies to develop an ever more elaborated and unified sense of self." SDT focuses on meeting three psychological needs—autonomy, competence, and relatedness—that can lead to "enhanced performance, persistence, and creativity." Their theory also stresses the importance of the social context in which people develop, pointing out that,

> *To the extent that the needs are ongoingly satisfied, people will develop and function effectively and experience wellness, but to the extent that they are thwarted, people more likely evidence ill-being and non-optimal functioning. The darker sides of human behavior and experience, such as certain types of psychopathology, prejudice, and aggression are understood in terms of reactions to basic needs having been thwarted, either developmentally or proximally.*[11]

Richard Barrett, an English author and philosopher whose work also builds on Maslow's, confirms that failure to move beyond survival needs can lead to highly dysfunctional behaviors.

> *When an individual holds deep insecurities about survival, anxiety becomes pervasive in their life. Such individuals easily get upset or angry. Whenever something goes wrong they see it as a personal threat. They believe they live in a hostile and brutal world. They are always on guard, and feel that if they don't look out for themselves no one else will. Consequently, to feel safe they must control everything around them. They micro manage their lives and have great difficulty in trusting anyone.*

*For these people time is of the essence. They are driven.
They need to be super efficient, so if they think they have
the answer they will stop listening. They are not good at
giving other people the time they need to process. They are
very focused on their own needs and find it difficult to put
themselves in somebody else's shoes. The anxieties they hold
keeps them focused in survival consciousness.*[12]

Going beyond Maslow, theorists in the basic-needs field also try to understand the relationship between unsatisfied needs and social conflict. Indian economist and philosopher Amartya Sen (Development as Freedom, 1999) for example, introduced the capabilities approach in the 1980s, a theory that focuses on human functioning, or what people are actually able to do with what they have. Other theorists, including American philosopher Martha Nussbaum (Creating Capabilities, 2011), have built on Sen's approach, compiling lists of universal needs that apply across countries and cultures. Both Sen and Nussbaum draw heavily on Aristotle's concepts of human flourishing, ideas which have also deeply influenced positive psychologists who study human strengths and virtues. No matter the approach, all would appear to agree that fulfilling basic human needs is fundamental, and vital if development is to move beyond simple survival.

Nearly one person in five—1.2 billion men, women and children—are living in a situation of extreme poverty by surviving on the equivalent of less than one dollar a day. Half the people in the world are trying to manage below the poverty level of two dollars a day. The need to put people to work in places where they can meet their basic needs is therefore a global imperative with both moral and practical implications. The global situation is only being made worse by cur-

If there were only 100 of us living on this earth, then the 20 richest would consume nearly 90% of the wealth and the 20 poorest just 1%.[13]

rent financial instability, increasingly unequal distribution of wealth, regional conflicts and wars, and climatic changes that are producing droughts and other conditions that impact survival.

According to the United Nations Development Program, "The cost of eradicating poverty is 1% of global income, while 0.5% of annual global income would ensure universal access to basic social services (basic education, health, nutrition, access to water and sewerage disposal)."[14] Not addressing these issues in a way that contributes to the development of the people is even costlier.

> *Unemployment, underemployment or badly-paid employment have a direct effect on people's ability to secure vital needs— food, health, drinking water, energy, and so forth. People who have been thrust aside or marginalised sometimes lose their self-respect and, in the long-term, risk being excluded from the social and cultural life of their community. Without money, people's lives are severely restricted and they are often caught in a vortex: with no job and not enough money coming in, it is practically impossible to get on in life and escape from poverty.[15]*

Unfortunately and often, these are the people whose vulnerability can be exploited. Terrorist groups, fundamentalists, and human-traffickers recruit individuals either for money or for the promise of rewards in the hereafter, by tapping into their need for a certainty they can believe in, or merely for simple survival. Even for those living in relatively stable cultures that are able to meet their basic physiological needs, current conditions are challenging their ability to experience safety and security in their workplaces, and their need for self-esteem and belonging in their communities. Millions are unemployed, underemployed, or fearful of losing their means of livelihood. The resulting stress, anxiety, depression, and physical illness costs organizations billions of dollars in healthcare and associated expenses, as well as the contribution of employees whose presence, commitment, expertise, and creativity are needed now more than ever.

Meeting Basic Needs in the Workplace

Production by the masses as a way of reducing poverty, and empowering people to take responsibility for their own and their children's growth and development, is not unique to Creative Handicrafts. This approach to development is evolving—with many variations—from the use of micro-loans made famous by the work of Muhammad Yunus and the Grameen Bank in Bangladesh, to myriad forms of social entrepreneurship all over the world.

Impact sourcing is a newer form of creating work with the potential for transforming lives, shifting the view of people in poverty from potential consumers to producers. Two such organizations, Digital Divide Data and Samasource, were founded by former management consultants determined to make a contribution to the alleviation of poverty. Each takes into account the development of the people along with the performance of the enterprise, and counters the abuses often seen in traditional out-sourcing approaches that focus on lowest-cost production at any cost to human lives.

Samasource, which is based in San Francisco, partners with independently-owned outsourcing firms in Haiti, India, Kenya, Pakistan, Uganda, and South Africa, who parcel out "microwork" to over 1,600 workers in those countries. According to David Borstein, author of *How to Change the World* (2007),

> *Samasource requires that partners adhere to an ethical code*
> *of conduct. They must reinvest at least 40 percent of revenues*
> *in training, salaries, and community programs. They must*
> *hire workers who were earning less than $3 a day. (Once*
> *employed, they generally earn $5 a day, and often more.) To*
> *date, the company has distributed $1.2 million in salaries.*
> *Seventy percent of its workers are the primary breadwinners*
> *in their households and support at least two other people.*[16]

Digital Divide Data (DDD) employs 900 people in Cambodia, Laos, and Kenya. The company hires high school students under a four-year work-study program, through which they spend six hours a day working and the rest pursuing their education. According to Borstein, DDD has graduated about 400 people who earn four times the average income in their countries. Because DDD spends more time with employees, it can provide them with more comprehensive skills training. This allows them to take on more complex work, such as electronic publishing. Jeremy Hockenstein, one of DDD's co-founders, reports, "The difference we see between when people walk in and when they walk out after four years is so powerful. They feel that they can control their future."[17]

These and thousands of other enterprises are providing a profoundly important service that goes well beyond economic development. They are creating conditions in which those employed and in poverty can meet their most basic needs. By any developmental theory, this step is critical to (a) meeting physical needs as well as beginning to build one's sense of self-worth and mastery, (b) building one's sense of having a role in the larger scheme of things, and (c) having some level of belief in the possibility of creating a life that goes beyond mere survival.

Fostering Basic Needs in the Workplace

Fostering basic needs in the workplace is revealed in the story of Creative Handicrafts of Mumbai. For thirty years, this organization has lifted up the lives of the city's slum women by offering them the opportunity for productive work that provides them a living wage, and allows them to take care of their own and their family's physiological needs, as well as providing the resources needed to ensure an education for their children. The women work in a safe and secure environment, knowing that their young children's needs are being taken care of at the organization's nearby crèche. They enter the work with minimal skills and partake in a training program in a fun-loving, flexible, communal environment. However, the Creative Handicrafts program also demands the attainment of a high level of performance. When the women are adequately prepared, they become a part of a cooperative team that supports them in their lives and their work, and in accomplishing shared goals that pay off in fairly distributed rewards.

Through their work, the women of Creative Handicrafts develop the self-esteem that comes from knowing that what they produce with their own hands meets the requirements of discerning buyers around the world. They earn the respect of their neighbors and their community for their accomplishments, as well as the prestige that comes from earning their own way. Their work releases them from the harsh realities of slum living—and, often, the abuses of their intimate relationships.

As the story of Creative Handicrafts so beautifully illustrates, organizations that create conditions where people can meet their basic needs are rewarded with employees who are loyal, hard-working, and committed to the mission and to the goals of the enterprise. Their people develop the capacity for adapting to changing circumstances, stepping up to higher levels of performance, mentoring novice employees, working collaboratively with others, taking pride in their work, and sharing responsibility and rewards. Once they have met their own and their family's minimum physiological needs, they can develop a stronger sense of identity, self-worth, and self-esteem, and take steps toward living a better life. They are poised to address their higher-level needs and develop ways of being that attend to their well-being, and develop their highest potential as fully aware and conscious participants in the evolution of life on our planet.

Cultural anthropologist and author Angeles Arrien, one of our most beloved teachers and mentors, often talked about the belief among traditional peoples that we travel through life with two companions—one on our right called Death, and one on our left called Destiny.

Death continually asks us, "Are you using the great gift of life well? Are you using the great gift of life well?" Destiny, on our right, is asking another question: "Are you doing what you've come here to do? Are you doing what you've come here to do?"[18]

These are questions that can only be heard and addressed by people who have been able to meet their basic needs. Perhaps there is no greater purpose than for organizations to create workplaces which allow this to happen.

The Zen Master poured his visitor's teacup full, and then kept pouring.

The visitor watched until he could no longer restrain himself.

"It is overfull. No more will go in!"

"Like this cup," the Zen Master said, "you are full of your own opinions and assumptions.

How can you learn truth until you first empty your cup?"[1]

— TRADITIONAL ZEN KOAN

We must revolutionize our thinking, revolutionize our actions, and must have the courage to revolutionize relations among nations of the world. Clichés of yesterday will no longer do today, and will, no doubt, be hopelessly out of date tomorrow.[2]

— ALBERT EINSTEIN

TWO

CHALLENGING ASSUMPTIONS

The Story of VBNK

We first encountered Graeme Storer in 2004, when Carole and Meg Wheatley worked with him and his staff to design and co-facilitate a five-day retreat in Bangkok, Thailand for CARE: USA. At that time, Graeme was the Director of Learning and Organization Development at CARE, and was responsible for managing the global retreat for senior staff and country directors. The retreat was intended as a turning point for CARE, engaging leaders in a process that would shift both their assumptions about development work and their practices in the field. When we renewed our friendship with Graeme in Phnom Penh, during our sabbatical travels in Southeast Asia, he was serving as Director of VBNK, a leadership development nonprofit. At VBNK, Graeme used his experience, expertise, and dynamic personality to engage development facilitators in learning experiences intended to "take the pulse of their current practice; to illuminate their values and assumptions; and to uncover the power dynamics behind their approaches."[3]

Graeme recently left VBNK in the able hands of Cambodian leadership, a transition that reflects the story of development work in this post-conflict society. To understand this work, it is first necessary to understand something of the country and its decades-long history of violence and cultural brutality, including the devastation imposed on the country by the Khmer Rouge regime, led by the infamous Pol Pot.

Beginning in 1975, and determined to return Cambodia to a utopian rural life of peasantry and simplicity, this Communist regime herded every single citizen of the country's cities and towns—including its capital, Phnom Penh—into the countryside. They were forced to live under new rules that banned religion, money, and private ownership; eliminated all communications with the outside world; and, dismantled the family and other social relationships necessary for cultural cohesion. Over the next several years, hundreds of thousands of people—perhaps as many as 1.7 million—died from genocide, starvation, forced labor, and disease. For decades after the routing of the Khmer Rouge in 1979, the people of Cambodia continued to suffer from civil war, constant regime change, economic impoverishment, and complete social instability.

Perhaps even more devastating to Cambodia's future than the loss of life was the impact of decades of trauma on the psyche of its people. Graeme described this impact in a 2009 article about VBNK's work:

> *Most significantly, the Khmer Rouge regime (1975–1979) systematically shattered social and family structures. The result was the destruction of almost all social bonds outside of the immediate nuclear family, with an extreme distrust of individuals and institutions alike rising in the general population.*
>
> *This history left Cambodians feeling generally suspicious of change. Not surprisingly, Cambodians have come to exhibit extreme cautiousness in public activities, and a general fear of speaking up or stepping out of the bounds of accepted practice. This fear, coupled with traditional conformist and "face saving" behaviours, has resulted in a tendency for self-monitoring activities and risk avoidance.*[4]

This context for development work is complicated by the fact that traditional authoritarian leadership approaches are still prevalent in the current government, which is trying to rebuild the country. As Graeme writes,

A main area of concern is that interventions into situations
of injustice and poverty are not empowering communities
to break out of patterns of the past. Nor are they enabling
communities to develop their capacities to have greater control
over their lives. Rather they encourage gratitude and reinforce
an expectation that those who have knowledge, resources and
power should give advice, manage and control.[5]

In this context, beginning with the Paris Peace Accord of 1991 and the establishment of the Transitional Authority between 1992 and 1993, the number of non-governmental organizations (NGOs) proliferated at an exponential rate. Generally funded by Western governments, these NGOs have worked in every conceivable area of development, including work with refugees, orphans, and victims of devastating injuries from landmines, as well as in the areas of microfinance, agri-business, gender equity, human rights, democratic elections, and public health. These NGOs have been almost entirely led by Western expatriate CEOs and administrators, and many have been highly critical of the rampant corruption in the nation's governmental ranks. The NGOs themselves have been accused of existing only to perpetuate themselves, and to line the pockets of those in charge. This situation has led to a highly contentious relationship between the public and civil sectors of society, alongside the need to develop highly competent and effective local leaders and managers in both sectors.

This development work is the role of VBNK, the Phnom Penh-based NGO, led by Graeme Storer from 2008 to 2011, and now headed by a Cambodian executive director in a move that was both desirable and necessary under Cambodian law. According to Graeme, one of the greatest challenges to rebuilding Cambodian society and its institutions continues to be the restoration of the people's faith in their own ability to lead and bring about positive change. Because of the events of the last decades, he says, the very concept of change represents loss and trauma to many. Thus the training, coaching, and other learning experiences offered by VBNK address the inner lives and belief systems of participants, as well as the external skills and practices needed for positive impact in their work. Central to VBNK's work is the understanding that "the link between personal change and social change is inseparable, for if we ignore the need to change ourselves it is unlikely that we will be able to stimulate change in others."[6]

VBNK programs, offered publicly as well as internally to governmental, social, and civil sector organizations, help participants to

- Increase their confidence in exercising leadership.
- Enhance their inter-personal communication skills.
- Gain practical experience in working holistically with teams and communities.
- Learn to work with the incongruence between development values and traditional values.
- Understand the cultural and social helps and hindrances to learning.
- Recognize power, patronage, trauma, and development processes in the Cambodian context.[7]

The challenge that VBNK has faced is helping development practitioners to see that the beliefs and assumptions underpinning their own ways of approaching their work are the same beliefs and assumptions held broadly in the country. If, writes Graeme,

> *practitioners are unable to liberate themselves from their own mindsets, they will be unlikely to be able to work in liberating ways with others. There is, thus, a compelling need to locate innovative approaches to leadership development that challenge conventional development wisdom.[8]*

In additional interviews during our visit, Cambodian VBNK staff members and trainers Mor Lean and Seoung Sothearwat acknowledged the great challenge in developing new leadership skills among Cambodians who have been raised and schooled in an extremely hierarchical society. They emphasized the importance of helping people recognize the human tendency to repeat the behaviors that have been modeled for them all of their lives. Mor told the story of a training participant who had become extremely fearful, as a result of being yelled at and intimidated by members of the Khmer Rouge. During the group process, he was able to recognize the degree to which he was perpetuating that behavior by yelling at his grandchildren. In her own development, Mor recognized the power of that same process by stating, "My personal development is the best contribution to society's development."[9]

Research shows that through VBNK's approach to leadership development,

> *participants have a deepened awareness of self along with increased confidence (self esteem); have sharpened their critical thinking skills and the ability to analyse and work with different types of power; have an increased ability to recognise and engage with others around issues of conflict and change; and have increased confidence in stepping out and challenging social norms that block learning and development.*[10]

A cultural, political, economic and social transformation in Cambodia may be a long time coming, but lessons learned at VBNK have implications not only for large scale transformations, but for change initiatives taken in any environment.

Challenging Assumptions and Transformation

There is nothing more essential to the process of transformative growth and development than our capacity for challenging our own deeply-held beliefs and assumptions. Lacking that capacity as individuals, we may remain stuck in an unrecognized and unexamined view of the world, even when it causes dysfunction and misery in our lives, our relationships, and our work. When organizations, communities, or societies lack that capacity, they may be blind to shifts in the environment that require them to change or die.

One compelling theory about how challenging assumptions functions in our growth and development is called "transformative learning." In defining that term, Edmund O'Sullivan, author of *Trans-*

formative Learning: Educational Vision for the 21st Century, clearly distinguishes transformative learning from simple mastery of a skill, or taking in new information.

> *Transformative learning involves experiencing a deep, structural shift in the basic premises of thought, feelings, and actions. It is a shift of consciousness that dramatically and irreversibly alters our way of being in the world. Such a shift involves our understanding of ourselves and our self-locations; our relationships with other humans and with the natural world; our understanding of relations of power in interlocking structures of class, race, and gender; our body awarenesses, our visions of alternative approaches to living; and our sense of possibilities for social justice and peace and personal joy.[11]*

Quite obviously, these profound shifts of consciousness are not something most of us experience on an everyday basis, and they are not shifts that come about through most of our ordinary experiences. According to adult learning theorists, they are inevitably precipitated by an encounter with "otherness" of some kind, for which our current way of thinking, acting, or interacting are inadequate. Such encounters must be followed by the surfacing and challenging of assumptions if they are to lead to new ways of being in the world. Patricia Cranton, Professor of Adult Education at the University of New Brunswick in Fredericton, Canada, describes transformative learning theory:

> *At its core, transformative learning theory is elegantly simple. Through some event, which could be as traumatic as losing a job or as ordinary as an unexpected question, an individual becomes aware of holding a limiting or distorted view. If the individual critically examines this view, opens herself to alternatives, and consequently changes the way she sees things, she has transformed some part of how she makes meaning out of the world.[12]*

Cranton goes on to articulate a process through which transformative learning occurs, as "a rough guide to helping us set up a learning environment to promote transformation," as follows:

1) An activating event that typically exposes a discrepancy between what a person has always assumed to be true and what has just been experienced, heard, or read.

2) Articulating assumptions: recognizing underlying assumptions that have been uncritically assimilated and are largely unconscious.

3) Critical self-reflection: questioning and examining assumptions in terms of where they came from, the consequences of holding them, and why they are important.

4) Being open to alternative viewpoints.

5) Engaging in discourse, where evidence is weighed, arguments assessed, alternative perspectives explored, and knowledge constructed by consensus.

6) Revising assumptions and perspectives to make them more open and better justified.

7) Acting on revisions: behaving, talking, and thinking in a way that is congruent with transformed assumptions or perspectives.[13]

While it may well be possible to go through life without transformative learning experiences that lead to elevations of consciousness, it is hard work to isolate ourselves from such experiences, or to refuse to engage in the process outlined by Patricia Cranton and other adult development theorists. Not only is it hard work, but living such an "unexamined life," as Socrates stated long ago, is probably not worth living or worthy of our humanity. From Socrates' point of view, the very purpose of life is reflection on who we are in the world. He was willing to sacrifice his life for this principle, and for his dedication to teaching his students to think for themselves. It seems obvious that people who are able to think for themselves and become increasingly conscious not only lead vastly more satisfying lives, but make far greater contributions to their organizations, their communities, and their societies.

Challenging Assumptions in the Workplace

The idea of "thinking for ourselves" is the basis of the work that Maryse Barak and others do with major organizations all over the world. Through an introduction by Angeles Arrien, we were fortunate to spend an afternoon with Maryse in Cape Town, South Africa, and to learn more about her work. As a consultant and executive coach with long experience in both South African and multi-national corporations, Maryse has employed a number of theories and methodologies in helping clients to survive and thrive. None, however, have so clearly connected with her personal beliefs and purpose in life than what is called the Thinking Environment, an approach developed by Nancy Kline, author of *Time to Think: Listening to Ignite the Human Mind* (1999).

The Thinking Environment approach is based on the simple idea that our ability to think for ourselves, and the quality of our thinking, is dependent on how we are treated by others while we are thinking. This idea suggests that thinking for ourselves comes about when we are engaged in dialogue with others. Kline's methodology, practiced by Maryse Barak and others, teaches people a principle-based, structured form of dialogue through which individuals and groups are able to surface hidden and limiting assumptions—replacing them with "liberating assumptions" that free them to accomplish their goals and aspirations. As we talked with Maryse, she shared with us her belief that "everything we do—the quality of it—is dependent on the quality of the thinking we do first. If that is true, then it is an extraordinary leadership invitation to generate businesses where human beings think well for themselves."[14]

Maryse shared with us a client story that points clearly to the power of the Thinking Environment approach, and how replacing limiting assumptions with liberating assumptions has the potential for shifting

---

It is not necessary to change. Survival is not mandatory.[15]

—W. EDWARDS DEMING

cultural dynamics, even in a place as challenging as post-apartheid South Africa. Maryse's client, the board of a large organization, included a black South African woman. As part of the dialogue process, board members were asked to examine their multiple identities and to identify their own, or culturally underlying, assumptions that might be limiting their ability to perform as they desired. The identity chosen by the woman was "Bantu-educated woman," referring to her own education in the apartheid-era schooling system for blacks, established in 1953 through the Bantu Education Act. Typical of the assumptions on which the apartheid leaders based the system was this from the Minister of Native Affairs at the time, Hendrik Verwoerd, who stated that, "There is no place for [the Bantu] in the European community above the level of certain forms of labour . . . What is the use of teaching the Bantu child mathematics when it cannot use it in practice?"[16]

For Maryse's client, the assumptions underlying the term "Bantu-educated woman," included being less intelligent, not really having made it, and not being able to deal with complexity. Consistent with the Thinking Environment approach, Maryse asked the woman if she thought those assumptions were true and, if not, what was true for her. In response, the executive began to tell her story and the determination, resilience, strength, insight, and other attributes it took to become educated under the apartheid laws, and what it had taken for her to rise to her current position of responsibility and respect.

Maryse then posed the type of question that seems to have such power in this approach. "If you knew—really knew—that Bantu-educated women were resilient and see things the way they really are, what would change for you?" In this moment, the woman turned to her colleagues and vowed to herself and to them to claim her own

What we think, we become. All that we are arises with our thoughts. With our thoughts, we make the world.[17]

— THE BUDDHA

knowledge and wisdom in their presence, and to speak out from her own truth.

Another approach to challenging assumptions in organizations is based on the work of Harvard-based psychologists Robert Kegan and Lisa Lahey. The approach is grounded in constructive development theory, a model that views adult development as a progression through five stages of mental complexity, or what Kegan has termed "orders of mind." Progression through those stages, according to Kegan, occurs when we are able to make explicit or objective those beliefs, assumptions, and mental models that, while currently hidden from our view, are the drivers of our behavior. Once we are able to look objectively at those assumptions, we are able to choose other assumptions that are more appropriate in our current circumstances, and thus shift our actions and interactions. Kegan is identifying the same dynamic that other adult development and transformational learning theorists we have talked about here are articulating. When we, as adults, encounter situations for which our current ways of making meaning or behaving are inadequate or ineffective, we have the opportunity to grow and develop by making those outmoded ways of being explicit and by choosing new ways of being that meet new challenges.

In their book *Immunity to Change: How to Overcome It and Unlock Potential in Yourself*, Kegan and Lahey lay out a four-column "change map" that they use to help individuals and groups move beyond situations in which they may be stuck, to more complex stages of mental complexity that can help them achieve their personal and professional goals. Using this map and with guided facilitation, Kegan and Lahey—along with others they have trained to use it—individuals or teams identify

1) their primary desired goals or commitments,
2) the behaviors they engage in that distract them or take them away from working on those goals,
3) the "hidden" or competing commitments that underpin those behaviors, and
4) the "big assumptions" behind those hidden commitments.[18]

"What a man believes may be ascertained, not from his creed, but from the assumptions on which he habitually acts."[19]

— GEORGE BERNARD SHAW

One example, among many cited in *Immunity to Change* and in their 1998 book, *In Over Our Heads*, relates to a leader having difficulty meeting a commitment he had made to delegate more responsibility to other team members. The leader was able to identify what he was doing or not doing that kept him from meeting that commitment, what competing commitments he was choosing, and what "big assumptions" he was making about what would ensue if he shifted his commitments. Among those assumptions were, "If I am dependent on others and unable to do many things well, I lose my self-respect," and, "If I don't have a way to get things done, I'll stop being valuable." Once able to make those assumptions "objective," rather than being "subject to" them, the leader was able to choose the commitments that were most important to him and to his team.[20]

Kegan and Lahey have a message for leaders who are interested in improving their own performance and the performance of their teams and their organizations:

> *If you are leading anything at all, you are driving some kind of plan or agenda, but some kind of plan or agenda is also driving you. It is out of your awareness. You cannot yet take responsibility for it. And most of the time, that agenda will limit or even doom your ability to deliver extraordinary results. If you do not attend as much to "development" as you do to "leadership," then your leadership development will always be directed to the plan or agenda you have. It will not be about the plan or agenda that "has you," and therefore your capacity for change will inherently be limited.[21]*

Organizations, and even entire industries, can fall prey to the same failure to challenge assumptions as individual leaders, blinding them to shifts in the marketplace, or making it impossible for them to take advantage of opportunities for innovation, growth, and development. Demetrius Madrigal and Bryan McClain, co-founders of Metric Lab, a research-based product development company located in California, point to a number of such examples, including the current challenges of the newspaper industry.

The two make a distinction between safe and risky assumptions: safe assumptions being those that need to be challenged, and risky assumptions being those that need to be verified. Safe assumptions are those that keep companies stuck and unable to innovate, while unverified risky assumptions can lead to catastrophic failures in the introduction of new products or services. The distinction becomes clear as they describe the experience of Xerox and the personal computer industry.

> One of our favorite examples of safe assumptions and missed opportunities is the Xerox Alto personal computer, which Xerox developed at PARC in 1973. The Alto was the first computer to use a graphic user interface, a desktop metaphor, and a mouse as its input device. Though Xerox developed the Alto several years before the Apple II—the first commercially successful personal computer—came out in 1977, they never brought the Alto to market—despite its having features Apple was unable to replicate until it developed the Lisa in 1983.
>
> Xerox finally acted on its innovations, creating the Xerox Star and bringing it to market in 1981. But, unlike the Apple II, the Xerox Star focused on office use and was part of a larger office system. Xerox required its customers to build an early version of an office network, purchasing a minimum of two Stars at $16,000 apiece—along with other equipment. The Apple II flourished, as did its successor the Macintosh, while the Star was considered a failure, and Xerox soon exited the personal computer market. Rather than capitalize on the Alto's innovations and develop a product for the consumer market, Xerox chose to play it safe and focus on the business market.

As a result, they missed out on an opportunity that could have resulted in enormous growth for Xerox.[22]

Toyota's challenge of the then Big Three during the late 1970s and early 1980s is another prime example of an organization's willingness to challenge safe assumptions, one that resulted in dramatic shifts in both buyer responses to purchasing smaller, more fuel efficient cars, and the global auto industry landscape.

Fostering the Challenge of Assumptions in the Workplace

Those who believe, as we do, that how we act and interact is a function of how we think, will understand that transforming organizations, communities, and societies rests on our ability to shift underlying assumptions. While shifts in the environment create plenty of opportunities to challenge assumptions, it is also possible to purposefully create the conditions for engaging in a transformative learning process. As evidenced by the work of Maryse Barack, the duo of Kegan and Lahey, and others, there are tools and methodologies available for creating those opportunities.

In our own experience with the Jackson Comm*Unity* Transformation Project, we were able to engage over 5,000 citizens in such a process, using the Interactive Design methodology of Dr. Russell Ackoff and Jamshid Gharjedaghi. The essence of the project was to create opportunities for residents to surface the widely-held assumptions that kept the community stuck, doing the same things over and over again while expecting a different result; to articulate alternative assumptions that would better serve the future of the community; and to design an ideal new Jackson based on those assumptions. In gatherings held all over the community, the set of assumptions on the next page were surfaced.

From the new assumptions generated, participants were able to design a community that we came to call a "learning democracy," or " . . . a mode of organizing human enterprise in which all people freely choose to bring about and continually renew the systems and structures

Old Assumptions	More Valid Assumptions for the Future
We need strong leaders to take care of us and make decisions for us.	Leaders can be developed everywhere to create the conditions for citizen responsibility and democracy.
Citizens are powerless to change the main systems that effect their lives.	Citizens can make and influence choices, take responsibility for the consequences, and learn.
Citizens outside our personal circles need to take care of their own problems by themselves.	Citizens can use their talents and work together to vastly improve the whole community for all citizens.
If we had enough time and money, new laws and better enforcement, we could fix any problems.	Citizens can be deeply motivated to understand and take action on complex problems with very little money.
If citizens gained the right job skill, they could have long-term security.	The changing nature of work requires the resources and availability of lifelong learning for all citizens.

through which they meet their own needs, the needs of others, and the needs of the larger systems of which they are a part."

Transformative change at any level—from the individual to the global—requires challenging the assumptions that are driving current ways of being and replacing them with more "liberating assumptions" for the future. As Abraham Lincoln said in an 1862 message to Congress, "The dogmas of the quiet past are inadequate to the stormy present. The occasion is piled high with difficulty, and we must rise with the occasion. As our case is new, so we must think anew, and act anew. We must disenthrall ourselves, and then we shall save our country."[23]

High levels of well-being mean that we are more able to respond to difficult circumstances, to innovate and constructively engage with other people and the world around us. As well as representing a highly effective way of bringing about good outcomes in many different areas our lives, there is also a strong case for regarding well-being as an ultimate goal of human endeavour.[1]

— NATIONAL ACCOUNTS OF WELL-BEING

THREE

ATTENDING TO WELL-BEING

The Story of Nic Marks

To this day, we are bowled over by the serendipitous and surprising good fortune that characterized our stay in Costa Rica. One such surprise was our encounter with Nic Marks, who served as the lead author of the Happy Planet Index (HPI), the global measurement methodology that in 2010 identified Costa Rica as the "happiest country on earth." Nic was leading a seminar at the University for Peace at the same time we were taking the BePeace® course there, and we were fortunate enough to spend a pleasant afternoon in conversation with him on the lush grounds of the campus. That experience, along with attending his Five Ways to Well-Being workshop the following day, opened our eyes to a new way of thinking about well-being: from an individual to a planetary perspective.

Nic has worked for many years with the New Economics Foundation (NEF), a self-described "think-and-do tank" in the UK that aims to "improve quality of life by promoting innovative solutions that challenge mainstream thinking on economic, environment, and social issues." The organization's stated purpose is "to bring about a Great Transition—to transform the economy so that it works for people and the planet."[2] The Happy Planet Index was launched in July 2006 as a radical departure from the world's dominant benchmark, Gross Domestic Product (GDP), which measures the total market value of a country's products and services. The HPI alternative uses a formula based on people's self-reported experience of well-being, their life expectancy, and their country's resource consumption or ecological footprint. The rationale for the measure is that a successful society is one that "can support good lives that don't cost the Earth."[3]

As Nic describes the rationale for the HPI, the idea was to try and show that quality of life was not the same as economic growth, and to start thinking about how nations should really think about creating great lives for their citizens, but also to think about doing that within the environmental limits of the planet we live on. That's the idea: "Happy People, Happy Planet."[4]

For Nic, the index is a powerful catalyst for creating positive change, an idea that comes from studying the work of systems theorist Stafford Beers. From Beers' cybernetics theory, Nic says that he "became fascinated in thinking of indicators as systemic feedback loops that allow a system, whether it be an individual, an organisation, or the whole of society, to positively adapt to changes in the external environment."[5] In other words, data from indicators such as the HPI provide us with the information required to understand the performance of a system (or our own lives), to inspire action, and to monitor progress toward desired outcomes.

Translating the idea of the HPI to the level of individual and organizational transformation was another of Nic's roles at NEF. Subsequent to his work on the HPI, he was responsible for founding the organization's award-winning Centre for Well-being, and leading the organization's well-being program. In that role, Nic served as an advisor to the UK Government Office for Science's Foresight Project on Mental Capital and Well-being. That project's researchers reviewed the work of over 400 global scientists, with the aim of identifying a set of evidence-based actions to improve well-being that individuals would be encouraged to build into their daily lives. One spin-off of that work was the NEF report, "National Accounts of Well-being," which gained extensive media coverage when launched in late January, 2009.

The National Accounts of Well-Being report set forth five evidence-based positive actions individuals could undertake to improve their well-being:

Connect – *Invest your time in your loved ones, in your friends, family, and acquaintances. Meet people. Talk to them. Understand how they improve your life, and also how you improve theirs. Knowing that you mean something to someone can be one of the most powerful positive forces in the world.*

Be active – *When exercising, the level of serotonin in your body rises and you get a powerful feeling of well being. Something as simple as kicking a ball or throwing a Frisbee around a garden with a friend can knock both this and the previous point off in one go. If you're feeling down, go for a brisk walk and get some air. You'll soon feel better.*

Take notice – *Keeping an eye on what's going on around you keeps your brain running smoothly. If you see an application for planning permission pinned to a lamp-post, and even the tiniest part of your brain wants to know what it says, then go and read it. On a train or bus, rather than burying your nose in a book or your mobile phone, look out of the window and see what's happening outside.*

Keep learning – *Humanity's relentless curiosity is behind almost every single one of our species' accomplishments. Once you've finished your formal education, that's no reason not to stop learning. Actively seek out different viewpoints. If you don't understand them, find someone knowledgeable to explain them to you.*

Give – *Finally, be generous. A survey gave £100 to two groups of people, instructing one group to spend it on themselves, and another to spend it on other people. Afterwards, the latter group's spirits were significantly higher. If you don't have cash, give your time, your attention, or your expertise instead.*[6]

These individual actions may seem overly simplistic. However, taken together and taken seriously, they form an interesting prescription for becoming responsible for one's own growth and development toward functioning as a human being at a higher level.

Taking those ideas directly to the workplace, Nic Marks has founded an organization called Happiness Works that offers services directly to workplaces. A Happiness At Work survey instrument designed by Nic helps organizations take a holistic approach to assessing satisfaction and engagement in the workplace. The free (as of October 2013) survey looks at the functionality of workers' personal resources and their work environment, as well as their overall experience at work.[7]

This more recent work is a reflection of Nic's background as a psychotherapist and his belief that people are moved to create change through a positive vision of the possible. It is, to him, a

> *transformational paradigm, rather than a managerial paradigm. That's why we focus on happiness. It gives an emotional tone to our work. We are emotional, and some would say spiritual, beings and we need some vision of how we're going to become, what we're going to be, and we need to have our whole selves respected.*[8]

Nic's own vision of a "high well-being, low carbon" world is an example of a straightforward, understandable vision that can speak to as many people as possible. It is one, he says, that

> *every nation can start to think about, and we can transform that into our own lives, as well. We don't need all the material goods to be happy. So maybe we can start to work our way out of this mess, if we start to realize that happiness and well-being is very relational, very 'between-us.' It's from our relationships, our communities, our family, our organizations, that we actually get well-being, as we relate with other people. Then, I think we can begin to see our way to a better future.*[9]

UK Prime Minister David Cameron agrees, stating that, "Improving our society's sense of well-being is, I believe, the central political challenge of our time."[10]

Nic Marks is fully aware of the challenges in using new measures of well-being and happiness as indicators of success. When we asked him about his views of the pressures companies face from Wall Street, and the need to demonstrate quarterly financial performance, he said,

> *One of the issues we face is short-termism in our financial systems, in our governments elected for the short-term, in our businesses thinking about their quarterly profits exclusively. That is something we all need to work on systematically. We have to understand that short-term, quick gains are not worth risking long-term issues for. We learn this as children. It's called delayed gratification. We seem to have lost this in our adult lives. We need to have systems that manage that tension between the short-term and the long-term. The whole financial system needs to start putting people and planet before profit.[11]*

Given that "delayed gratification" is an indicator of maturity and emotional intelligence, Nic is suggesting that we grow up and take on our role as responsible adults seeking to live well on a healthy planet.

Attending to Well-Being and Transformation

Contemplating the urge to live well goes back at least as far as Aristotle, who saw the realizing of our human potential as our true reason for being. This idea, much debated and studied across disciplines, has been prominently featured in the field of humanistic psychology and, more recently, the field of positive psychology. Noted American psychologist Carl Rogers called this developmental urge the "actualising tendency—a fundamental motivation towards growth," which he described as

> *man's tendency to actualize himself, to become potentialities. By this I mean the directional trend which is evident in all organic and human life—the urge to expand, develop, mature—the tendency to express and activate all*

the capacities of the organism and the self. This tendency
may become deeply buried under layer after layer of
encrusted psychological defences, it may be hidden behind
elaborate facades that deny its existence. It is my belief,
however, based on my experience, that it exists in every
individual, and awaits only the proper conditions to be
released and expressed.[12]

Abraham Maslow later noted that these defenses included the "fear of one's own greatness," or the "evasion of one's destiny," or the "running away from one's own best talents." A reflection by Marianne Williamson, often incorrectly credited to Nelson Mandela, beautifully speaks to these defenses and what becomes possible when they are overcome.

Our deepest fear is not that we are inadequate. Our
deepest fear is that we are powerful beyond measure. It is
our light, not our darkness that most frightens us. We ask
ourselves, Who am I to be brilliant, gorgeous, talented,
fabulous? Actually, who are you not to be? You are a
child of God. Your playing small does not serve the world.
There is nothing enlightened about shrinking so that other
people won't feel insecure around you. We are all meant
to shine, as children do. We were born to make manifest
the glory of God that is within us. It's not just in some of
us; it's in everyone. And as we let our own light shine,
we unconsciously give other people permission to do the
same. As we are liberated from our own fear, our presence
automatically liberates others.[13]

Among those who believe in the possibility of activating our actualizing tendencies in the workplace are Gretchen Spreitzer and Christine Porath, along with their research partners at the University of Michigan's Ross School of Business Center for Positive Organizational Scholarship. Using the term "thriving" to describe overall well-being, they report in the *Harvard Business Review* that there are "two integral components of this concept: vitality, 'the sense of being alive, passionate, and excited'; and learning, or 'the growth that comes from gaining new knowledge and skills.'"[14] Thriving benefits both employees and their organizations, say the authors.

> *The combination of vitality and learning leads to employees who deliver results and find ways to grow. Their work is rewarding not just because they successfully perform what's expected of them today but also because they have a sense of where they and the company are headed. In short, they are thriving, and the energy they create is contagious.*[15]

Martin E. P. Seligman, former president of the American Psychological Association and commonly known as the father of positive psychology, has come to use the term "flourishing" to describe his theory of well-being. Having disavowed the term "happiness" to describe well-being—in spite of the fact that it has spurned an entire happiness industry—Seligman encourages individuals and organizations to "increase flourishing by increasing positive emotion, engagement, positive relationships, meaning, and accomplishment," or PERMA.[16] PERMA is now the basis for a U.S. military program called Comprehensive Soldier Fitness, which is designed "to build resilience and enhance performance of the Army Family: soldiers, their families, and Army civilians."[17]

While not without his critics, Seligman is widely regarded as having shifted the focus of psychological study from illness to wellness. Those who are following his lead are providing research-based tools that can help awaken the actualizing tendency present in all of us.

Heeding our own actualizing tendencies can be extremely difficult, however, given the complexities of life for those in the developed world, let alone for those who are trying to survive from day to day. The stresses and strains of daily life leave little energy or space for our own pursuit of happiness and well-being. In fact, the reason for writing this book is a call for our workplaces to become containers for the work of becoming more of who we are meant to be in the world. The workplace is where we can, if we are fortunate, express

positive emotions, become deeply engaged, develop positive relationships, create meaning, and experience accomplishment.

Attending to Well-being in the Workplace

Fortunately, a growing number of organizations, communities, and
societies are already doing a great deal to promote their constituency's
attention to well-being. Later in our Costa Rican travels, for example,
we encountered a fascinating set of well-being indices, developed by
National Geographic researcher and journalist Dan Buettner, and a
team of the world's top experts in longevity. The team identified five
"blue zones" in the world where people live healthy lives well past
100 years of age. On our trip, we were delighted to visit one of those
blue zones, Costa Rica's Nicoya Peninsula. The others named include
Italy's Island of Sardinia, Japan's Island of Okinawa, California's Loma
Linda, and the Greek Island of Icaria. In Buettner's 2008 book, *The
Blue Zones*, he describes how people function in these areas.

> **Move naturally:** *your home should go along with the natural
> way you move. Concentrate on things you like to do, such as
> gardening, walking, swimming or spending time with family
> and friends.*
>
> **Express your ideas** *with a positive attitude and allow time
> for rest.*
>
> **Eat wisely:** *forget those diet trends that force you to consume
> 20% less than normal. Do not consume processed foods and
> have a few glasses of red wine daily. Please remember: do not
> over indulge.*
>
> **Be part of the right tribe:** *put those you love first and try
> and reconnect with your religion or connect to one you wish
> to explore.*[18]

On a global scale, other organizations are now measuring and
publishing international happiness indices similar to NEF's Happy

Planet Index, which was first made public in 2006. As of this writing, the most recent World Happiness Report was introduced just prior to the 2013 UN General Assembly meeting in New York City. The report was originally commissioned for a 2011 UN conference on happiness, based on a General Assembly resolution that encouraged member nations "to pursue the elaboration of additional measures that better capture the importance of the pursuit of happiness and well-being in development with a view to guiding their public policies."[19]

The growing interest in measuring and promoting happiness and well-being on a large scale originates in large part from the adoption of the term "gross national happiness," which was first introduced in 1972 by Bhutan's King Jigme Singye Wangchuck. The king was searching for a way to transform the country's economic system, while maintaining its Buddhist values. The resulting survey instrument, developed by the Centre for Bhutan Studies, consists of four pillars:

1) fair socio-economic development,
2) conservation and promotion of a vibrant culture,
3) environmental protection, and
4) good governance.

These four pillars further measure nine domains:

1) psychological well-being,
2) living standards,
3) health,
4) culture,
5) education,
6) community vitality,
7) good governance,
8) balanced time use, and
9) ecological integration.[20]

Although Buthan's new Prime Minister, Tshering Tobgay, is said to be setting aside his predecessor's happiness indicators for more concrete measures and actions, the idea is one that has now caught on around the world.[21]

Meanwhile, organizations and communities are also beginning to focus on attending to well-being and happiness, in addition to more traditional economic indicators of success. Many are experiencing success in improving health and well-being indicators, and significant financial savings and rewards. In a *Harvard Business Review* article titled, "What's the Hard Return on Employee Wellness Programs?," the authors report that companies like Johnson & Johnson are enjoying substantial savings due to their wellness programs. At J & J that amounts to "$250 million on health care costs over the past decade; from 2002 to 2008, the return was $2.71 for every dollar spent."[22]

In their research, the authors conducted interviews in ten organizations to discover what they call "six essential pillars of a successful, strategically integrated wellness program, regardless of an organization's size." The pillars include:

Multilevel Leadership — Creating a culture of health takes passionate, persistent, and persuasive leadership at all levels—from the C-suite to middle managers to the people who have "wellness" in their job descriptions.

Alignment — A wellness program should be a natural extension of a firm's identity and aspirations. Don't forget that a cultural shift takes time.

Scope, Relevance, and Quality — Wellness programs must be comprehensive, engaging, and just plain excellent. Otherwise, employees won't participate.

Accessibility — Aim to make low- or no-cost services a priority. True on-site integration is essential because convenience matters.

Partnerships — Active, ongoing collaboration with internal and external partners, including vendors, can provide a program with some of its essential components and many of its desirable enhancements.

Communications — Wellness is not just a mission—it's a message. How you deliver it can make all the difference. Sensitivity, creativity, and media diversity are the cornerstones.[23]

One organization with an award-winning approach to well-being in the workplace is Bright Horizons, a childcare organization with 750 child care centers in the U.S., the UK, Ireland, the Netherlands, India, and Canada. The company has partnerships with over 850 employers for whom it provides "a complete family of employer solutions, including child care, back-up care for children and adults/elders, and educational advising for employees and their college-bound dependents," along with "complete consulting services to assess, identify, and respond to work/life and dependent-care challenges among an organization's employees."[24] For these efforts, Bright Horizons has been recognized in multiple years by *Fortune* magazine's "100 Best Companies to Work for in America" list, and *Working Mother* magazine's "100 Best Companies" list.

The array of services offered by Bright Horizons is truly staggering. Offerings include comprehensive medical, dental, and vision insurance for employees and their families (including same-sex partnerships), retirement planning, gym memberships, tuition reimbursement and academic advising, savings on commuter costs, a full-service credit union, retail discount programs, generous paid time off, adoption assistance—the list goes on and on. A Well-Being Help Center helps employees

> *reduce stress and manage life issues outside of work, [with] a comprehensive support system [that] offers 24/7 assistance with many areas of daily life. Get support referrals for personal problems, event planning, or general life-management issues. On-staff attorneys offer legal assistance on an array of issues (e.g., divorce or bankruptcy), and financial professionals assist with money management such as budget creation, retirement planning, and saving for college.*[25]

The William Baun et al. research mentioned above notes that "results of comprehensive programs" that go beyond "passes to fitness clubs and nutrition information in the cafeteria," are impressive, including lower costs, greater productivity, decreased attrition, and higher morale. The MD Anderson Cancer Center program, for example, decreased lost work days by 80% and modified-duty days by 64%, resulting in savings of $1.5 million, while Workers Compensation insurance premiums declined by 50%.[26]

Fostering Well-Being in the Workplace

Organizations seeking to activate the inherent "actualizing tendency" of people in the workplace will find a great deal of guidance from research, books, articles, and even the popular press. Traveling in Budapest, we were fortunate to interview Imre Lovey, one of the authors of a fascinating book, *How Healthy is Your Organization* (2007), which seeks to help leaders "cure corporate diseases and promote joyful cultures." Lovey is an internationally acclaimed organization development consultant, writer, and lecturer. He and his co-authors point to diseases including distrust, lack of communication, alienation, workaholism, suboptimization, and self-centered leadership, among others, and suggest ways in which "organizations can uncover negative influences in the corporate culture, root them out, and prosper with newly committed, energized employees."[27]

Likewise, Gretchen Spreitzer and Christine Porath, in their HBR article, "Creating Sustainable Performance," offer four methods that create the conditions for thriving employees:

Method 1: Providing decision-making discretion. "Employees at every level are energized by the ability to make decisions that affect their work," note the authors. They point to companies like Southwest Airlines and Facebook as places that have made this fundamental to their organizational culture.

Method 2: Sharing information. "People can contribute more effectively when they understand how their work fits with the organization's mission and strategy." So, sharing not just plans but progress, especially at a granular level, allows empowered employees to act locally on the organization's broader strategy. The authors point to Alaska Airlines and Whole Foods as two companies with an "open book" policy.

Method 3: Minimizing incivility. The authors found "half of employees who had experienced uncivil behavior at work intentionally decreased their efforts. More than a third deliberately decreased their quality of their work." Companies that establish a tone of civility as part of their corporate culture start by focusing on candidates in their hiring process.

Method 4: Offering performance feedback. "Feedback creates opportunities for learning and the energy so critical for a culture of thriving," note Sprietzer and Porath. "Feedback keeps people's work-related activities focused on personal and organizational goals. The quicker and more direct the feedback, the more useful it is." Some companies, such as Quicken Loans, use a ticker with panels showing organizational and personal metrics comparing progress against daily goals, and coaching is used to provide assistance. [28]

The authors say that leaders cannot choose among these mechanisms, but rather that all four are mutually reinforcing. The payoffs can be great. They report that

Happy employees produce more than unhappy ones over the long term. They routinely show up at work, they're less likely to quit, they go above and beyond the call of duty, and they attract people who are just as committed to the job. Moreover, they're not sprinters; they're more like marathon runners, in it for the long haul.[29]

Furthermore,

Across industries and job types, we found that people who fit our description of thriving demonstrated 16% better overall performance (as reported by their managers) and 125% less burnout (self-reported) than their peers. They were 32% more committed to the organization and 46% more satisfied with their jobs. They also missed much less work and reported significantly fewer doctor visits, which meant health care savings and less lost time for the company.[30]

Throughout this discussion on well-being in the workplace, we have frequently thought about how often one of our most treasured friends and mentors, Dr. W. Edwards Deming, spoke about the need for people to be able to experience joy in work. It is said that Deming originally spoke of "pride in work" but changed to "joy in work" when David Kerridge, a professor at the University of Aberdeen, let him know that "joy" was mentioned in two verses of the Book of Ecclesiastes.[31] Given Dr. Deming's deep love for liturgy, he quickly changed his tune. One of those verses, Ecclesiastes 8:15 says, "So I commend the enjoyment of life, because there is nothing better for a person under the sun than to eat and drink and be glad. Then joy will accompany them in their toil all the days of the life God has given them under the sun."[32]

This is, perhaps, a blessing that can one day be bestowed on every one of us.

Autonomy . . . is different from independence. It's not the rugged, go-it-alone, rely-on-nobody individualism of the American cowboy. It means acting with choice —which means we can be both autonomous and happily interdependent with others.[1]

— DANIEL PINK

Freedom of action is a tremendous advantage because in freedom-based companies, employees facing a sudden surge in competition, a downturn, a new government regulation, or an inadequate business process don't simply wait for their higher ups or some new policies to tell them what to do. Instead, they take action that they—not their bosses—deem is best for the company and they do it right away—not when it's too late.[2]

— BRIAN CARNEY AND ISAAC GETZ

FOUR

ACTING AUTONOMOUSLY

The Story of the Chaeli Campaign

Imagine being a 17-year-old girl living in the Cape Town suburb of Plumstead, South Africa, and receiving a letter from Mikhail Gorbachev, former President of the Soviet Union and Nobel Peace Prize Winner, that reads in part:

> *This year Nobel Peace Laureates have decided to select, within the world of social activism, a woman or a man for their commitment in society, with the aim of spreading solidarity as a source of inspiration throughout the world.*
>
> *I have the honour to inform you that you have been selected as the recipient of the 2012 medal for Activism, as an acknowledgement of your active commitment to peace and human rights, particularly through your actions for the rights of children with disabilities in South Africa, with the establishment of your professional organization: the Chaeli Campaign.[3]*

This was the experience of Michaela (Chaeli) Mycroft when she received the news that she would be traveling to Chicago, Illinois to receive the award during the 2012 World Summit of Nobel Peace Laureates. Just four months earlier, Chaeli traveled to Amsterdam, where she received the prestigious International Children's Peace Prize. All because she decided, when she was nine years old, that she wanted the freedom and mobility that a motorized wheelchair could give her!

Michaela's birth was greeted by her parents, Zelda and Russell, with all the joy that parents of newborns experience. The parents named her Michaela, which to them meant, "a gift given by God." When Michaela—who came to be called Chaeli—was eleven months old, her parents noticed that she was not standing normally. After consulting their doctor, Zelda and Russell learned that their child had been born with cerebral palsy. When Chaeli was six years old and had been confined to a wheelchair for a number of years, she was also diagnosed with congenital degenerative neuropathy.

At the age of six, Chaeli was enrolled at the same school as her sister Erin and their friends Tarryn, Justine, and Chelsea Terry. The five girls, whose parents were long-time friends, had been together since birth, even being cared for by the same "day mom" while their parents were off to work. The school adjusted to meeting Chaeli's needs, her classmates were eager to be of service, and her friends adapted their games so that she could participate.

Then one day, when she was nine years old, Chaeli entered a repair shop that sold assistive devices. She learned about motorized wheel chairs that could be customized for young children. When Chaeli and her family learned that the chair would cost R20,000 (around 2,600 USD), the shop owner suggested that Chaeli get her friends together for a cookie selling fund-raiser.

That was all Chaeli needed to set her imagination in motion. She called her sister and the Terry girls for a brain-storming session about how they could raise the required funds. After a number of options were rejected by their parents as being a bit too dangerous, the girls came up with a plan. Soon they were selling Erin and Chaeli's artwork on greeting cards, making do-it-yourself Sunshine Pots for growing sun-flowers, and going door-to-door taking orders for Saturday morning muffins. When one man offered them R5 if they would just go away, the girls were thrilled to know that there would be one less muffin to bake!

It took just seven weeks for the girls to raise the necessary funds, and Chaeli became the beaming and proud owner of a motorized wheelchair. Zelda Mycroft reflected on the experiences of the Mycroft and Terry girls, who were ages six through twelve at the time.

> *When the money started rolling in, that just affirmed what they were doing, it affirmed their relationship, their empathy for Chaeli and the acknowledgement of Chaeli needing to be more independent. And they gave life to the fact that disabled people need the dignity of being given a mobility aid that is going to change their lives in order to be more functional in an able-bodied world.*[4]

The team of friends didn't stop there. Once they achieved their initial goal, the two families decided to help other children achieve independence and mobility. By 2005, they officially formed the Chaeli Campaign, a non-profit organization with the tagline, "Hope in Motion." We had the opportunity to sit down with Chaeli and the girls who make up the Chaeli Campaign Founders Committee, along with their mothers Zelda and Diane, at the Chaeli Cottage. By this time the organization was running a wide range of programs to achieve their vision "to mobilise the minds and bodies of children with disabilities and to normalise society through advocacy and education programmes and events."[5]

The Campaign's services include

- a therapies program offering physiotherapy, speech and occupational therapy sessions for children from disadvantaged communities,
- an inclusive education program serving the Early Childhood Development sector as well as the formalized schooling sector, and
- an assistive devices program that secures custom-made devices that help children become "more comfortable in their own bodies, whilst trying to improve functional use of hands and fingers as well."[6]

In recent years, the Chaeli Campaign added a pay-it-forward ambassadors program that engages groups of children ages 10–12 in

a one-year commitment to offer input to Chaeli Campaign program-
ming, as well as learning about social entrepreneurship and developing the skills and knowledge to grow their own service projects.
Zelda says,

> I think the most important thing that they get out of it is that
> they know that the most important story they are ever going
> to tell is their own life story and that they claim who they are,
> where they come from, and what they have to offer the world.
> They suddenly realize that they have something powerful to
> offer the world.[7]

Hearing the group speak about the origins of the Chaeli Campaign
and how it is organized made us realize how deeply acting autonomously runs through everything they do. Zelda and Russell Mycroft,
along with Diane Terry, make up an executive committee that reports
to a management committee, which functions as a typical board of
directors. Unlike many non-profits, however, Zelda says that she and
her colleagues do not have

> to wait for their management committee to give things the
> nod. We go from the premise that we are responsible and we
> are decision-makers and that is our job. We need to report
> to our management committee and be held accountable,
> but people who do not work on the ground do not have the
> vision and the day-to-day knowledge of what is needed.
> That is our decision and our role and we just want to know
> that the management committee has a great deal of trust
> in what we do, and that we are being held accountable as
> decision-makers. We have that freedom. We don't have that
> bureaucratic process of waiting for a nod.[8]

Both Zelda and Diane also speak of the varied skills among the
executive committee's members, and the appreciation they have for
what each contributes to the functioning of the whole.

Zelda and Diane are well aware that one of their challenges as
parents is to encourage their daughters to pursue their work of choice

as they become young adults, and to balance that "letting go" with expectations about how they continue to fulfill their roles in the work of the Chaeli Campaign. As Zelda says, "When they reach a certain age, you have to let them go, and give them limited functions because they are dealing with their own lives." Otherwise, she continues,

> *You run the risk of forcing them to be more involved.*
> *It's a matter of balance and letting them know that you*
> *understand that they are at a point where they are claiming*
> *their own lives. We need to recognize, as moms, that it's okay*
> *for them not to do this and that there are other things they*
> *need to do.*[9]

At the Chaeli Campaign there is a highly coherent consistency among the beliefs, behaviors, and values, and the mission, structure, and ways of working that is, in our experience, almost impossible to find in an organization. The central theme that came up over and over in our visit was the focus on acting autonomously. That theme is reflected in the Campaign's origins: Chaeli's desire for increased freedom and mobility, and the five young girls focusing on a goal and taking its accomplishment into their own hands. It is expressed in the creativity that flowed from their hands when given free reign by their parents to reach a seemingly impossible fund-raising goal. It is evident in how the management, executive, and founding committees function and interact, and how the ambassadors program ensures that the voices of youth will be heard. From this program there will be a steady stream of young people who know who they are and what they care about, with the knowledge and skills to create their own entrepreneurial service to the world.

The deeply held value of autonomy seeded in this program is heard in Zelda's description of her own daughter. "I think what makes me proudest of Chaeli," she says, "is that she is comfortable in her own skin, she knows who she is, and I think, more importantly, she knows what she has to offer to the world around her. She feels that she can make her own way, she has a wonderful contribution to make, and she believes in herself."[10]

Acting Autonomously and Transformation

Increasing the capacity for acting autonomously is clearly a central goal for those who work with people with disabilities, and some researchers claim that it is, perhaps, the most essential goal for all human development. Valery Chirkov of the University of Saskatchewan and Nadezhda Lebedeva of the State University-Higher School of Economics, Moscow, Russia, believe that, "instead of striving for happiness, people should strive for psychological autonomy," and that "autonomy has to be the goal of psychological development, education, social and economical practices and policies." Their thesis is that "maximizing psychological autonomy is the only way to make people feel themselves the agents of their destiny, of their life, and of their authentic happiness." Further, they believe that when people act autonomously,

> *their happiness will inevitably come as a natural by-product of their exercising of the highest and the most powerful capabilities given to them by evolution; awareness/ mindfulness, reflection and rational choice. If we exercise these capabilities in our lives we inevitably become more optimally and fully functioning and, correspondently, more happy individuals.*[11]

According to Chirkov and Lebedeva, people who act autonomously are:

- Aware of their own needs and aspirations and where they come from: they are able to make conscious decisions to pursue them.
- Mindful of potential limitations and expectations: they are able to decide whether to follow, ignore or fight them.
- Discerning about what will make them happy and set their own life goals: they establish their own ethical standards for pursuing what they want.
- Sensitive to the goals and needs of other people and the larger society: they take them into account in the pursuit of their own.[12]

It may be that acting autonomously leads to happiness because it is a way of being in the world that allows us to live from the essence of who we are as human beings. Acting autonomously, according to Mark Piper of Virginia's James Madison University, is about an individual's ability "to reflect critically on their natures, preferences and ends, to locate their most authentic commitments, and to live consistently in accordance with these in the face of various forms of internal and external interference." Those who possess this ability are said

> to possess heightened capacities for self-control, introspection, independence of judgment, and critical reflection; and to this extent personal autonomy is often put forth as an ideal of character or a virtue, the opposite of which is blind conformity, or not "being one's own person."[13]

While the drive toward autonomy is universal, it is not an ideal that can be achieved independent of one's social, cultural, geographic, and economic context, and without consideration for one's internal and external limitations and constraints. This recognition is borne out in the research of Carolyn Ells of the Dalhousie University's Department of Bioethics in Halifax, Nova Scotia. Ells affirms that the capacity for acting autonomously is not achieved in the absence of context and interdependence. In essence, she finds that:

- None of us are "self-contained choosers." We are not capable of making decisions without the influence and support of the world.
- None of us has complete authority over and control of all aspects of ourselves and our lives. All of us need to negotiate our pursuit of desires and goals based on our own situations and relationships.
- All of us experience changes in ourselves and in our circumstances that shift our reasons for action, and our hopes, dreams, expectations, and goals. Changes in circumstances and our life plans impact the degree of autonomy we can achieve.[14]

Currently, an emerging area of research called Self-determination Theory (SDT) is making a new contribution to our understanding of autonomy. The originators of this theoretical approach are Edward Deci, Professor of Psychology at the University of Rochester, and his colleague, Richard Ryan. They identify autonomy as the most significant of three basic human needs, the other two being the need for competence and the need for relatedness, all of which are highly interrelated. The pair has inspired a great deal of research in this area, including that of Valery Chirkov. Daniel Pink, author of the business best-seller, *Drive: The Surprising Truth About What Motivates Us*, focuses heavily on Deci and Ryan's concept of SDT. In an edited excerpt from his book, Pink writes:

> *Autonomy, as they see it, is different from independence. It's not the rugged, go-it-alone, rely-on-nobody individualism of the American cowboy. It means acting with choice—which means we can be both autonomous and happily interdependent with others. And while the idea of independence has national and political reverberations, autonomy appears to be a human concept rather than a Western one. Researchers have found a link between autonomy and overall well-being not only in North America and Western Europe, but in Russia, Turkey, and South Korea. Even in high-poverty non-Western locales like Bangladesh, social scientists have found that autonomy is something that people seek and that improves their lives.*[15]

The capacity for acting autonomously has implications for resolving global issues as well. From their research on human autonomy from a cross-cultural experience, Valery Cirkov and his colleagues believe that it is "a fundamental pre-condition for both individuals and groups to thrive," and that "without understanding the nature and mechanisms of autonomous agency, vital social and human problems cannot be satisfactorily addressed."[16]

Acting Autonomously in the Workplace

While the Chaeli Campaign is a very small organization, and one largely built on relationships among family and friends, it is not alone in fostering the capacity for acting autonomously. Perhaps the best known organization that intentionally and enthusiastically encourages employees to act autonomously is Google. Google grants employees 20% of their time to work on projects of their own choosing, a practice that has resulted in a number of the company's best known offerings, including G-mail. Julie Clow, a former Google employee and author of *The Work Revolution: Freedom and Excellence for All*, tells an interviewer about her first impressions of the company.

> *The first day of work at Google was like a dream. I walked into the brightly decorated office with open floors, and I was led to my workstation outfitted with a huge monitor, a laptop and docking station, ergonomically adjusted chair and desk, a few books of interest, and balloons to celebrate my start. I wore jeans my first day, and it wasn't even a Friday. I indulged in breakfast, lunch, and dinner, the gym, the drinks and snacks in the microkitchen, the warmed toilet seats, and even the medicine cabinet. I marveled that there were so many perks, I could never keep track of them or even fully realize what they had to offer.*
>
> *But it wasn't the perks that fueled my joy. It was the freedom. I could show up when I wanted, and leave at night whenever I needed. I could go for a run on my lunch break and not worry whether it took more than an hour. My manager gave me a great starter project, and she set me free to own it. In those first few weeks, I kept waiting for the email to show up asking me to log my time or report my hours worked. It never happened. Instead, I was evaluated based on the impact I created for Google.[17]*

Clow says that she chose to write her book because

> *when I was treated like a responsible adult at work and empowered to do work in the way that best suited me, I was awakened. I felt like a new person, like I could finally spread my wings and do great work with very few constraints. I want to share this with the world and I want to change the world so that work isn't so terrible for everyone anymore.[18]*

Semco is another organization that has become known globally for what some would call its radical approach to workplace autonomy. The Brazilian conglomerate grew out of a small machine shop started by founder Antonio Curt Semler in 1954. Today, under the highly hands-off guidance of Semler's son, Ricardo, the company produces high-tech mixing equipment and cooling towers for commercial properties, engages in facility management and environmental consulting, and operates a number of high-tech ventures. Ricardo Semler has, to many people, become a bit of a poster child for leading a successful company where autonomy is valued more than almost anything else. Semler has written two best-selling books that describe how the operation functions, including *Maverick: The Success Story Behind the World's Most Unusual Workplace* in 1995 (which has been translated into 33 languages), and *The Seven Day Weekend: Changing the Way Work Works* in 2004.

Semler grew up with the expectation that he would take over the reins of the company one day, even though that prospect became increasingly distasteful as the time for his father to retire approached. He did take over, however, when his father agreed to give him the freedom to make over the company as he saw fit. He did just that, immediately firing most of his father's senior managers, although he is unlikely to take credit for the organization's subsequent success. In describing how the company is organized, Semler writes:

> *Semco has no official structure. It has no organizational chart. There's no business plan or company strategy, no two-year or five-year plan, no goal or mission statement, no long-term budget. The company often does not have a fixed CEO. There are no vice presidents or chief officers for information technology or operations. There are no standards or practices. There's no human resources department. There are no career plans, no job descriptions or employee contracts. No one approves reports or expense accounts. Supervision or monitoring of workers is rare indeed.*[19]

To Semler,

On-the-job democracy isn't just a lofty concept but a better, more profitable way to do things. We all demand democracy in every other aspect of our lives and culture. People are considered adults in their private lives, at the bank, at their children's schools, with family and among friends—so why are they suddenly treated like adolescents at work? Why can't workers be involved in choosing their own leaders? Why shouldn't they manage themselves? Why can't they speak up— challenge, question, share information openly?[20]

One of the more interesting ideas implemented at Semco is the Retire-A-Little initiative. The program gives employees who have been with the company more than two years the freedom to exchange one day a week to pursue the passions they might otherwise leave until their retirement years, for time given back after they reach retirement age. According to Semler,

the program borrows time for the future so employees can live a more fulfilled life while they are younger and healthier. In exchange, they can give that time back to the organization after they retire—an added benefit that allows the organization to take their wisdom while allowing retirees to continue contributing and participating.[21]

Somewhat to the surprise of the company, most people have chosen to use their time for personal growth and development, rather than adventure or leisure.

In "First, Let's Fire All The Managers," a 2011 *Harvard Business Review* article, noted business writer Gary Hamel asks the reader to ponder the possibility of an organization where

no one has a boss; employees negotiate responsibilities with their peers; everyone can spend the company's money; each individual is responsible for acquiring the tools needed to do his or her work; there are no titles and no promotions; and, compensation decisions are peer-based.[22]

His query is a prelude to the story of the Morning Star Company of Woodland, California, the world's largest tomato processor. The company, founded by Chris Rufer when he was an MBA student at UCLA, has a set of practices that Hamel says is "one of the most delightfully unusual companies" he has ever come across (and he has seen a lot of companies in his career). According to Hamel, Morning Star employees (called colleagues), "are ridiculously empowered yet work together like members of a carefully choreographed dance troupe."[23]

That level of autonomy comes from company practices at Morning Star, which include (a) the requirement that every employee write a personal mission statement outlining how he or she will contribute to the company's goals, and (b) negotiating a "Colleague Letter of Understanding" or CLOU with other relevant employees that defines their voluntary agreements about the work to be done, and how their performance will be measured. Other policies allow staff to purchase what they need to get their jobs done, to initiate a hiring process when additional staff are required, and to take the lead in making improvements across operations. Compensation is also established collaboratively based on the CLOU, as Hamel explains.

> At the end of each year, every colleague develops a self-assessment document outlining how he or she performed against CLOU goals, ROI targets, and other metrics. Colleagues then elect a local compensation committee; about eight such bodies are created across the company each year. The committees work to validate self-assessments and uncover contributions that went unreported. After weighing inputs, the committees set individual compensation levels, ensuring that pay aligns with value added.[24]

Hamel's interviews with Morning Star employees suggest that the company's business model produces greater initiative, expertise, flexibility, collegiality, and loyalty, and leads to better decision-making and judgment. None of this is surprising to Chris Rufer, who shared with Hamel his belief that, "If people are free, they will be drawn to what they really like as opposed to being pushed toward what they have been told to like. So they will personally do better; they'll be more enthused to do things."[25]

Rufer would not agree with the "fire all the managers" theme of the article, however, as he believes that his organization is "manager rich." As he sees it,

> *The job of managing includes planning, organizing, directing, staffing, and controlling, and everyone at Morning Star is expected to do all these things. Everyone is a manager of their own mission. They are managers of the agreements they make with colleagues, they are managers of the resources they need to get the job done, and they are managers who hold their colleagues accountable.*[26]

Another approach to a more autonomous workplace that appears to be gaining followers is called "results-only work environment," or ROWE. ROWE is an initiative that began at Best Buy as the brainchild of employees Jody Thompson and Cali Ressler. ROWE is now being embraced by companies that are using the pair's consulting services to try the approach in their own organizations. The approach is based on a simple idea: given the opportunity to choose when and how their work is accomplished, most people will not only get the work done, but they will be happier, more loyal, more satisfied with their work, and more committed to the organization. Research by University of Minnesota sociology professors Erin Kelly and Phyllis Moen has now provided evidence that this has, indeed, been the case at Best Buy. Their study, based on over 600 employees, found that participants reported "an increased sense of schedule control and a reduction in work-family conflict which, in turn, improved their sleep quality, energy levels, self-reported health, and sense of personal mastery while decreasing their emotional exhaustion and psychological distress." The company also benefitted, reducing "turnover by 45 percent—after controlling for multiple factors like job level, organizational tenure, job satisfaction, income adequacy, job security, and other turnover intentions."[27]

Fostering Autonomy in the Workplace

The principles and practices highlighted in this chapter are based on deeply held beliefs and assumptions about people. The managers and leaders who foster them in their workplaces are secure enough in themselves and trusting enough in others to be able to let go of the traditional top-down, command- and-control mentality that is so prevalent in organizations today. Thus, the first step managers and leaders must take to increase the autonomous functioning of leaders and teams in their organizations is self-reflection and self-examination. Managers and leaders should aim toward becoming more conscious, more able to appreciate the inherent goodness and competence in the people around them, more able to recognize the value in experimentation and learning from mistakes, and more able to move from a "power over" to a "power with" people orientation. Once that shift in consciousness occurs, the many available models and methods appropriate to the organization can be identified and put into practice.

The capacity for acting autonomously is an ability that enriches our personal and professional lives. Autonomy also serves organizations that support its development through employees who have passion for their work, loyalty to the organization, and commitment to its mission. Moreover, autonomous employees tend to be

- self-aware,
- goal-oriented,
- persistent,
- confident in their own abilities,
- flexible,
- reflective,
- sensitive to the needs of others,
- collegial, and
- mindful of reasonable constraints.

Autonomous employees show more initiative and make better decisions, in addition to being happier and more enthusiastic. People who act autonomously use their intrinsic motivation to exercise creativity and bring their best selves to the workplace. They know how to work collaboratively with others, how to make best use of the resources available, and how to ask for help when they need it. Their organizations are able to rely on them to live up to well-understood expectations, and to go beyond expectations when the situation requires innovation and imagination. It is difficult to imagine an organization that can function successfully in these times without people who are in possession of these values and capacities.

OTHERNESS

If we are too busy, if we are carried away every day by our projects, our uncertainty, our craving, how can we have the time to stop and look deeply into the situation—our own situation, the situation of our beloved one, the situation of our family and of our community, and the situation of our nation and of the other nations?[1]

— THICH NHAT HANH

In the attitude of silence the soul finds the path in a clearer light, and what is elusive and deceptive resolves itself into crystal clearness.[2]

— MAHATMA GANDHI

FIVE

PRACTICING INNER REFLECTION

The Story of the Brahma Kumaris

Traveling from London to the Brahma Kumaris (BK) World Spiritual University's Global Retreat Centre in Oxford, England with Sister Jayanti Kirpalani was an opportunity to reconnect with her, as well as with Neville Hodgkinson, both of whom we first met while attending a conference at the BK's global headquarters in Rajhastan, India, in 1987. We were aware that our interviews with Sister Jayanti and Neville were a privileged opportunity. We wanted to refresh and deepen our understanding of their organization's remarkable history, its leadership, and its approach to elevating the consciousness of its members, students, and others who have chosen to develop a reflective spiritual practice under their guidance.

BK had its humble beginnings in 1936, when a small number of people became followers of wealthy Indian jeweler Dada Lekhraj after he experienced visions related to the nature of the soul. Since then, the Brahma Kumaris organization has grown into an influential spiritual movement through which millions of people study and practice meditation in over 8,500 centers in more than 100 countries around the world. The organization's headquarters is located in an impressive campus called Madhuban (meaning "Forest of Honey") in the Aravali Mountains of Rajasthan, India. It serves as a center for retreats, conferences, and the teaching of the BK approach to Raja Yoga. Along with two other nearby campuses, Madhuban attracts over 2.5 million students and visitors every year from all ethnic and religious backgrounds. Madhuban was the site of our own first dedicated experience with meditation and protracted silence, when we attended a global peace conference at the invitation of a dear friend and spiritual mentor, Rita Cleary.

As we sat down to interview Sister Jayanti in her sitting room at the BK's London headquarters, we were reminded of our experience with her many years ago at Madhuban. Sister Jayanti is an example of a human being who exudes a completely loving, peaceful, and spiritually focused way of being in the world. She is also a well-educated and well-traveled woman of the world, who serves as the BK's European Director, coordinating the university's activities in more than eighty countries. She also represents the BK's consultative status with the Economic and Social Council of the United Nations in Geneva. Together with Dr. Peter Senge, she is a co-chair of the Call of the Time Dialogues, which brings together world leaders in dialogue about the spiritual dimension of current crises. Sister Jayanti has also been deeply involved in initiatives around the world related to her lifelong dedication to the empowerment of women. The BKs are themselves a fascinating study in women's empowerment, given that nearly all of the organization's leaders are female, including the current administrative head of the organization, Sister Dadi Janki, who took over that role several years ago at the age of 92!

During our conversation we were reminded that the BKs are far from being an unapproachable and esoteric religious sect, but rather an organization that is deeply engaged in practical and innovative initiatives around the globe. Among other things, the BKs operate a number of hospitals in India that serve needy populations free of charge, and are conducting ground-breaking research in spiritual approaches to healthcare. The environment is also an area of deep involvement for the BKs, through which the organization researches, builds, and uses alternative sources of power in their operations. The BKs are now India's single largest user of solar energy, and are undertaking a remarkable project called India-One, which will feature construction of a 1-megawatt solar thermal power plant that will generate enough heat and power for the campus of 20,000 people.[3]

On a smaller scale, the BKs have adopted nearly twenty gardens in and around the city of Mumbai, transforming them into peace parks. In the 1990s, we were privileged to play a small part in an inspiring initiative called "Global Cooperation for a Better World," a project in cooperation with the United Nations through which people in 129 countries were asked to share their visions of a better world. These visions, offered by "princes and prime ministers, aboriginal elders in central Australia, shoe-shine boys in Brazil, and lepers in the Philippines,"[4] were presented to the UN in New York City in the book *Visions of a Better World*.

The primary work of the Brahma Kumaris is to play a role in elevating the consciousness of people around the world through its educational programs and the teaching of Raja Yoga. To Sister Jayanti, this work is critical for our times. "People recognize," she noted, "that the problems of today's world cannot be solved just on the level of action and physical resources, such as people or technology or money or information, but they need a different way of seeing, of perceiving, a different attitude, a different consciousness." She went on to share what is perhaps the simplest explanation of the BK perspective on how the inner life impacts the outer world.

> *Whatever is my attitude or what I carry in myself is going to determine my awareness. And whatever is my awareness is going to determine the way in which I see something, my vision, my perception. And accordingly, our perceptions determine the quality of our actions. The quality of our action is the world we create.*[5]

This is what the BKs refer to as the "spiritual trajectory." Through this process, Sister Jayanti concluded, "You become aware and you see what it is you need to do as a human being, in order to be able to contribute in a more positive way to all the things that are going on around you and in you."[6]

This view was reinforced by Neville Hodgkinson when we had the opportunity to reconnect with him at the BKs' Global Retreat Centre in Oxford, England. The Centre is an extraordinarily beautiful mid-eighteenth century villa built on 55 acres overlooking the banks of the Thames River south of Oxford. When we first met Neville at Madhuban during the 1987 BK retreat, he was serving as the medical correspondent for the *Sunday Times* of London. Little did he know at the time that he would eventually leave life as he knew it to join the BKs on a full-time basis. Today he lectures, writes, chairs the Janki Foundation for Global Health Care—a UK-registered charity supporting research and awareness in the field of health and spirituality—and fulfills other responsibilities for the BKs. When we met at Oxford, he was helping to organize the Spirit of Humanity forum, a 2012 global gathering in Reykjavik, Iceland. The purpose of the forum was to create a kind of "spiritual Davos," at which leaders from around the world would "explore the role of higher human values and spirituality in empowering effective decision making at personal, community, national, and international levels."[7]

Neville first encountered the BKs in the early 1980s while writing his book, *Will To Be Well: The Real Alternative Medicine,* and has been a practitioner of inner reflection ever since. In a 2005 conversation with *The Oxford Muse*, Neville explained the role that inner reflection has played in his own life.

> *I have learned that through the practice of turning inside*
> *you can connect to a place of silence that fills you with more*
> *of a sense of peace about the way events flow. This is more*
> *than just a faith that feels comfortable. You develop a deep*
> *sense that there is a reason for everything that happens,*
> *and that we can make a difference, but that the best way*
> *to make that difference is to move with the flow peacefully.*
> *This enables you to be more attuned to signals that come*
> *about what is the right thing to do at the right time. If you*
> *are distracted by too much noise, internal or external,*
> *whilst trying to right wrongs it is as if you cannot pick up*
> *the delicate signals that nature or God, however you like to*
> *look at it, are trying to give about what is really needed. The*
> *ego comes in, and messes things up.[8]*

This excerpt from Neville's article, "The Sound of Silence," further explains this Brahma Kumaris perspective:

You are what you think.

Patterns of thought we create have an impact on us physically. They say that you are what you eat, but a much more powerful understanding is that you are what you think. If you habitually think in anxious ways, angry ways, frustrated ways, feeling cheated ways, those kinds of feelings actually start to imprint themselves on your being, and you become a person who is rather like that.

The understanding within the teachings of the Brahma Kumaris is that this is not the natural state of human beings. The natural state is to be tranquil, loving, peaceful, and positive. From this position of strength, we can act in natural ways, but in today's world, cultural, emotional, and commercial pressures encourage us to become peaceless. In fact, we get so caught up in this peacelessness that sometimes there is a nervousness about letting the noise stop, because we realise that we are not actually in control of our mind. So, we may fill every little space in our lives with noise and stimulus in order to avoid facing up to the fact that we've lost control and we can't actually be truly still inside.

It works the other way round too.

If you habitually are experiencing thoughts of peace, strength, hope, confidence, then you become a person with that kind of positive power inside you. This is an amazing revelation, because it means that we can really change our characters if we feel the need to do that. Many of us don't, many of us are pushed to our limits and beyond with the challenges that life offers us these days. In a way, it's a good thing, because it's forcing us to realise that we've lost what is most human about us, our ability to choose how to be.[9]

Inner Reflection and Transformation

Jack Mezirow is the recognized founder of transformative learning theory, and Emeritus Professor of Adult and Continuing Education at Teachers College, Columbia University. Inner reflection, he says, is the very essence of the process through which we understand ourselves, shift our "habits of the mind," and change our way of being in the world over time.[10]

Lacking the capacity for practicing inner reflection severely inhibits our ability to develop into high functioning, fully conscious human beings. This concept, according to Professors Victor C. Wang and Kathleen King, is as old as Confucius. In comparing the wisdom of Confucius' teachings from twenty-five centuries ago in China with the transformational learning theory of Jack Mezirow, they note that Confucius "prescribed 'self-realization' as the ultimate goal of every learner." To Confucius, they write,

> *learning is both much more than the acquisition of empirical knowledge and more than another method of internalizing the proper manner of behavior in society. Confucius' definition of learning focuses on the cultivation of the* **inner experience** *so that learners can deepen their knowledge about how to be human and transform their lives into meaningful existences. As for critical reflection, Confucius describes it as follows: "to learn without silent reflection is labor in vain; to think without learning is desolation."*

They summarize Confucian beliefs in these three points:

- Learning results from reflection.
- Those who are incapable of reflection are less capable of learning.
- Hence, growth and development cannot emerge.[11]

In modern times, inner reflection can play another significant role in our lives: as a powerful means through which we are able to deal with the hardships that come our way. In general, the testimony of many who claim that meditation, yoga, mindfulness training, and other forms of inner reflection benefit employees as well as workplaces is borne out in research. One of the earliest researchers in the practice of mindfulness is Jon Kabat-Zinn, who is the founder of the Center for Mindfulness in Medicine, Health Care, and Society at the University of Massachusetts Medical School, and of the school's Stress Reduction Clinic. From its beginnings in 1979, over 18,000 people have taken part in the clinic's famed eight-week Mindfulness-Based Stress Reduction Program (MBSR), whose research-based results include

> *lasting decreases in physical and psychological symptoms, increased ability to relax, reductions in pain levels and an enhanced ability to cope with pain that may not go away, greater energy and enthusiasm for life, improved self-esteem, and an ability to cope more effectively with both short and long-term stressful situations.*[12]

The Clinic claims that

> *Restoring within yourself a balanced sense of health and well being requires increased awareness of all aspects of self, including body and mind, heart and soul. Mindfulness-based stress reduction is intended to ignite this inner capacity and infuse your life with awareness.*[13]

These results have enormous implications for healthcare costs as well. According to the Centers for Disease Control and Prevention in the US, depression is estimated to cause 200 million lost workdays each year at a cost to employers of $17 billion to $44 billion.[14] According to IMS Healthy, at least 27 million Americans take antidepressants and more than 164 million prescriptions for antidepressants were written in 2008, totaling nearly $10 billion in U.S. sales, and $20 billion globally.[15] Moreover, according to the National Institute for Occupational Safety & Health, all stress-related ailments cost companies about $200 billion a year in increased absenteeism, tardiness, and the loss of talented workers (Der Hovanesian 2003).[16]

Mindfulness therapies may well reduce those costs dramatically. One recent study conducted at the Centre for Addiction and Mental Health in Toronto, Ontario, and published in the *Archives of General Psychiatry*, compared the results of patients with depression who took antidepressant medications, and those who participated in mindfulness therapy. Their finding that those who practiced meditation fared just as well as those who medicated could have far-reaching effects on both the suffering and costs of treating those with depression.[17]

Another research approach has focused on what is called "loving kindness meditation" and its impact on positive emotions. Loving kindness meditation is generally related to the Buddhist tradition of wishing happiness for oneself and others, including all sentient and non-sentient beings. This form of meditation has been popularized by Sharon Salzburg, teacher and author of a number of books on the topic, including *Lovingkindness: The Revolutionary Art of Happiness*. The methodology has been widely used and extensively researched. Barbara Fredrickson, Professor at the University of North Carolina at Chapel Hill and author of *Positivity*, is a leading researcher in the field of positive psychology, and has become known for her "broaden and build" theory of positive emotions evoked from loving kindness meditation. As Fredrickson notes,

> *I've encapsulated two classes of these benefits into my broaden-and-build theory. First, when we experience a positive emotion, our vision literally expands, allowing us to make creative connections, see our oneness with others, and face our problems with clear eyes (a.k.a. the broaden effect). Second, as we make a habit of seeking out these pleasing states, we change and grow, becoming better versions of ourselves, developing the tools we need to make the most out of life (the build effect).*[18]
>
> *Put simply, the broaden-and-build theory states that positive emotions widen people's outlooks in ways that, little by little, reshape who they are.*[19]

Inner Reflection in the Workplace

The Brahma Kumaris and other organizations with a spiritual mission are not the only ones convinced that better leadership, performance, and decision-making come from the practices of inner reflection. In the article "Spirituality and Ethics in Business," Corinne McLaughlin, Executive Director of the Center for Visionary Leadership, notes that companies such as Medtronic, Apple, Google, Yahoo, McKinsey, IBM, Hughes Aircraft, Cisco, Raytheon, and others offer meditation classes. Apple, Avaya, Prentice-Hall, and Sounds True in Colorado (among others) have meditation rooms and encourage employees to take time during the day for silence and inner reflectio8.[20] Michael Carroll's book, *The Mindful Leader*, mentions a number of other companies that provide training programs in mindfulness, including Raytheon, Procter & Gamble, Monsanto, General Mills, Comcast, Bose, New Balance, Unilever, and Nortel Networks.[21]

The Tower Companies of Rockville, Maryland, a large and highly successful organization, has enthusiastically embraced another well-known form of meditation, Transcendental Meditation (TM), as its technique of choice for inner reflection, as well as funding independent research as to its efficacy. Tower is a three-generation, award winning, family-owned real estate development company, the largest Green Developer in the Washington, DC area, and one of the largest purchasers of Green Energy in the country, buying 100% wind energy for their electrical energy needs. The Tower Companies is one of only thirteen carbon-neutral companies in the U.S.[22]

Tower's mission is "to create eco-progressive spaces that transcend traditional approaches to the built environment, teach people how to engage with their surroundings, promote the balance of body and mind, optimize human achievement, and treat the planet with respect." The company builds office buildings, apartment buildings, office parks, shopping centers, hotels, and industrial complexes. Among its accomplishments is the design and building of Tower Oaks, a 200,000 square foot LEED Platinum certified office building based on "Vedic Architecture" principles that are thousands of years old. Partner and grandson of the founder, Jeffrey Abramson, explained in a recent article that Vedic Architecture is "architecture in accord with natural law" that espouses over 100 design principles including the building's siting on the land, the orientation of its entrance, and where its center point is located. What Abramson has to say about the importance of principle-based architecture reflects his values regarding human peacefulness and well-being.

> Buildings affect people. And if buildings can affect people, they can affect their behavior, their outcomes, and their success. Buildings can elevate life and if you can figure out those architectural principles that can uphold the life of the occupant, make them more successful, brighter, and smarter, it can be very useful. The built environment can enhance productivity of the company and collectively this is going to have huge ramifications on the health and economic development of the US, reduce pollution, create new jobs and new technologies. It's not an intellectual concept, it's not like there's a sign that says you are about to experience something. But people come in and say they feel peaceful and energized. It has nothing to do with style, it can be any style the architect chooses.[23]

Initially drawn by scientific research related to Transcendental Meditation, Abramson began his own practice more than thirty-five years ago. He introduced training into the company over a dozen years ago when he came to realize that

> creativity was really a product of the stillness of the mind, the quiet of the mind. The quieter the mind, the more coherent the mind. The more coherent, the more intuitive. The more intuitive, the more flexible. And I thought, "I don't know anyone who couldn't use that."[24]

Since taking part in the program, Tower's staff members report far better health indicators, eating and sleep habits, and are more positive, relaxed, peaceful, focused, energized, clear, optimistic, able to put things in perspective, and to more readily prioritize their work. They say that they simply "work smarter, not harder."[25]

Abramson and his wife Rona, through the Abramson Family Foundation, support independent research on TM. The research includes a two-year randomized controlled study conducted at American University on the effects of the TM technique for improving the health, well-being, and performance of students. This research has been recognized by the Center for Complimentary and Alternative Medicine at the National Institutes of Health for its importance to the healthcare of young adults. They have also funded the implementation of TM programs for students at risk, college students, and other onsite programs.[26]

Fostering Inner Reflection in the Workplace

During our visit with Neville Hodgkinson, he shared a story that speaks to the role leaders can play in modeling a mindful approach in the workplace. When the Brahma Kumari's first acquired their Oxford property and opened the Global Retreat Centre, there were challenges for those who took responsibility to keep the place running smoothly for the 10,000 guests and visitors it serves every year. These newcomers felt somewhat uncertain, insecure, and territorial about their responsibilities. They were almost, in his terms, "little tyrants" in their areas of responsibility. Neville related an instance when he was actually chastised by the heating administrator for turning on the gas fireplace in a chilly room where he was meeting with a group of guests, because he lacked the authority to do so! Over time, however, as the administrators grew in their own dedicated spiritual journeys, they came to serve together in far greater harmony.

Neville attributes this greatly to the guidance of Dadi Janki, the current head of the BKs, who was in those days based in London as the leader of international operations. He recalled that on her visits to the Centre, she would receive complaints from administrators about the performance of colleagues by asking them what they were doing to resolve the situation. She would say,

You are making it worse by being upset like this. Look to yourself. You can improve things externally not by force or demands, but by your example. If you can contribute some quality to the situation, that example is going to be a much more powerful way of getting things right than making people behave according to certain rules that you might set from outside.[27]

According to Neville, "It was because of this constant focus, when there is a friction or a problem that rather than dwelling on the problem, we dwell on how we can reframe our approach to it. It is a very powerful approach to addressing problems and, in time, surmounting them."[28]

The BKs have another simple practice that could readily be adopted by individuals, departments, or entire organizations. It is the global initiative called "Just-A-Minute," which is designed to "shift consciousness in our busy, noisy world by introducing regular one-minute pauses and breaks, when individuals can re-connect with their core self, their strengths and their values."[29] This project is based on a traditional pause for one minute every hour at all BK locations, during which music plays and everyone stops what they are doing for a few moments of inner reflection. As Sister Jayanti explained, "Pausing every hour for just a few moments of silence—we call it 'traffic control' to stop the traffic in our minds—is extremely beneficial for peace, for clarity, to be able to know the way forward"[30]

No matter what one's religious convictions, spiritual orientation, or views about such practices as mindfulness, yoga, and meditation, nearly all of us are aware of the increasing deluge of sensory stimulation, particularly the constant noise of both inner and outer chatter. It is little wonder that for many people any planned or accidental encounter with silence can be deeply disconcerting, considering the siege of media, technology, machinery, traffic, and human voices. Quite often, the first experience of silence from the noise of the external world is replaced by the increased noise of very disturbing inner thoughts—thoughts we have been trying to silence by those external stimuli all along.

The absence of silence in our lives, however, is the source of great loss to our individual and collective lives, both in public and in private. On the flip side of that coin, there is much to be gained from deliberately inviting silence into our lives and our workplaces. The practice of inner reflection is of the essence for learning, personal happiness, and professional performance, as well as for an elevated consciousness through which transformation becomes possible.

There are rewards for organizations that provide support and training in inner reflection and mindfulness practices: employees who are more physically and psychologically healthy, more able to relax, more energetic and enthusiastic, and more able to deal with the stresses and strains of daily work life. These employees bring greater self knowledge, self-esteem, and confidence to the workplace, and influence others through positive emotional well-being.

While it is difficult to carve out this time in our lives and in our workplaces, ingenuity can play a role. It is claimed by one of the biographers of James D. Newton that the great inventor Thomas Edison sometimes fished without bait on his hook. Edison, he wrote, "was not interested in catching fish; he was after time to think. As he sat at the end of his dock with a line in the water, no one (and no fish) would bother him." (*Uncommon Friends* 1989).[31]

Everybody needs beauty as well as bread, places to play in and pray in, where nature may heal and give strength to body and soul.[1]

— JOHN MUIR

Looking for and enjoying beauty is a way to nourish the soul. The universe is in the habit of making beauty. There are flowers and songs, snowflakes and smiles, acts of great courage, laughter between friends, a job well done, the smell of fresh-baked bread. Beauty is everywhere.[2]

— MATTHEW FOX

Is it possible for business leaders to realise that the dilemmas they are facing cannot be solved by their traditional management behaviour, their traditional management tools? And that they are going to need to dwell in the deep domain of human experience and things like faith, courage, friendship, love, compassion, all of those emotions, grief, loss, which are only expressed in the arts.[3]

— MARGARET WHEATLEY

SIX

APPRECIATING BEAUTY

The Story of Oleana

In honor of their company's fifth anniversary in September 1997, the co-founders of Norwegian knitwear maker Oleana, Signe Aarhus and Kolbjorn Valestrand, rented out the famed Grieg Hall in Bergen for a performance that would celebrate the renewal of traditional Norwegian culture and design. At the time, they had only fifteen employees in their small factory in Espeland, but they managed to secure the hall and fill all 1,500 seats for the extravaganza. With some minimal funding from a Norwegian culture-related export program, they brought together the country's finest musicians, dancers, and choreographers on one stage, along with a fashion show featuring their knitwear. To Signe and Kolbjorn the scale of the event was a tribute to the grand visions of their namesake, Norway's world-renowned violinist Ole Bull. But it was also a brilliant business strategy. This celebration of beauty, excellent performance, and the power of story (Olean's motto is "the future belongs to the story-tellers") is the driving force for this extraordinary company.

Oleana is Norway's premier textile manufacturer, and the maker of what may be the most stunningly beautiful knitwear in the world. Signe is originally from Norway's capital of Oslo and was educated as a textile engineer in England. Unable to find a position she wanted in a textile industry that was dissolving in Norway, she became a lecturer at the National College of Art and Craft in Bergen, an institution that taught both craft and industry. Kolbjorn's background is in management, marketing, and organizational behavior. Prior to starting Oleana, both Signe and Kolbjorn were division managers in the largest textile mill in Norway, which was bought and sold five times in six years. Signe says both were "squeezed between our own ideas and the ideas of new owners and the new owners over and over again." Kolbjorn adds, "We didn't agree with a great deal of what they were doing, their strategy, and how they treated people."[4]

At the time the pair and their partner, Hildegunn Møster, decided to start Oleana, the textile industry was struggling in Norway as it still is in most Western countries. Mills were closing down and production was moving to low-wage countries around the world. Kolbjorn describes the context for the business start up.

> People said it wasn't possible to have a textile industry in
> Norway. There was also a finance crisis in 1991, so the banks
> were almost bankrupt, and it was difficult to get a loan to
> start the business. Unemployment was also at the highest
> level since the last world war. We decided to start an "ideal
> project," to create jobs, and to show that it was possible to run
> a textile business in Norway. We thought there was a market
> for good design, and that there would always be a market for
> good products. We said our main goal was not to be as rich
> as possible, but to make a beautiful product and to be nice
> with people.[5]

There are many reasons for the success of Oleana, but none is more apparent than the beauty of their knitwear. As one journalist wrote in the Norwegian American Weekly,

> I don't remember when I first saw an Oleana design,
> but I do know that it made me dream. I could imagine
> stepping into the forest scene, emerging into the amazing
> outfit, replacing the woman wearing it, as if I had stepped
> into a fairy tale. Without reading a word about Oleana, I
> knew from their advertising that they exemplified quality,
> uniqueness, and beauty.[6]

Another article about Oleana put it this way:

*White flowers are bursting open on a cobalt blue background
and the waist is slightly cinched with a knitted midsection in
two shades of pink, making this, like all Oleana sweaters, look
like a painting. Oleana is definitely art. Art you can wear.[7]*

In that same article, Signe said, "Good design is not a result of
compromising. It's like art," and goes on to describe one of Oleana's
most valuable relationships, the partnership with their sole designer,
Solveig Hisdal, whose inspiration draws on cultural design traditions
from around the world. Signe explains.

*Countries and cultures have always borrowed from each
other. The silk in the Norwegian folk dresses, the bunads,
was imported, for instance. Solveig has been following the
Silk Road and found inspiration from places as far away
as China. Some of her patterns are inspired by the German
Meissner porcelain, so it's not all that Norwegian.[8]*

The article's author observes,

*Little things like that are what Oleana is all about: subtle but
beautiful details. A button is never just a button—it's pretty, it
has a history. There are patterns on the insides of the sweaters
which can only be seen by the one who wears it, unless she
folds it a bit to reveal it. Though Oleana's designs are inspired
by textiles and patterns from the past they still have a distinct
modern feel, something Michelle Obama has also recognized.
While her husband picked up his Nobel Peace Prize in Oslo,
the First Lady picked up a couple of Oleana sweaters.[9]*

The story of their business strategy is one that Kolbjorn was rightly
proud to share with us during our visit:

*I have been through many theories about human behavior,
and we think it is not so complicated as many people think it
is. We look at people as people. And we think the people want*

to work. Some others think that people have to be controlled all the time, that you have to make control structures because they don't want to work. We say we don't build up structures, we build up people. We are working for a common goal. We have a profit-sharing through which we distribute 30%–40% of profit to all of our employees as a kind of bonus. The rest we put back into the company. It is the same for all of us. There are different wage scales for different jobs, but the bonus is the same for all. It is an important sign that all of us are important to get a jacket out of this house. The people who are planning, sewing, knitting, washing dishes, making coffee, washing the floors, everybody.[10]

Oleana's success is also built on the value of relationship, both internally and externally. "We like to invite our customers here, from Europe and the United States, to see production, to see Bergen, to take a little sight-seeing tour to Hardanger, to serve them food. And we tell about our business philosophy,"[11] says Kolbjorn. Signe adds that they often bring home-baked bread to their visitors, based on an old recipe of her mother's, a gesture that is long remembered. In our interview, Signe also spoke of what may be one of the most remarkable employee development/supplier relations programs we have ever encountered.

We close the factory once a year for a study trip with everybody, sixty people, more or less. We have been visiting many of our suppliers. This year we went to Vienna where we buy quite a few of our buttons from and visited that button-maker. Two reasons: first of all, they get to know us better, and we get to know them better. We get to learn about the country, eat food from where we are going. We have been to Italy to see two of our spinning mills way up in the mountains, the Alps. It is so interesting for people who have this yarn through their hands every day at work. So now they have a picture in their heads of where it is spun, what was important, what did they learn there. It is a way to try to widen their perspective, because it is lots of tedious work in this industry. But we believe if you have a bigger rainbow over the whole thing, it is more interesting, and you understand more. So we have also been to many of the places where Solvieg finds inspiration for her designs, such as Istanbul. We may have lectures before we go about Muslims, for example. Many of the people haven't been in a Muslim country before. It's a small education project, but it's an important education project.[12]

Signe and Kolbjorn have an environmental sensibility that is unique in their industry. Most obviously, they use materials that are entirely renewable, from wool to silk to alpaca. Their entire business strategy is based on consuming fewer, but more beautiful, long-lasting and more meaningful apparel. They say,

People all over the world are becoming more aware of what they buy. By thinking more about the choices we have when we shop, we can share in taking care of our planet. Clothes made from natural fibres, like wool and silk, are good environmental choices. It is becoming more important for us to buy clothing that is produced in a responsible manner. We can no longer accept the humiliating circumstances that many women and children work under in order to produce inexpensive textile products.[13]

Shopping, in Signe's view, "is a political action."[14]

Signe and Kolbjorn believe whole-heartedly that wearing a jacket or sweater as beautiful as those designed and produced by Oleana creates social connections between people. Customers write them letters describing the compliments they receive when wearing an Oleana jacket, and the conversations that are started as a result. One customer wrote that having an Oleana sweater is like having a dog, referring to the similarities in their ability to get a conversation going! "What initially draws one to Norwegian Oleana's sweaters and blankets," wrote one journalist,

is of course visual—with such splendor and colors, how can
it not be?—but wrap yourself in one of those sweaters or tuck
your child into one of the blankets and what you will also be
doing is making a subtle life style choice. By buying Oleana
you'll support women through this company which doesn't
outsource; you'll support a company that will probably help
reduce your carbon footprint. You'll most definitely get loads
of compliments.[15]

Clearly, the appreciation of beauty is a theme that permeates everything about Oleana in:

- the design of its knitwear drawn from the art and design of many cultures,
- the elegant look and feel of the knitwear,
- the extravagant celebrations linking the tradition and renewal of Norwegian culture and the arts,
- the destinations and experiences shared with employees that enhance their appreciation for the history and source of the natural materials they touch every day,
- the harmony that Signe and Kolbjorn seek in relationships with each other and among employees, suppliers, customers and visitors,
- the sense of vision and idealism in their connection with the larger-than-life mythology of their beloved namesake, Ole Bull, and
- the magic of the stories they tell about their adventures in creating an enterprise that leaves a small footprint on the earth and a very large impression on those with whom they interact.

Appreciating Beauty and Transformation

What has beauty and its appreciation to do with the evolution of more conscious human beings? This subject has been studied and explored since Plato and Aristotle. To Plato, to experience beauty was to appreciate the proportion, harmony, and unity in objects, while Aristotle pointed to the elements of order, symmetry, and definiteness. German philosopher Friedrich Schiller believed that beauty connects us to the potential for social harmony, and makes us capable of becoming good citizens, while Hegel believed that art could make us capable of better understanding ourselves.[16] According to Voltaire, "Appreciation is a wonderful thing. It makes what is excellent in others belong to us as well."[17]

According to Denis Dutton, the late philosopher and author of *The Art Instinct*, Darwinian evolution has given humans a "permanent, innate taste for virtuoso displays in the arts," and that, "We find beauty in something done well." Beauty, to Dutton,

> *is a gift handed down from the intelligent skills and rich emotional lives of our most ancient ancestors. Our powerful reaction to images, to the expression of emotion in art, to the beauty of music, to the night sky will be with us and our descendants for as long as the human race exists.*[18]

In Abraham Maslow's later versions of his hierarchy of human needs, the appreciation of beauty—along with the need for continuous learning—falls between the need for self-esteem and self-actualization, and leads to "a feeling of intimacy with nature and everything beautiful."[19] To positive psychologists, including Martin Seligman, the appreciation of beauty and excellence creates connections to the larger universe, and helps to provide meaning in our lives. A Seligman colleague, Ben Dean, writes that

> *Awe is the emotion that most frequently accompanies this strength. Its behavioral manifestations include wide eyes, open mouth, goose bumps, tears, or even a lump in the throat. When we exercise this strength, we feel uplifted. Viewing an artistic masterpiece or reading about a heroic, selfless act in the newspaper does not make us feel small in comparison. Rather, it instills within us a sense of awe and connection to something larger than ourselves.*[20]

This experience of awe and elevation has the power to motivate self-improvement, personal change, altruistic actions, and devotion to others. To integral theorist Ken Wilbur, our capacity to perceive beauty is "a tribute to the existence of perfection."[21]

To Jamshid Gharajedaghi of Interact in Philadelphia, one of our most wise mentors, beauty is essential for the development of individuals, communities, and societies, and covers a far more expansive field than the aesthetics of objects or material goods. It is also the joy and excitement experienced in recreation. Thus, beauty is not only about that which is creative, it is also about the recreative, or that which is experienced for sheer pleasure. To Jamshid's long-time friend and colleague, the late Russell Ackoff, beauty "recreates creators" by providing "the pause that refreshes."[23]

> To sense beauty is to be inspired. To awaken to beauty means to become inwardly active and to be present in the moment. To be touched by beauty is to feel the breath of the spirit in our soul.[22]
>
> — BRONWEN HARALAMBOUS

Appreciating Beauty in the Workplace

Given all that is evoked in human beings by appreciating beauty, it is surprising that it has taken so long for it to be recognized by organizations as a way to inspire their people. Nevertheless, there are now more and more enterprises using the arts as a means of personal and organizational transformation.

One such enterprise is the much-acclaimed Catalyst Project at Unilever. The project was started in 1999 by James Hill, who was then Chairman of the Lever Brothers unit of Unilever when the company was attempting to increase its competitiveness by creating an "Enterprise Culture." It was Hill's idea to use "artists, arts organizations, and the artistic process as a means to solve business problems and explore critical issues." This somewhat radical approach, says Hill, came out of "a sense that our existing efforts were reinforcing the current ways of doing things, not changing them."[24]

Hill and the designers of the project began by investing in a collection of art by British artists, which were chosen by staff and prominently displayed in the company's public spaces. This step provoked a great deal of conversation, in which links were made between art and the design process at Lever Brothers. In another step, a product development unit hired a "poet-in-residence" as a means of spurring creativity. Another dimension of the project, called Live + Direct, employed a team of actors to enact the dysfunction in the company's culture, related to giving and receiving feedback. Live + Direct was also linked to workshops that used artistic themes as metaphors for business issues.

When Lever Brothers merged with Elida Fabergé into Lever Fabergé, the Catalyst Project became the means to create a new culture for both companies, rather than simply trying to meld the two together. As Hill tells the story,

> *Both senior management teams were going into unknown*
> *territory together. Everyone was in the same place outside*
> *their comfort zone. For example, theatrical workshops in the*
> *workplace were very different for all of us. But Catalyst events*
> *(which are open to everybody) compelled the different teams*
> *to mix and network. At the time we had no other relevant*
> *forum for this. I remember Catalyst staging a debate at a*
> *gallery about whether advertising was more potent than art,*
> *and I saw members of staff from both sides of the business*
> *realizing they held common beliefs about this subject. In a*
> *different way, Catalyst would focus on a skills area, such*
> *as writing, and people came together over that because*
> *they wanted to be better writers. This, in turn, became a*
> *signal of our developing culture. Learning will be at its*
> *heart. Of course not every project brought people together*
> *in the anticipated way. Catalyst put up some risky high*

art photographs from the art collection that had everyone demanding they be taken down. We came together to push against Catalyst. That was important.[25]

Shifting the culture at Unilever Ice Cream and Frozen Foods (UICF), where Hill later served as CEO, was a bit more challenging. Given its more conservative orientation, Catalyst interventions, which began by making some fairly radical changes in the physical environment, were greeted with a great deal of skepticism and derision. Gradually, however, Hill says that

people grasped the permission that had been presented and started to transform their own areas, be prouder and more explicit of who they were and what they were working on. This permission point is very important. People began to ask themselves, "if Catalyst is allowed to do this, why can't I?" So now we have an office environment that is much richer in its diversity and people are constantly thinking about how they can move it on yet again.[26]

According to Hill, the award winning project has "helped us develop by drawing on the energy and the creative power of the arts. It is my belief that it has worked, it has speeded up the change process and made people more open minded, helped them embrace creativity."[27]

While the practice is still relatively rare, other organizations and projects that embrace the transformative powers of beauty in their work are chronicled by Ingrid Fetell, a multidisciplinary designer and design researcher at IDEO in New York. Fetell keeps a blog and a book-in-progress called *Aesthetics of Joy*, through which she explores and shares her insights about "the intersection between design and positive emotion."[28]

One project Fetell chronicles is the work of Danish artists Jeroen Koolhaas and Dre Urhahn. Their work together began in 2005 when they were filming a documentary about hip-hop in the favelas, or slums, of Brazil. One of their first projects, in collaboration with local youth, was to paint a gigantic mural (2,000 square meters) featuring a

Japanese tattoo-style fish along a concrete staircase extending up the hill in the Vila Cruzeiro favela, Rio de Janeiro's most notorious slum. When the mural received local and international acclaim, the duo created the Firmeza Foundation to continue the work. The purpose of the foundation is to "support the creation of striking artworks in unexpected places. It collaborates with local people to use art as a tool to inspire, create beauty, combat prejudice, and attract attention."[29]

The Foundation's most recent project in Rio's Santa Marta community, according to the artists,

> *involves employing the inhabitants of a favela to paint their*
> *own houses according to a pre-arranged pattern. It will*
> *turn their community into an artwork of epic scale and*
> *will produce an explosion of color, joyfully radiating into*
> *the world. Visible from the center of Rio, "O Morro" will*
> *draw attention to the city's deplorable social situation, while*
> *instilling pride and joy at the bottom of the social hierarchy.*
> *The project will transform the community into a landmark,*
> *a tourist attraction, and, most of all, an inspirational*
> *monument that assumes a place as an essential part of*
> *Rio's image, alongside the Sugarloaf and the statue of Christ*
> *the Redeemer.*[30]

Local residents learned about a variety of materials, safety measures, and painting techniques, and earned money while participating in the project. The artwork they completed covered 7,000 square meters of the hillside slum, and spanned more than 30 buildings, including houses and the local school. Ingrid Fetell writes that projects like this

> *are a signal that someone cares about a place, that the*
> *condition of that environment matters to someone. Someone*
> *is paying attention to the details. To make something*
> *beautiful is to invest time and energy in it, and these two are*
> *the most valuable, limited resources we have. We perceive*
> *this signal of caring and passion, often unconsciously,*

and we typically follow in kind. We read our landscape for cues about how to treat it, we draw inferences about the inhabitants, and we subtly alter our behavior to maintain this condition—or enhance it. These aesthetic signals often become a discourse of community, a conversation between the denizens of a place that leads, via a subtle form of one-upmanship, to the organic growth and improvement of our favorite places to call home. Alain de Botton has written (I'm paraphrasing here) that one of architecture's purposes is to inspire us to be better people, and I would say the same for any of these urban interventions. We see improvements, and they unconsciously motivate us to improve ourselves.[31]

These examples of fostering beauty in the workplace offer lessons in how creating beautiful (or at least useful) products, services, organizations, and communities, joined with a mission of "being nice with the people," can be a winning strategy for any organization.

Fostering the Appreciation of Beauty

Creating a workspace that makes the appreciation of beauty a central theme is a tall order. Organizations that are not focused on the arts or culture may not have considered the appreciation of beauty to be an important part of their peoples' development. However, almost any organization or community can take a few simple steps to foster the appreciation of beauty in their workplaces, including the enhancement of their physical environment. Open spaces, greenery, natural light, color, artwork, cleanliness, and order can all make the workplace less

> The only reason to employ people in the future will be to benefit from the qualities that raise them above machines, the qualities of inspiration, creativity, imagination, commitment, enterprise and ambition.[32]
>
> — SIR ERNEST HALL

stultifying and more satisfying. Sounds, sights, and smells all impact our senses and help us to feel energetic and productive at work—or lazy and lethargic. The physical environment creates an identity that sends a message to employees as well as to customers, suppliers, visitors, and other stakeholders about the organization's self-image and how it hopes to be seen by others. A beautiful space can let others know that the organization takes pride in what it does and what it offers to others.

Appropriate entertainment and social events can play a role in generating camaraderie and well-being. Field trips, customer visits, attending workshops, conferences, and trade shows can pay off in employees who are more engaged and likely to stay with the organization. As Oleana has demonstrated, work that is tedious need not take place in a tedious culture or environment.

The appreciation of beauty in our lives inspires us to tap into our own creative capacities, and moves us to continually reach for unattainable perfection in what we do. At the same time, it provides deep satisfaction in simply being present to what is. It creates social cohesion and connection by urging us to share our positive experiences with others. It expands our horizons by opening us up to the outer expressions of the creator's inner vision. The appreciation of beauty entertains us, lifts our spirits, and produces joy, excitement, and fun. It helps us to perceive harmony and unity and to see the deep patterns of order in chaos.

In conclusion, we present a story that should give us all pause. In 2007, as the story goes, the *Washington Post* entered into an experiment with violinist Joshua Bell, heralded as "the best classical musician in America." Bell agreed to descend into the L'Enfant Plaza Metro Station in Washington, D.C., carrying his $3.5 million instrument (handcrafted in 1713 by Antonio Stradivari), and there to perform a number of compositions that are known to be among the most difficult in the world. Wondering what might happen, the *Post* did a bit of scenario planning.

> *Their most widely held assumption was that there could*
> *well be a problem with crowd control: In a demographic as*
> *sophisticated as Washington, the thinking went, several people*

would surely recognize Bell. Nervous "what-if" scenarios abounded. As people gathered, what if others stopped just to see what the attraction was? Word would spread through the crowd. Cameras would flash. More people flock to the scene; rush-hour pedestrian traffic backs up; tempers flare; the National Guard is called; tear gas, rubber bullets, etc.[33]

What actually happened? It took six minutes for any passerby to stop and listen even for a moment.

Things never got much better. In the three-quarters of an hour that Joshua Bell played, seven people stopped what they were doing to hang around and take in the performance, at least for a minute. Twenty-seven gave money, most of them on the run—for a total of $32 and change. That leaves the 1,070 people who hurried by, oblivious, many only three feet away, few even turning to look.[34]

Only a couple of people appeared to recognize the quality of the performance, and only one person actually recognized the world-renowned artist. Bell experienced a number of reactions to the scenario, including the humor of it all. Regarding the $32 take, he said, "That's not so bad, considering. That's forty bucks an hour. I could make an okay living doing this, and I wouldn't have to pay an agent."[35]

The *Washington Post* experiment obviously raises many questions, but one seems to stand out for us: "What is it that we miss when we fail to appreciate the beauty in all forms that surrounds us in every moment of every day?" There can be many answers to that question, but one of the most significant is that we fail to be present in our own lives, and aware of our very existence in the larger world.

Work is about a search for daily meaning as well as daily bread, for recognition as well as cash, for astonishment rather than torpor; in short, for a sort of life rather than a Monday through Friday sort of dying.[1]

— STUDS TERKEL

If one wanted to crush and destroy a man entirely, to mete out to him the most terrible punishment . . . all one would have to do would be to make him do work that was completely and utterly devoid of usefulness and meaning.[2]

— FYODOR DOSTOYEVSKY

SEVEN

ENGAGING IN MEANINGFUL WORK

The Story of Nature Air

If ever there was a person who exemplifies a life engaged in meaningful work and creating that possibility for others, it would be Alex Khajavi, CEO and Chairman of the Board of Nature Air Holding Company. When snow in the Midwest delayed our departure from Costa Rica, we had an opportunity to interview a Nature Air executive. This was a last-minute appointment and we had no idea who would be the subject of our interview. But it was Alex Khajavi himself who warmly greeted us and invited us to join him in his conference room for a conversation. We were immediately entranced by the story of his personal journey from his Persian roots to the founding of Nature Air, and the story of what has become the world's first carbon neutral airline.

Mr. Khajavi's career has included a fascinating mix of assignments. After moving to the United States as a young man, he worked for many years on Wall Street, first as an investment advisor, and later as CEO of the Triad Group of companies, where his responsibilities included development projects from Africa to the Middle East. In 1979, he founded Western Architectural Systems, a company that manufactured architectural shading and passive energy devices, and which eventually became Hunter Douglas. In 1990 he founded Naturegate, a San Francisco-based nature tourism consulting group with projects all over Central and South America, including Costa

Rica, a country known for its spectacular beauty and extremely poor transportation infrastructure.

During his tenure as an investment advisor, Mr. Khajavi's passion for preservation compelled him to leave his job in pursuit of a different approach to development. In preparation, he took courses in ancient farming methods including permaculture, and looked for ways that village life, ancient knowledge, and cultural heritage could be preserved. He once explained to the *Beach Times* what heritage had come to mean to him. "Heritage is not just the sites, there's also an invisible heritage . . . clothing, songs, recipes, respect, shyness, mystery, the stories handed down mouth to mouth." He went on to explain his vision—a vision he began to see in the days before eco-tourism was even a word—a kind of low-impact tourism that might be "a good way to bring hard currency into those countries."[3]

Khajavi's vision began to become reality when he and Naturegate consultants working in Costa Rica discovered that Travel Air, a tiny airline founded by two Alaskan bush pilots a decade earlier, was available for purchase. Purchasing Travel Air in August 2001—which only owned a single airplane—was a risky venture at best. Not one to back away from a challenge, however, Mr. Khajavi and his family packed up their belongings and took up permanent residence in Costa Rica. The post-9/11 exit of investors posed a particular challenge, but in less than a decade the company had won the highly esteemed Tourism for Tomorrow award, presented by the World Travel & Tourism Council.

In just over a decade, Nature Air grew from flying under 20,000 passengers a year to 150,000 today, flying 62 routes to 17 destinations in Costa Rica, Panama, and Nicaragua. The airline has grown by more than 35% compounded annually, and is predicted to be one of the fastest growing companies in Latin America. The Nature Group now includes Naturegate, Nature Vacations, a flight school, a travel magazine, and NatureKids, a non-profit educational foundation. The company has become a prize-winning global success story, and a model for sustainable development.

During our conversation, Mr. Khajavi was quick to point out to us that, "We are not in a traditional sense an airline. We are connecting people and trying to create rare experiences for people when they travel. Our pedigree, our background, is in preservation, creation of jobs, and bringing up the GDP's of local communities. That is a belief that goes deep in us as a practice."[4]

One example of that practice is the role that Nature Air plays in the preservation of the Osa Peninsula. The company makes the extraordinary bio-diversity of this area accessible to tourists eager for a rare experience. A recent study by the Center for Responsible Travel describes the Osa this way:

> The Osa Peninsula has been hailed by National Geographic as the most biologically intense place on the planet. It holds scores of rare and endangered plants and animals, including jaguars, puma, ocelot, white-lipped peccaries, tapirs, and harpy eagles, as well as Costa Rica's largest population of the endangered scarlet macaw and Central America's largest population of squirrel monkeys. It is also home to more than 375 species of birds (18 are endemic), 124 species of mammals, 40 species of freshwater fish, approximately 8,000 species of insects, and 117 species of reptiles and amphibians. In a total area of less than one million acres, the Osa contains thirteen distinct tropical ecosystems and, remarkably, hosts two and one-half percent of all the existing flora and fauna species on earth.[5]

Alex Khajavi has had a great passion for this part of the world since he was a very young man, and the Osa is a prime example of the development approach of Nature Air. One major contribution has been the establishment of the company's NatureKids Foundation, which is dedicated to "working with low-income families to develop the tools they need for self-reliant futures." He described the Foundation's programs to interviewer Stefanie Slater.

> One of the things we found out in 2003 was based on a study conducted by the University of Costa Rica—those Costa Ricans that speak English earn on average 40% more than those that

do not. In addition, we are constantly working with our hotel partners and tour operators in the destinations we fly to, and the lack of English proficiency within the destinations was something that both the hotel operators and the community members wanted to improve. Therefore, in 2003 we opened up our first school in a small village outside San Jose, the capital city of Costa Rica. Based on the programs early success in teaching English, we had over 107 graduating students the first year, ranging from 5 years old to 62; we opened a second school in the Osa Peninsula of Costa Rica, one of the most isolated and biologically diverse areas on the planet. Since 2004, this second program has taught over 500 students of all ages. The program helps give people the skills to speak conversational English, which makes finding employment, especially in tourism (hotels, restaurants, tour operators, fishing, transportation, guides, boats, etc.) much easier.[6]

A further contribution to development and preservation is Nature Air's mission of carbon neutrality. In pursuit of that ideal, the company joined forces with Costa Rica's Forestry Financing Program (FONAFIFO). The backbone of Nature Air's program is that for every ounce of carbon emissions produced, the company purchases carbon credits from FONAFIFO. Eighty percent of Nature Air's carbon offsetting contribution is paid directly to landowners, who have voluntarily agreed to conserve their land in exchange for yearly financing. The other 20% goes toward administration, analysis, and auditing of the lands. Through its efforts, the company has compensated for nearly 20,000 tons of carbon dioxide though the protection of more than 500 acres of tropical forests, offsetting more than 6,000 tons of carbon emissions each year.

The approach to travel and tourism taken by Nature Air is in direct contrast to what Mr. Khajavi describes as the dominant industry approach around the world. In that approach,

People come, high rises are built, beaches become accessible. Then the dirt comes, the crowds come. In my life, I always

believed that mass tourism is not the answer to a country's issues. You need to have a tourism in which the money that comes in trickles down very quickly to the people in that country. Too often, they bring in big hotels, where the tickets are sold somewhere else, pilots are paid somewhere else, the plane lease is paid someplace else. People come in and they close the door and they don't even know where they are. There is no touch, there is no idea of the culture. I think that the experiment in Costa Rica is to get the money flowing down to that vendor of fruit that you meet on your walk.[7]

Asked about the rationale for Nature Air's work, he told us,

I believe that the destruction of nature and the problematic issues of preservation are economic. If you do not have a job and if you don't know how to feed your child, then you are going to cut a tree and sell it. You will take protein out of the jungle in the shape of poaching. So we set out to say that if we can bring up the level of earnings of people in the field, people in these very hot bio-diversity areas, then we could help to preserve the land. I am against buying huge pieces of property, maybe even by NGO's—some famous ones—and saying I am saving something. I am not saving anything. You are just putting something away that some people are using for their living. They are not allowed to live in it any more. You have created a problem that is going to be there. So, we started doing lodges and small hotels to create jobs, and, at the same time, to do other businesses like fishing or growing vegetables, and to train them to be able to do these businesses themselves.[8]

As one would expect, those who work for Nature Air are not simply pilots, cleaners, baggage handlers, accountants, ticket agents, or teachers. They are a vital part of something much larger than themselves or their individual roles in the company. As Nature Air's Chief Operating Officer, Robert Kopper, told us during our visit,

It's the team! I love the people here. During the high week of Christmas, for example, it's all hands on deck. We have to double our capacity in terms of transporting passengers. We go up to 700–750 passengers a day and the turnaround of the aircraft is fifteen minutes. They see me jumping into one of the aircraft, taking a broom, cleaning the aircraft, putting the seat belts away, putting the little bags on the back rests, putting extra bags in there. It's the team that makes it all happen.

The individual's initiative is one of the key factors. It's not what are my ideas, what are Alex Khajavi's ideas, and how do we permeate that down into the organization. It is how each individual person or team member will come up with an idea to make the system even leaner, even better, more efficient. How do we make the repair systems better, how do we keep the windows cleaner, how do we keep the aircraft smelling nicer. That isn't something that I can come up with. It is people that are on the line all the time.[9]

For Alex Khajavi—ever the visionary optimist—the people, the purpose, and the prospect of prosperity and peace continue to drive him well past the time many would consider retiring. "We are in the right position in this country," he says, "to be the crucible for the changes that the rest of the world is looking for. We cannot let it fail. We need to get everyone on our side to make this small experiment in something very radical but very necessary, to work. We need to be an example to the rest of the world."[10]

Meaningful Work and Transformation

The concept of meaningful work has been much studied by social, political, and economic scientists over the years. Currently, there appears to be general consensus about its constituent parts. Michael Steger, PhD, a prominent researcher and faculty member at Colorado State University, points to three "central components" of meaningful work. "First," he writes,

Your vocation is where your greatest passion meets the world's greatest need.[11]

— FREDERICK BUECHNER

the work we do must make sense; we must know what's being asked of us and be able to identify the personal or organizational resources we need to do our job. Second, the work we do must have a point; we must be able to see how the little tasks we engage in build, brick-by-brick if you will, into an important part of the purpose of our company. Finally, the work that we do must benefit some greater good; we must be able to see how our toil helps others, whether that's saving the planet, saving a life, or making our co-workers' jobs easier so that they can go home and really be available for their families and friends. A growing body of evidence shows that meaningful workers are happy workers, more committed workers, and, in some tantalizing ways, better workers.[12]

Steger, whose research focuses on the "foundations and benefits of living a meaningful life," explains that

Humans appear to have a strong desire to be able to understand their experiences, gain some clarity about their own identity, and identify some sense of purpose in their lives. In other words, people want to know what their lives are all about and how they fit into the grand scheme of things and the world around them. When we talk about meaning in life, we are talking about knowing these things. Meaning in life refers to the feeling that people have that their lives and experiences make sense and matter.[13]

Further, he says, "People who feel this way, who have a sense of meaning in life, also report feeling more happy, more satisfied with their lives, less depressed and anxious, and more satisfied with their jobs." In his research, those who "feel like they've found an occupational path infused with a sense of higher purpose and spiritual calling report more well-being and more investment in their career development."[14]

In his study "Work as Meaning: Individual and Organizational Benefits of Engaging in Meaningful Work," Steger and colleague Bryan Dik report:

> *Providing people with a clear understanding of their unique role in fulfilling the purpose of their organization automatically connects them with the interests of something greater than themselves. First, we contend that as people deepen their understanding of who they are as workers, what their organization is about, and how they uniquely fit within and contribute to their organization, they will develop a sense of comprehension about themselves as workers that will generate a purpose for their work. As they work toward a purpose in their work—whether self-generated or fostered by clear leadership from their organization—they will feel a sense of transcendence that encourages their identification with their organization and its mission. Thus, organizational purpose would seem to drive transcendence. As people are drawn out into their organization, they are more likely to be drawn out into their broader social contexts, increasing the chances that they will develop the desire to have their work serve the greater social good.*
>
> *Second, employees driven by a sense of self-transcendence (i.e., who are working to address salient social needs) will desire to use their organization as a source of support and a facilitator of that work. Successfully working toward a greater social good will deepen comprehension about self, organization, and organizational fit, and thus transcendence would seem to deepen both comprehension and sense of purpose. Similarly, transcendence also will drive employee commitment to an organization's purpose. Organizations, therefore, can encourage employees who are not initially inclined toward considering interests beyond*

*their own to develop increasing levels of transcendence,
and also to encourage employees already attuned to
transcendence to commit to the organization's purpose.
Thus, viewing work as meaning is expected to benefit both
employees who hold such views and the organizations they
work for.[15]*

Some philosophers go beyond the concept of meaningful work to address work that can actually be a calling or vocation. Matthew Fox, author of the fascinating book, *The Reinvention of Work*, distinguishes between a job that produces a paycheck, and work or vocational calling. In an interview, he spoke to the difference. "Jobs are legitimate, at times, but work is why we are here in the universe. Work and calling often go together. Work is something we feel called to do, it is that which speaks to our hearts in terms of joy and commitment."[16] Further,

*Work also connects us to the universe. If we thought less
anthropomorphically, we would realize that our whole
universe is at work. There is an ancient affinity between the
great work and our daily lives. The great work is the work of
the universe, it is the unfolding of creation. Somehow, our
work, our daily life, should contribute to that. We should
feel that we are connected to the great work of the universe.
Without that, we lose meaning in our work and the only
meaning is a paycheck.[17]*

Fox goes on to describe the kind of deep personal questioning that can lead to meaningful work. "Why," he asks, "are you here?"

*It has taken fifteen billion years to get you here. That is
scientific fact. We are not just the products of our parents.
Sixty percent of our body is hydrogen atoms. The hydrogen
atoms in us go back to the fireball fourteen billion years
ago. We have been around a long time, and it has been a
great birthing process to bring us forward. So you have to
presume there is some reason for being here, other than
going shopping. We have to probe that reason. What are*

*our talents? What is the pain in the world that speaks to us
that we want to respond to? What gifts do we have, whether
material goods or power to influence? What gifts do we have
to make a difference?[18]*

This is the kind of "self-transcendance" of which researcher Michael Steger speaks, and a way of being in the world through which we are able to embrace an ever larger sense of identity by becoming more aware of who we are in the larger scheme of things. Recalling Richard Barrett's words in our chapter on "Work That Transforms," being engaged in meaningful work offers us

*an increasing sense of connectedness to the world that shows
up as an expanded sense of identity. We feel a sense of oneness
with ourselves, with our family, with our community, with the
organization we work for, with our nation, with humanity
and the planet, and eventually with the whole of creation.[19]*

Meaning in the Workplace

The phenomenal growth of social entrepreneurship all over the world is a prime example of finding and meeting the world's great need with an individual's unique gifts and talents. Some believe that this on-the-ground approach to solving the world's "big problems" leads to a spirit-fulfilling way of being, and is the only way that these problems can be solved. One such believer is Pooja Warier, co-founder and Director of UnLtd India, an organization in Mumbai that provides incubator support and collaborative space for early-stage entrepreneurs. During our visit with Pooja at the Hub, the organization's laboratory and co-working space, she shared with us her personal belief that "the world is not going to change because of nonprofits or the government. It's going to change when each one of us takes action about stuff we care about, and when we stop expecting that someone else will come and solve it." She goes on to say that "viewing a problem from a different lens shifts something within you. And it remains within you throughout your entire life, because you'll never see the problem as a passive person again."[20]

UnLtd India is modeled after UnLtd London, where Pooja once worked, and functions in a mode similar to many support organizations around the world. Pooja, her co-founder Robert Alderson, and her team help potential entrepreneurs with good ideas to

- focus their attention on effective action,
- act as a sounding board,
- offer encouragement and feedback,
- provide access to resources and seed-funding,
- provide training and coaching, and
- facilitate connections with investors and mentors.

Through their co-working and incubation space, they offer affordable rentals and equipment, as well as the social support of a community of peers and fellow adventurers. While the offerings of UnLtd India are quite similar to other such providers, their uniqueness is in the "investees" they seek out and support. Their niche is working with those in the first three years of their project lifecycle, typically before any legal enterprise has been established, and well before they are able to attract investors who generally look for an already established track record of success.

The ideas that potential entrepreneurs bring to UnLtd India run the gamut of Mumbai's monumental social problems and issues. One young group of investees, Raj Janagam, Jyotika Bhatia, and Jui Gangan, sought out the services of UnLtd India in order to develop Cycle Chaloa, a subscription-based bicycle sharing business. The business focuses on the transportation needs of nearly 9 million Indians who commute from the countryside via train. These commuters need to secure transportation to their job sites, which can be a significant distance away in the most congested traffic city in the world. Another entrepreneur, Vijaya Pastala, founded an organization called Under the Mango Tree that connects reliable suppliers of high quality organic foods to urban markets. As she explored the problem, she focused on the need for small beekeepers to bring their indigenous varieties of honey to market. Since implementing the organization's "Bees for Poverty Reduction" strategy, the company has moved from sourcing honey to providing beekeeping training, capacity-building, and ensuring market access to nearly 3,000 farmers across six states, impacting more than 15,000 rural lives. Working primarily with small farmers in tribal areas, the organization has trained over 1,400 farmers, provided a similar number with direct market access, increased suppliers' annual income by 25%, brought eight metric tons of honey and five metric tons of beeswax to market, and prepared more than fifty Master Trainers to take the strategy to scale.[21]

The worldwide economy is currently incapable of providing work of any kind to growing populations, and millions of workers are unable to find meaning in their current work. It is therefore not surprising that more and more people around the world are seeking alternatives. Two new books, both intended to inspire people to leave meaningless work behind, provide stories of social entrepreneurs who are creating work for themselves and others that both feed the spirit and serve the larger world.

Making Good: Finding Meaning, Money, and Community in a Changing World is primarily written for the younger generation of what the authors call "rebuilders," or those who are taking a different pathway toward engagement in meaningful work. The book was written by Billy Parish and Dev Aujla, both successful and inspirational entrepreneurs and rebuilders in their own right. The pair's analysis of rebuilders' stories and interviews revealed common pathways, and four stages along the way:

1. "the wilderness," or acknowledging the stuck and uncertain place that keeps us from moving forward;
2. "finding your own special powers," or the unique edge we can find in our own personal histories;
3. "the kin," or finding one or more communities of like-minded/ like-hearted people; and
4. "the tests," or meeting "moments of truth" with our own powers of persistence and perseverance.

Their book describes a kind of hero's journey that can lead to meaning and belonging, as well as financial rewards.[22]

Walk Out Walk On: A Learning Journey Into Communities Daring to Live the Future Now, by our friends Meg Wheatley and Deborah Frieze, invites readers to join the authors in visiting seven communities in seven countries (Mexico, Brazil, South Africa, Zimbabwe, India, Greece, and the United States), where those who are choosing a different path toward meaning are "experimenting with what it means to live the future now." These visitations reveal "how much becomes possible when we abandon hope of being saved by the perfect leader or the perfect program, and instead look inside our community to notice that the resources and wisdom we need are already here." One of the book's journeys, to Joubert Park in Johannesburg, South Africa, is one we also took in our travels. We were accompanied by Mabule Mokhine, director of the GreenHouse Project, which is one of the indigenous enterprises that have emerged in the park in response to the needs of a suffering neighborhood.[23]

Meg and Deborah beautifully describe these enterprises, which include the Photographers Association, the Lapeng Family and Childhood Center, the Creative Inner City Initiative, the Youth Empowerment Network, the Joubert Park Neighborhood Network, and the Joubert Park Public Art Project. These and other ventures create energy and aliveness in spaces smaller than a football field, and with sordid histories of violence, crime, and homelessness. The story of Joubert Park and the others related in the book illustrate the mantra: "Start anywhere. Take it everywhere." The idea is a simple one for those who would seek meaning in work with others.

Fostering Meaning in the Workplace

Of course, workplaces already exist that create the conditions in which people can find themselves engaged in meaningful work. Most others, given the proper motivation, could realize the rewards of such practices through fairly minimal efforts. However, as suggested by the research, success requires

- an enterprise and leadership that offer specificity about what the work requires,
- access to necessary resources,
- clarity regarding how the work relates to the organization's overall purpose,
- the opportunity to use unique skills and talents to experience progress in the work,
- providing for establishment of community sensibilities,
- demonstration of values alignment, and
- evidence that the work serves the greater good.

Rajendra Sisodia, David Wolfe, and Jagdish Sheth, authors of *Firms of Endearment*, have proclaimed that we have already entered a new era, one they refer to as the Age of Transcendence. The term signals that people everywhere are increasingly "looking for higher meaning in their lives, rather than simply looking to add to the store of things they own." This "search for meaning is changing expectations in the marketplace, and in the workplace. Indeed, we believe it is changing the very soul of capitalism."[24]

And well it should. Those who engage in meaningful work are healthier, happier, less depressed and anxious, more motivated, more creative, more satisfied and absorbed in their lives and with their jobs, and more committed to serving the greater good. Their workplaces experience fewer turnovers, absenteeism, and the enormous costs that go with those losses in productivity. It should be obvious that creating the conditions in which work engages the heart, as well as the body and mind, pays off for everyone, and helps to create a world that works for all.

While leaders and managers have a responsibility and a role to play in making work meaningful, we are also reminded of the famous story of the three stone masons and its lessons about our private responsibility for creating meaningful work in our own lives.

As the story goes, three stone masons in the middle ages were hard at work when a visitor came along and asked them what they were doing.

The first stone mason's brow was beaded with sweat. "I am cutting this stone," he grumbled.

The second stone mason, though less distraught, responded with a deep sigh. "I'm building a parapet."

The third stone mason replied with a radiant face, "I am building a beautiful cathedral that will glorify God for centuries to come."[25]

You are what your deepest desire is.
As your desire is, so is your intention.
As your intention is, so is your will.
As your will is, so is your deed.
As your deed is, so is your destiny.[1]

— UPANISHADS

Once you make a decision, the universe
conspires to make it happen.[2]

— RALPH WALDO EMERSON

EIGHT

MANIFESTING INTENTION

The Story of Sankalp at Syngenta India

When we sat down to interview Prakash Apte, we had no idea that we were about to uncover a fascinating story of organizational transformation. We did know that Prakash was president and managing director of Syngenta India, a relatively young global enterprise formed in 2000 by the merger of the agri-businesses of Novartis AG and AstroZeneca. Prakash generously drove the ninety miles or so from Syngenta's headquarters in Pune to meet with us at our hotel in Mumbai. Prakash has, perhaps, the most infectious laugh of any CEO in the world, and was just one month from retiring into a position as non-executive chairman of Syngenta, a role that would take up 25% to 30% of his time. Asked what he planned to do during this transition, he said that his first intention was to spend time trekking in the Himalayas, and that as director of the Syngenta Foundation he would be spending more time working on humanitarian projects. One such project is an agricultural project supporting the Maharogi Sewa Samiti Leprosy Service Society, which works for rehabilitation and empowerment of leprosy patients. That should have been our first clue that this was no ordinary CEO.

Prakash is no ordinary person. Beginning in 1980, he spent most of his career working for the legacy companies of Syngenta, including Novartis, a large multi-national pharmaceutical company. His first positions were on the technical side, but in the mid-1990s, at the invitation of management, he moved to the business side of Novartis operations, a move he welcomed for its learning opportunities. When Syngenta was formed in 2000, CEO Prakash was instrumental in leading the merger of the two companies and cultures, a process that took nearly two years. The dramatic story of how the companies integrated their product portfolio's transformation is worth telling in Prakash's own words.

> *In the year 2002, we made a decision, a right decision, about modernizing our portfolio. We had some products that were extremely popular with farmers, and I said we should simply get rid of the old stuff. These products were on the market for 25 years. The salesmen liked them; they had become a household name. We approached farmers asking them if we should establish a new brand. They said no. But, I said, if we are convinced that there are better solutions, then we must take these products off the market. It meant cutting about 25% of our turnover at that point in time. Many people said, "You have gone crazy," but I said, "Look here, there is one truth. If there is a better product, you better start establishing it. Why would you want to live off that legacy? Why don't you create something of your own?"*
>
> *It was a drastic step, but top management agreed. We got the product out and our company grew by about 1.5% in that year, while our competitors grew by about 14%. The Indian market was growing, the agricultural market was growing everywhere, and the competitors came in with a good portfolio ahead of us, because we were not yet ready to bring in our new portfolio. At the same time, a new technology arrived which introduced a discontinuity, and two of our largest competitors merged together. These events unrolled one after the other. We were in a very tight spot, like in a trap, surrounded by emerging technology on one side, and a new stronger post-merger competitor on the other side. Our entire channel of distribution was unhappy with us, because we had taken away 25% of their most popular brands.*

The question was, "How do we get out of this?" One way was just looking at an escape route, save your life. The other way was to say no, why did we do all of this? We have the technology, we have the capability, we have the people. Getting out of this should not be our objective, it should be, "How do we rise to the top and become a winner once again?" In taking that target, our chances of failure were very high. The easy way would be to set an escape route, climb out of the ditch and celebrate it. But we said, we are made for something bigger than this. Why not envision something greater. Let us look at that future, and then we'll work backwards. All of us, the senior managers, decided that we would go for the second one, the risky path. All of us might lose our heads.[3]

If ever there was a triggering event from which transformative learning might emerge, this was it for Prakash, his management team, and for the entire company. It could not have been more clear that the current way of operating was not sufficient and that alternatives must be identified and pursued. This led Prakash to dig deep for a way forward that many might see as radical, or even reckless. As he explains:

Then we asked, "How can we improve our chances for success?" I said we should use something from our cultural and religious background, old Indian traditions to help us, and suggested the tradition called Sankalp. *Sankalp is an old traditional concept that means to do something great, where you want to make a large commitment to something. Then you really focus your mind on that, and you declare your intention. It is a process of conscious willing, if you like. You consciously will that this is what I am going to do, this is what I am committed to do, and this is what I have to achieve. This is not only an internal commitment, but you proclaim it to the rest of the world that I am standing for this and say that I am going to work for it.*

Then you find that the whole environment and the support systems will slowly align with your actions and your mind, and you will find a way. As you progress you will find a way. If you say exactly what you are going to do, you will not be able to know, but eventually you will find the way. We said we would all take a Sankalp, which is like an oath. It is much bigger than a goal, because it is a holistic concept. Sankalp is not to be taken for some small thing or some small achievement or some transactional success. It has to be something that will have a larger positive impact than your immediate goal. It has to be something good for everybody. It has to be a positive good intention and a good intentioned approach. So it is bigger than what we normally analyze as a goal. It is much deeper than a simple desire, which is fleeting, it comes and goes. It is sustaining, meant to bring about a transformation. As you aspire, so you achieve. If you have a sincere aspiration and your goal is positive, then the whole world and its energies will support it, and you will achieve it. But you must have such a lofty goal. We had such a lofty goal. We wanted to help the farmers and wanted to improve the productivity of Indian agriculture, and to bring in the modern products. And we intended to do it in a transformative way.

So we started a Sankalp project. On the one hand we used this traditional, cultural approach and on the other hand we used all the modern techniques. Before we went to our people, we needed to be clear about our situation and our current assumptions, what we think it is possible to do. We did a study that showed that while it would be difficult, it would not be impossible. It is not out of this world. What we are talking about is feasible. We can increase our market share from 9% or 9.5% to 15% in approximately four years time. We did all of our portfolio analysis, which markets we will go after, what approaches we will need to take. In the process, as we studied the landscape, we used all the professional techniques that

*they teach in management schools. Thus, on the one hand
there was the traditional approach, in which we were saying
that we wanted to do something great and we are committed
to it, and on the other there was the rigor of systematically
analyzing it. What are the market drivers, what we will be in
a position to do, how much time it will take, what resources
will it take, what do we need to do differently?*

*What we found was that at a strategic level in the
traditional management sense, we needed to completely
transform the way we ran our business, our systems, our
processes, our go to market strategy, and the way we ran the
business at the organizational setup. All of this would have
to be transformed; it would have to be changed completely.
We were, for example, rolling out a pan-Indian strategy, a
one India strategy, and we knew we would have to change
that. India is far too diverse and we can't have one solution
from one end of India to the other. In some places, the market
is not as well developed, where farmers have very, very tiny
pieces of land, they do not have the knowledge, and they
have only 100 rupees in their pocket. So we will have to have
another approach there. In other places they are driving
tractors, their children are studying overseas, many of them
know English, and half of them have studied agriculture
science in the universities. We identified five areas and
organized around five strategic business units. Each had to
have its own strategy, its own bottom line responsibility, its
own structure. In order to do this in a systemic way, we had
to change our reporting systems, our control systems, the
works, everything.*

*Then we asked, "How will our people take it? Are
they ready for this?" This is a solution coming out of our
experience, out of our text books and all of that, but if we
make such a radical change, what will happen to all these
people who constitute this company today, who on the
one hand may feel that management has given some very*

unrealistic targets, that increasing market share to 15% in four years is crazy, and at the same time they are going to change everything. People may not be ready for the change. Sankalp means holistic, systemic change. You can't achieve something gigantic, something different by doing things in the same way in which you have been doing it in the past. Just running faster is not going to work. People need to develop new abilities, to develop themselves, to learn new skills. It is a development opportunity for the people.

We said, "Let us go back and put this before the people." So we went back to our people, first the management committee of about eight or ten people, then to about forty of our senior managers, saying this is what we want to do. The session was going on for three days. We explained the whole thing to them and said that if at the end of this all of us are convinced that this is the right thing to do, even though it is a risk we're taking, then we will stand up and take a Sankalp. There was one Sankalp for the company, within the company there will be five units with their own Sankalp. We asked if they were ready for it. On the last day, we invited the spouses also and told them the story. This is what the company is facing, this is the situation, this is what we have thought about and if we go stand up and say this is a Sankalp it might mean anything. It might mean some sacrifice but for a good cause. And without your support, it is not going to be possible. Then we asked them what they thought about it. Most of them said this is great, we will support it. At the end, this group said we are going to go with a Sankalp.

So then we did the reorganization, reengineered all of the processes. Then I personally went across the country talking to people, explaining the concept of the Sankalp as a conscious willing, because a Sankalp cannot be given from me to you. I would say the company has taken a Sankalp and I have taken a Sankalp, and asked what part of this they felt they could contribute. If you are willing to take the Sankalp, then you will pronounce it. I explained that when you make a lofty goal, part of you thinks that you have gone crazy, you should not do this, this may not happen, there is only a fifty percent chance. You don't cut off the concern, but you set it aside, and you say, "I am going to do this!" And in going through this dialogue, you actually get help from your second mind, your second sense. This is an approach of acceptance of a second heart, learning from it, without getting diverted from your goal. I didn't know a lot about this in the beginning, I am not a cultural expert. But as I experienced it, read more about it and practiced it, and then discussed it with the people, I learned. So everyone took a Sankalp very willingly.[4]

In three years, the company reached 95% of its goal. Feeling confident that they would achieve it, everyone agreed to go for a much higher goal, the next horizon, a larger Sankalp. Syngenta involved people in a widespread visioning process, asking each individual to write one or two things they wanted to leave behind, and one or two things they wanted to embrace or do more of, and asked them to participate in a reflection exercise on what they had written. When they were clear about their writing, each person posted paper leaves on the branches of a symbolic tree for what they wanted to achieve as a Sankalp, and put the potential obstacles that they would leave behind at the roots, so that the learning from those things given up would enrich the tree.

The time we spent with Prakash surely piqued our interest in the concept of Sankalp. We wondered what definitions, explanations, or applications we might find by doing a little research. What we found essentially affirmed what Prakash shared with us. The term comes from combining the Hindi word *san*, meaning altogether, and *kalpa*, meaning idea. One source said,

Sankalp is a pledge, a commitment, an undertaking, a vow, which is made by a person making Ishwar (meaning God) a witness to it. It is much stronger than a resolution. Sankalp is at a much higher level; it involves and engages

the person both at the physical, emotional, intellectual, and spiritual level.[5]

Another wrote, "Sankalp is like an unwavering vow, pledge, or commitment and has a deep spiritual significance. By making a pledge a person becomes committed towards the accomplishment of his goal."[6]

Prakash summed up these ideas in a presentation at the Indian School of Business "Igniting the Genius Within" conference, defining Sankalp as:

A "conscious willing," a robust declaration of intent, realized only by harmonizing the impulses of body, mind, and heart.

MORE than simple DETERMINATION

BIGGER than RESOLUTION

GREATER than GOAL

HIGHER than COMMITMENT

DEEPER than DESIRE[7]

Manifesting Intention and Transformation

What Prakash Apte and his Syngenta colleagues were tapping into in their powerful story of transformation is what becomes possible when the leaders of an organization have complete trust and faith in the power of their peoples' shared intentions. They knew that the lofty goal of increasing their market share from 9% to 15% in four years was only achievable through the combined will and effort of their employees. They simply went to the people and asked them to reach into the depth of their hearts and minds, revealing to each other their most profound aspirations, weaving them together into a set of inter-related goals, and putting themselves on the line in order to fulfill their commitments to themselves, to each other, to the organization, and to their customers and other stakeholders.

The Sankalp process was tapping into what some researchers believe to be the very essence of what makes us human—our capacity for shared intentionality. That capacity, simply defined as "collaborative interactions in which participants have a shared goal and coordinated action roles for pursuing that shared goal,"[8] actually develops from a very early age. Researchers led by Michael Tomasello, a developmental psychologist and co-director of the Max Planck Institute for Evolutionary Anthropology in Leipzig, Germany, have conducted

> Once every one has agreed, a pool of wills is formed and individuals are then jointly committed. That pool of wills is greater than the sum of individual commitments, and it gives rise to certain obligations and entitlements. Members of the group have a right to expect that other members will follow through on their commitments.[9]
>
> —MARGARET GILBERT

studies in which they observe young children as they collaborate with one another, and with adults, to accomplish a shared goal such as building a tower of blocks. By comparing what they see to what they observe in our closest relatives, the ape family, they concluded that shared intentionality is the primary distinction to be made between man and ape. Primates engaged in hunting monkeys together, for example, are each trying to capture the prey for themselves, while humans "can actually put their heads together. They can put their minds together to collaborate and do things that neither one of them could do alone."[10] Human cooperation also has unique motivations, according to Tomasello's research. "When we're working toward something together, part of my goal is that you also get your fair share of what we're working toward, and then in some situations, I can even do altruistic things for you. I can help you in various ways."[11]

Researchers claim that this capacity for shared intentionality and its resulting cooperation accounts for human creativity: from natural languages and mathematical symbols, to complex social institutions like governments and religions, to the rules and norms that constitute what we refer to as culture. Establishing and reinforcing these kinds of social rules and norms out of collaborative behavior define for us not just a right or wrong way of doing things, but a kind of "we-ness," or a sense of "the way we do things here." It is interesting to note that in addition to Syngenta's goal of increasing market share, they were also in the process of integrating two cultures from the merger of Novartis AG and AstraZeneca. Undoubtedly, the Sankalp process aided enormously in that process by helping to create a "we-ness," or shared cultural context of meaning about "the Syngenta way."

Prakash Apte's choice of the Sankalp was also grounded in a profound belief in free will which, according to researcher Eddie Nahmias, is "best characterized as the ability to know what you really want and to know how to act accordingly."[12] For Nahmias, professor of philosophy at Georgia State University, free will is "a set of capacities for imagining future courses of action, deliberating about one's reasons for choosing them, planning one's actions in light of this deliberation, and controlling actions in the face of competing desires."[13] And,

> by exercising our capacities for free will, we are able to discover the underlying consistencies among our desires, goals, and values that form our character. And these discoveries, of course, are crucial in shaping our future since they are manifested in our decisions. We do not create who we are from scratch; rather we discover who we are and in doing so we shape who we will become.[14]

Nahmias' ideas are consistent with those of another professor of philosophy, Dr. Timothy O'Connor of Indiana University. O'Connor refers to an

> ignored side of freedom of the will, which is self-mastery. A person acts freely to the extent that he has control of his appetites and impulses and is able reliably to direct his more significant actions towards larger aims. A self-mastered person perforce has a great deal of self knowledge, including

especially knowledge of the factors that incline him to this or that course of action. This concept of free will as self-mastery suggests that through practice we can, over time, increase our capacity for exercising our freedom to create what we desire to bring forth in our lives.[15]

Not everyone acknowledges the existence of free will, of course, but for those who do there can be a positive impact on satisfaction and performance at work. One study, conducted by Dr. Kathleen Vohs of the University of Minnesota and her colleagues, showed that workers who believed in free will scored higher on tests related to effort, reliability, consistency, positive social impact, and general workplace performance. "Free will guides people's choices toward being more moral and better performers," the researchers found. "It's adaptive for societies and individuals to hold a belief in free will, as it helps people adhere to cultural codes of conduct that portend healthy, wealthy, and happy life outcomes."[16]

The idea of increasing our capacity for making choices and decisions about the future we desire is also present in more than one recent popular book about the subject of willpower. In one of those publications, *Willpower: Rediscovering Our Greatest Strength*, psychologist Roy F. Baumeister and science writer John Tierney set forth the idea that willpower can be strengthened through practice. In an interview with National Public Radio's Audie Cornish, Tierney said that willpower "is like a muscle that can be strengthened with use," but one, he goes on to say, that "also gets fatigued with use."[18] As with other muscles, the authors claim, exercising our willpower can improve our capacities for self-control over time. This self-control gives us the ability to influence our own worlds and the

---

Collective will is the attractor that allows form to emerge from chaos.[17]

— TRACY HUSTON

world around us. Baumeister and Tierney write, "Willpower lets us change ourselves and our society in small and large ways,"[19] and "improving willpower is the surest way to a better life."[20] It is, according to these two, the "most significant factor in human success and contentment."[21]

We came away from the Syngenta story—and our exploration of manifesting intention—realizing that when we make a commitment to achieve something with others, we are making a commitment to our deeper selves and to our own development as human beings. Whether we achieve what we set out to do is, of course, highly relevant, but not nearly as important as the process of inner reflection and discovery that leads to self realization and actualization. We also came away recognizing that while Sankalp is a very Eastern conception, there is much to learn from Syngenta's experience that can inform those who would create conditions in the workplace for personal and organizational transformation.

Manifesting Intention in the Workplace

The Orpheus Chamber Orchestra, based in New York City, is an organization founded and operating on the very essence of freedom, responsibility, and shared intentionality. The Grammy Award-winning and highly acclaimed orchestra was founded in 1972 by cellist Julian Fifer and a group of friends, around the concept of shared and rotating leadership. The orchestra has made over seventy recordings, and presents an annual concert series at Carnegie Hall. The organization, through its Orpheus Institute, also works with college-aged musicians with an interest in their philosophy, as well as providing workshops and other learning opportunities for hundreds of students in the New York City public schools.

Unlike most conductor-led orchestras, which tend to be highly hierarchical and autocratic institutions, Orpheus organizes each of its performances around a mutually selected concertmaster, a core group of performers, and a process of highly participative interpretation of the score, along with painstaking practice and refinement. Alan Key, clarinetist, writes,

> By the time I became a member in 2002, the group had
> developed the Orpheus Process™, a system of artistic
> democracy and mutual respect in which musicians share the
> responsibilities of leadership, onstage and off. Playing with
> Orpheus, the difference is palpable. There is a heightened
> sense of collaboration, of personal commitment to each
> phrase and gesture. We strive to create vibrant, compelling
> performances in which the whole is greater than the sum
> of the parts. We hope this exuberance is contagious among
> listeners at Carnegie Hall and around the world.[22]

One listener and avid admirer is photographer Larry Fink, whose exhibit of black-and-white photos of Orpheus at Lafayette College's Williams Center for the Arts—where the orchestra is a resident ensemble—describes his own experience of the orchestra's performances. It is, he says,

> what it's like to be enraptured by music. It's absolutely
> impossible, but wonderful to try for. You're looking for beauty
> and dignity and grace and balance. The music is behind
> you, with this tremendous emotional fuel. You're swimming
> through these musicians, who are so invested in humanity,
> in decency, in exuberance. The sum part of the evidence is
> that they really enjoy themselves more than other orchestras
> because they really take control. It's amazing to see how hard
> they work and how fulfilled they are at the end of the day.
> God, how they have good times![24]

In a culture in which people hold each accountable for their impeccability, where commitments are taken seriously, there is trust, coordination, and efficiency.[23]

— FRED KOFMAN

Music Editor George Grella describes the orchestra's performance this way:

Musicality is the fundamental quality of the Orpheus Chamber Orchestra; they couldn't exist as a performing unit without it. Examining what they do and how they accomplish it brings us deep into an understanding of the word. Though they're best known for performing without a conductor, what really sets them apart is their chamber quality, which is more than just a measure of numbers. There are plenty of musicians who keep solid time and can navigate their way through tricky phrases and rhythms; conductors exist because they, ideally, do a great deal more than that, and the Orpheus does a great deal more than that. They play like a chamber ensemble in their unanimity of phrasing, their transparency, and their highly conversational manner. And they listen and respond to each other in ways an orchestra doesn't have to when a conductor is doing that for them. Most importantly, they come to a consensus on what the music means to them and communicate that directly to the audience.[25]

Another fascinating example of manifesting shared intentionality comes from the development of the Village at Market Creek Plaza in the Diamond improvement district near San Diego, California. This low-income, urban area is made up of several communities with nearly 90,000 residents who are African American and Latino, as well as of Laotian, Samoan, Filipino, and Somali descent. The project is organized and supported by the Jacobs Family Foundation and its Jacobs Center for Neighborhood Innovation (JCNI), a non-profit foundation that "operates on the premise that residents must own and drive the change that takes place in their community for it to be meaningful and long-lasting."[26]

From the beginning, the JCNI has worked with a network of neighborhood working teams, making it a renewal project as well as a community development and skill-building initiative that has engaged thousands of community residents and attracted national attention.

Members responsible for day-to-day implementation issues were paid a stipend for their contribution. The project began in 1997 with a multilingual, door-to-door community survey and neighborhood meetings conducted by the residents' Outreach Team. The team sought to find out what kind of programs, services, businesses, and employment the people wanted to see in their area. The most significant findings included a full-service grocery store, cleanup of a brownfield site, and jobs for local residents. As a result of the research, the first element of the project was the redevelopment of an abandoned twenty-acre aerospace factory site into the Market Square Plaza. The Foundation purchased the land and initiated a comprehensive strategy of community engagement, learning, and residential ownership.

> Market Creek is built on the belief that for change to be sustainable, residents must own it. Everyone must be willing to learn their way. Every voice matters. Testing ideas matters. Partners committed to learning matter. Success depends on it.[27]
> — 2010 SOCIAL AND ECONOMIC IMPACT REPORT

The teams involved in the project include the Construction Collaboration Team, which set and met their goal of having 69% of the Plaza construction contracts awarded to minority and women-oriented businesses. Through the process, a consortium of organizations developed a process for recruiting, training, and hiring laborers and contractors. One organization, the MultiCultural Contractors Group, created a mentor-protégé program to build the business skills of small contractors. A business development and leasing team made sure that the Plaza would have the right mix of both locally-based and national tenants. Businesses selected were expected to meet the needs of residents based on the initial survey, and to commit to local hiring and development of the community. The team, with financing from JCNI, developed a "patient-debt capital" program to help finance local businesses.

The Employment Development Team developed a program to develop employment opportunities and to prepare residents for the newly created jobs. When the first business opened in the Plaza, 91% of the employees of the Food 4 Less grocery store (the first major grocer to locate in the area in thirty years) were local residents who were able to join the union because of the work of the team. At the same time, the Resource Development Team, made up of representatives from each of the other working teams, set out to attract funders to the project. The team has attracted more than $3 million to the project. JCNI reports that

> *Being involved in the project from the start, these team members were able to uniquely share their stories from the heart about Market Creek Plaza and what it has meant to the community. When foundations, policy groups, and other interested organizations tour the Plaza, it is the members of the Resource Team who guide them through the process that brought the Plaza to life and share the victories and innovations from a first-hand perspective.[28]*

The Art and Design Team, working with the project's architects, was responsible for creating a look and feel for the Plaza and its public artwork that would reflect and celebrate the community's cultural and artistic heritage. The team asked participants to bring together artifacts, including textiles and clothing, that represented their cultures. These pieces were the inspiration for a series of three tile walkways at the Plaza, one from an African batik, another representing Samoan tapa cloth, and a third made up of Laotian colors. Another project team, the Evaluation Guide Team, works with independent evaluators to assess the project's impact, to document learning, and to feed data back into the project's teams and operations.

Perhaps the most innovative component of the project is its community ownership model. It took nearly six years to accomplish, but the Foundation and Ownership Design Team, involving more than 100 residents, worked to convince the California legislature to approve a community development IPO that would allow local residents to invest in the project. After dozens of proposal submittals and rejections, the state finally approved a plan in which residents with $2,000 in net worth or annual income could invest from $200 to $10,000, and resident shareholders could own up to 20% of the company. An additional 60% would be owned by the Jacobs Center, while 20% would be owned by the Neighborhood Unity Foundation, a 501(c) (3) nonprofit organization controlled by residents. The plan is for the Jacobs Center to retire its share by 2017, resulting in complete resident ownership by that time.[29]

Ultimately, the plan is to transform up to 84 acres, creating 1,000 affordable homes, 2,000 jobs and 250 new businesses, 5,500 linear feet of restored wetlands, and 1.6 million square feet of new construction. Recently, the project became only the third in the country to receive the U.S. Green Building Council's Leadership in Energy and Environmental Design for Neighborhood Development (LEED/ND) Silver level designation. In its award, the Council cited the project's walkability and transit connections, energy savings concepts, and environmentally sustainable practices. In 2010, the Village was named as one of only five "Gold" Catalyst Projects by the California Sustainable Strategies Pilot Program, and has received area-wide cleanup grants from the U.S. Environmental Protection Agency. It has taken on the role of a national demonstration project for local involvement in neighborhood revitalization, and currently attracts hundreds of visitors interested in learning more about the community-based approach to sustainable development.

> There is no power greater than a community discovering what it cares about.[30]
>
> — MARGARET WHEATLEY

The Market Creek project has, of course, suffered its share of disappointments, including the challenges brought upon local business owners by the current recession. What has been accomplished and what has been learned, however, authenticate the significant investments and efforts of the JCNI and local residents. The project's research partner, PolicyLink, in its case study, "Market Creek Plaza: Toward

Resident Ownership of Neighborhood Change," writes that "involving residents as ongoing partners requires a commitment to developing multiple engagement approaches and continuous outreach." The case study further notes that "bringing residents inside the complexities and tough decisions of the project is essential for forging ownership of the implementation and the results," that "partnering with residents in development activity can expand residents' perception of their own capacities," and that "helping to build and sustain community owner-ship of change requires asking questions rather than providing an-swers."[31] These themes are echoed in the words of Jennifer S. Vanica, Jacobs Family Foundation President and CEO.

> *Embarking on this journey was not a choice; it was a mission. This work is patient and personal, requiring risk and rethinking everything we thought we knew. Yet we encourage others to experience the gifts and talents of people coming together, feeling their pride, and seeing change take root. We hope these experiences will inspire and inform other efforts around the country. Our journey continues.*[32]

Fostering Intention in the Workplace

Given that the capacity for manifesting shared intentionality may be what makes us most uniquely human, it is remarkable how few work-places invite the full participation of all stakeholders. Far too many workplaces employ participative methodologies—including strategic planning, management by objectives, hoshin deployment or others—without embracing the underlying intention of full engagement. Even fewer undertake the use of these methodologies with the intent of al-lowing employees and other stakeholders to exercise and strengthen their capacities for a level of freedom and responsibility that leads to their own growth and development as human beings.

In our experience, an organization typically comes up against a major threat to its survival, gathers key executives to develop a coping strategy, and organizes a campaign that rolls-out the solutions to the rank and file. Perhaps many organizations fail to fully engage stakeholders because of a perception that the process is too time-consuming. Arriving at, acting on, and achieving shared intentions requires a process in which individuals can

- reflect on their own needs and aspirations,
- align or negotiate them with others,
- establish common goals and means of accomplishing them,
- understand their own and others' roles,
- monitor action as it unfolds,
- make adjustments in performance, and
- stand ready to assist others when needed.

It also requires a high level of attunement to what is going on with others psychologically and emotionally, sensitivity to what is required by other people, and the situation. Yet all of this becomes possible in an environment that invites or allows for the expression of a high level of freedom and responsibility. The payoff, as in the case of Syngenta's Sankalp process, can be achievements that far exceed expectations.

The idea of shared intentionality was so important to Peter Senge when he wrote his breakthrough book, *The Fifth Discipline*, that building shared vision was one of the five disciplines he thought necessary to create a learning organization—a form of organization that has gained much popularity since he first wrote about the idea. Entire organizational development approaches have been elaborated that create shared visions involving every stakeholder in an organization in a vision's creation—or at least a microcosm of those stakeholders. These new approaches stand in stark opposition to the traditional approach of creating the vision behind closed doors and "selling" it to the troops.

Fortunately, there are literally dozens of ways that organizations and communities can engage their people in these processes. They include World Café, Appreciative Inquiry, Gallery Walks, and Open Space Technology, as well as any number of methods for conducting dialogue, circle, and other conversational forms. We have personally used a great number of these methodologies, especially in a large community engagement project called The Jackson Comm*Unity* Transformation

Project (JCTP) in our own community. The project engaged over 5,000 individuals and 200 organizations through a three-level engagement strategy: first, organizing "community design teams" all over the community to create an ideal design for the community; second, supporting strategic initiatives, or collaborative approaches to bringing about the envisioned design; and third, an "each one, bring one" approach bringing citizens into the project's work one voice at a time.

Over a four-year period, the JCTP engagement strategy demonstrated to residents that this approach to community development was different, that it was about a sincere invitation to all persons to create a community that would work for everyone. Many residents began to see that this approach was about creating a shared understanding of the complexity of interrelated problems rather than focusing on single causes and effects, and that it was about people acting and reflecting together to create a better community.

A profound lesson related to the will of the people and shared intentionality came when one of our primary advisors and mentors, Jamshid Gharajedaghi, encouraged us to depend on the power of the shared vision created by the citizenry. He told us that the resources to bring about the vision would come to the community, that we would simply "find" the money from previously unavailable sources. He told us that the new perspective gained from the creation of the vision would help all of us to see new opportunities that we would not otherwise see.

Although we did not fully understand what he was telling us, we trusted him and went forward. Although there were many disappointments—just as with the Market Creek project—there were also many serendipitous successes. A dangerous concrete cap over the Grand River as it flowed through the city was taken off, an issue that had been discussed for decades. Consumers Energy, a statewide power company, decided to centralize their corporate offices in downtown Jackson instead of moving to Detroit. Those two actions helped to revitalize the downtown. A bond issue in an outlying township—previously considered impossible to pass—built a new township office and fire house. Many community organizations were created, recreated, or consolidated to improve their services to the community. They included the police department, the economic development enterprise group, a new youth education and athletics program, a community-wide respite care organization, and a new community center. All because of the power of shared vision!

Surely, the best of all possible worlds is created when the aspirations of individuals and organizations can be aligned in such a way that they can manifest their highest intentions.

WHOLENESS

Compassion is the desire that moves the individual self to widen the scope of its self-concern to embrace the whole of the universal self.[1]

— ARNOLD TOYNBEE

The compassionate mind is like an elixir; it is capable of transforming bad situations into beneficial ones. Therefore, we should not limit our expressions of love and compassion to our family and friends. Nor is the compassion only the responsibility of clergy, health care, and social workers. It is the necessary business of every part of the human community.[2]

— HIS HOLINESS THE DALAI LAMA

NINE

EMBODYING COMPASSION

The Story of the Desmond Tutu Peace Centre

In an address to members of the United States Congress on March 18, 2009, Nomfundo Walaza, Chief Executive Officer of the Desmond Tutu Peace Centre in Cape Town, South Africa, spoke about the three themes that provide focus for the Center's work: inspiring a commitment to peace, creating a space for the marginalized, and encouraging a leadership that serves. At the conclusion of her address, she told the Congress:

> *I started by saying I wanted to give you some context about the origins of Desmond Tutu Peace Centre. I'd like to conclude by sharing our vision. Unsurprisingly it was forged by our experience in 1994 and thereafter when, despite their history, the majority of South Africans demonstrated they had chosen dialogue over revenge, compassion over hate, and love over fear. They showed that despite tremendous odds forgiveness and reconciliation are possible.*
>
> *This is why we can imagine a world committed to peace. A world in which everyone lives together as a family, everyone is loved, heard, cared for, and unique. A world in which everyone matters and the essential good in everyone is manifested.[3]*

Nomfundo Walaza is a leader who embodies the themes and vision of which she spoke on that day. To hear her story is to witness the still unfolding life of a compassionate and accomplished woman, the evolution of an organization committed to human goodness, and the hope for peace that each brings to the world.

Although she has lived nearly all of her life in Cape Town, Nomfundo was born in Queenstown, South Africa, the place her heart most calls home and the place where her grandparents are buried. She attended both primary and secondary schools in the Langa Township, outside of Cape Town, and then studied as an exchange student in Niagara Falls, New York, before returning to study at the University of Cape Town to earn her qualifications as a clinical psychologist.

The influence of Nomfundo's grandmother accounts for much of her strength, resilience, and courage, but it is likely that her upbringing in the Langa Township, and her early career, were the crucibles for her later embodiment of compassion. Her direct experience of violence and oppression did not come up in our interview, but it is an issue she has addressed elsewhere in her writing, speaking, and in interviews. Speaking of her experience, Nomfundo once told an audience of 150 attendees at a workshop on nonviolence in Palestine,

> *I know what it is to live in a divided society; I know of the*
> *pain of being hounded every day; I know of the pain of*
> *having to carry little pieces of paper to be able to move in my*
> *land from one area to another; I know of the pain of seeing*
> *demolition of houses.*[4]

Surely those early experiences of violence, oppression, and suffering influenced her choice of career as a clinical psychologist, and influenced her work in a clinical setting at Cape Town's Valkenberg Hospital. After working at Valkenberg for several years, Nomfundo was recruited by the Trauma Center for Survivors of Violence and Torture. The Trauma Center opened its doors in 1993 in response to the dire mental health needs of survivors of apartheid atrocities. The Center took on the work of counseling victims of gang violence and rape survivors, while trying also to integrate political prisoners as they came out of Robben Island, the famed prison where Nelson Mandela was held for 18 of the 27 years he was incarcerated. Nomfundo was named executive director of that organization in 1996, just two years after Mandela was elected President of South Africa in the country's first non-racial elections.

Commenting on her service as director of the Trauma Center for Survivors of Violence and Torture, and her decision to leave after eleven years, Nomfundo told us, "Not many people had survived in those kinds of organizations for more than five years, because we were dealing with both our administrative duties, but also carrying the weight of the pain of the nation on our shoulders."[5] What she meant, of course, was that these were the years of transformation in South Africa, a transformation from the pain and suffering and oppression of the apartheid era into a fledgling democracy. Nelson Mandela, and others, gave everything they had not only to win their majority rights to determine their own destiny, but simply to be treated as fellow human beings in their native land. The "pain of the nation" to which Nomfundo referred was the pain of humiliation and degradation, as well as physical abuse, torture, and death suffered at the hands of the oppressors.

During Nomfundo's tenure at the Trauma Center, she also served as a support person to the Truth and Reconciliation Commission (TRC). The TRC was established by Nelson Mandela and chaired by Archbishop Desmond Tutu, with the purpose of holding hearings on human rights crimes committed during the apartheid era. Nomfundo explains that the dawning era of the South African democracy, and the role that the TRC played in it, came directly from the African cultural perspective on restorative vs. retributive justice. The essence of the TRC, Nomfundo told us,

> *was to get victims to say what was done to them, for*
> *perpetrators to account for their deeds, but the essence was*
> *in between the victims and the perpetrators. It was to find out*
> *if we could take the perpetrators who were de-humanized by*
> *their actions and find a way to re-humanize them, to bring*
> *them back to the fold of humanity.*[6]

Speaking of restorative justice, she told us:

At the end of the day, it is not us who judge. Everybody will go and face their Maker, whoever it is, whether God or Allah or whomever. I can stand in judgment of you, but I am not your Maker. You can have all the anger and frustration you have, but it was important for us to recognize that as people we were paying for the blood of those who harmed our people. You don't want the blood of your enemy on your hand. You don't want to retaliate and go and kill people. You want people to face what they have done, to say that in the final instance, "If you want to come back to humanity, the door will open for you."

When we say in my language, "ubuntu," we mean a person is a person through others, I am because you are, you are because I am. It is about that essence of humanity that asks of us to find whatever shreds of humanity that are still left in the worst of perpetrators and say can we salvage that for the greater good of our society.[7]

In another role as a lay member of the Joint Standing Committee for the Anglican Communion, Nomfundo was called upon to speak on behalf of the third Millennium Development Goal, which is to "promote gender equity and empower women." In her speech, she expressed the depth of her own embodied compassion. According to the Communion's report of her testimony,

She talked about a South African word, inimba. *It's the connection a mother feels with her child regardless of time and space. Ms. Walaza said that inimba is the pain that the mother feels when the umbilical cord is cut—and that pain for her child is always there because our world is so fragile. If the human family is not just to survive but flourish, then we all must feel that pain. Inimba connects us and makes those of us in the US care about the children in South Africa and they about us. Inimba makes us respond because the response is embedded in us. It is the catalyst to change the world.[9]*

> Like a mother who protects her child, her only child, with her own life, one should cultivate a heart of unlimited love and compassion towards all living beings.[8]
>
> — THE BUDDHA

Both during and after the TRC hearings, Nomfundo played a role in issues of restorative justice about which she was most passionate. These issues included her leadership in influencing the TRC to create spaces for women to speak to their own suffering and their role in reconciliation. By the time Archbishop Tutu invited her to serve as Chief Executive Officer of the Desmond Tutu Peace Centre, Nomfundo had already been instrumental in helping to heal the wounds of a nation, and had spoken around the world about what would become the Centre's vision: "A world committed to peace. A world in which everyone lives together as a family, everyone is loved, heard, cared for, and unique. A world in which everyone matters and the essential good in everyone is manifested."[10] Nomfundo would be the first to say that there is still much work to be done in South Africa to achieve that vision. "In order to help my country heal from the legacy of segregation and discrimination, I believe it is critical to address racism, xenophobia, sexism, and homophobia, and their impact on the lives of South Africans today."[11]

During our visit, we asked Nomfundo what she does to maintain her stamina, and how it is possible to be a leader in such challenging circumstances. In response, she shared the story of an encounter with a student on Berkley's campus in California, where she once served as a visiting scholar on human rights. The student stopped Nomfundo on the street one day to ask about her personal approach to leadership.

I told the student something very simple. When you walk down the street and you see homeless people after homeless people, some with cats, some with dogs, some selling little things, and asking for 'Change, ma'am,' you don't walk over that person as if you are walking over a banana leaf. Look at them in the eye; acknowledge that they are a fellow human being. Smile if you can manage to do that, because often it will lighten their day, and you say 'Hello, how are you doing?' You don't even have to go to your wallet, because that may not be what the person needs. They may ask you for money, but that is not what is essential. What is essential is an encounter with a human being who recognizes that they are in a hard place, and who can share something that is nothing about money, a connection of a human being to a human being. You say, 'Brother, I see you, I hear you. I may not be able to do something about your plight but, you know what? We are part of the same family.' I said to the student, 'If you can do that, then you can do the work that I do.' It's about leadership that sustains life. Leading with grace. And leading in a way that acknowledges that I am not above, but I am within a family of other human beings.[12]

As we reflected on our interview with Nomfundo Walaza, we felt privileged to have spent time with such a wise, bold, and compassionate leader. As journalist Tarryn Brien once noted regarding what it is to be in the company of this woman, "Her totem animal has to be a giraffe. There is no other option for this indescribably graceful woman, who walks silently into the room and yet demands your instant and full attention."[13] In her company, we had no doubt whatsoever that Nomfundo Walaza is up to the task as a global advocate for peace.

Compassion and Transformation

In reflecting on Nomfundo's story, one may wonder what compassion has to do with a transformative workplace, and how one could possibly have the experiences that lead to embodying compassion in one's own development. In response, we have learned that compassion has a great deal to do with the workplace and that it is possible for the places in which we work to be the contexts in which we can learn and practice our own compassionate becoming.

Research conducted by many scholars in the positive psychology field speaks to the value for organizations in creating a context in which people can embody compassion in their everyday work lives. In a March 2011 article titled "Understanding Compassion Capability," for example, authors Monica Worline, Jane Dutton, Jason Kanov and Sally Maitlis define compassion as "an empathic emotional response elicited by another person's suffering that moves people to act in a way that will ease the person's anguish or make it more tolerable."[14] They cite their own and others' research on the topic as follows:

> *Evidence suggests that compassion in organizations may shape people's commitment to their workplace (Grant et al. 2008; Lilius et al. 2008) and aid recovery from painful circumstances (Dutton et al. 2006; Frost et al. 2000). Compassion thus has clear performance implications for individuals and organizations. It may also have financial implications for organizations, given estimates that grief-related absences and productivity losses cost firms US$75 billion annually (Zaslow 2002). In sum, compassion capability may be an important but unexamined form of organizational strength and advantage.*[15]

The article's authors are members of CompassionLab, an organization co-founded by the late Peter Frost of the University of British Columbia (UBC) that examines the importance and effects of compassion in the workplace. A UBC article early on in the formation of the Lab quoted Frost's views on the significance of the research, saying,

> *These days we depend on people's intellectual and emotional capacity to get a competitive edge, so we need to look at people as an investment, not a cost. And if you're investing in people you must invest in the whole person, not just their hands or their brains.*[16]

And,

A growing body of research shows when organizations put people first, their performance on almost all indicators is better. In times of trauma, people aren't focused on their job or their organization—they're focused on the pain. But if people are cared for when they're vulnerable, it makes it possible for them to move on more quickly and become productive again.[17]

Compassion is also cited as a productive response to incidences of employee anger in the workplace. According to *Science Daily*, the research of Dr. Deanna Geddes of Temple University's Fox School of Business, and Dr. Lisa T. Stickney of the University of Baltimore, found that "more supportive responses by managers and co-workers after displays of deviant anger can promote positive change at work, while sanctioning or doing nothing does not." The researchers' article, "The Trouble With Sanctions: Organizational Responses to Deviant Anger Displays at Work," points out that, "Business codes of conduct are often about what we shouldn't do as an angry employee in emotional episodes, while few, if any, tend to address our role as observers of emotional episodes." According to the article, "Such guidelines, if available, could expand to include positive suggestions for those who witness, judge, and respond to angry employees—formally or informally."[18]

Another researcher, Sarah J. Tracy, Associate Professor at Arizona State University, speaks to the role of compassion in addressing rising instances of workplace bullying, stress, burnout, and even suicide. In an article titled "Compassion: Cure an Ailing Workplace?," Tracy cites the case of the Chinese company Foxconn, the world's largest maker of electronic components.

Just since May of this year, 16 of its factory employees have attempted suicide by jumping off factory roofs. Twelve succeeded and another 20 were stopped before they could jump. Why? According to The New York Times and ZDnet, Foxconn employees face long hours, average hourly pay of 51 cents, beatings by company security guards, and must stand for hours without talking, stretching, or taking a break. It's gotten so bad that management recently installed nets—strung between factory buildings—to thwart death for those who jump. According to Foxconn's CEO, Terry Gou, as reported in ZDnet, "It is a clumsy solution, but it may save lives."[19]

Tracy concludes that

working toward understanding and implementing positive organizational communication will take time, research, programs, and skills-based training. However, when we consider extreme cases like Foxconn, it's worth a shot. Teaching compassion-related skills like recognizing, relating, and responding is likely cheaper—and certainly "less clumsy"—than draping suicide catch nets between factory buildings.[20]

Recognizing, relating, and responding, the three skills Tracy refers to, are the three key components of compassion that she identifies and describes:

Recognizing refers to the processes of noticing and understanding details about another person so that one can (re)act most appropriately. Recognizing occurs through communicative behaviors such as observing nonverbal cues, listening, opening oneself up to feedback, and seeing individuals as "whole" people and not just organizational automatons. For recognizing to thrive in the workplace, employees must regularly interact, observe others' behavior in a variety of activities, listen to each other in a range of contexts, and be open to subtle nonverbal cues about potential pain, suffering, and burnout.

Relating refers to identifying, feeling for, and connecting with another through affective, relational, and embodied means. In the workplace, relating is fostered when employees are encouraged and rewarded for finding connections with others. Employees can better relate and move away from an "us-them" relationship with peers and clients when they try to put themselves in others' shoes and identify ways that they are not so different from themselves.

Responding refers to engaging in behaviors or communication that attends to another person's suffering or distress. Responding can be as simple as nonverbally acknowledging the presence of someone waiting in line, or more directly by providing praise, or lightly patting someone's back in a show of support. Such responses are especially important in care-giving situations, but also have the potential to improve a variety of workplace situations.[21]

Compassion in the Workplace

Another individual who speaks to the process of engendering compassion is Chade-Meng Tan, Google's Jolly Good Fellow. Yes, Jolly Good Fellow is Chade-Meng Tan's official title at Google. His business card reads "Chade-Meng Tan, Jolly Good Fellow (which nobody can deny)." Meng, as he is known, is also at the very top of the list of people we still hope to interview as a follow-up to David's sabbatical. Meng was one of Google's earliest engineers, serving in that role for eight years before moving to GoogleEDU (formerly Google University) as the head of Personal Growth. Meng, as reported by the *New York Times* (September 1, 2007) is the guy with whom nearly all famous visitors to Google's headquarters since 2003 have had their pictures taken. These visitors include Bill Clinton, Colin Powell, George Soros, Tom Brokaw, Muhammed Ali, Mikhail Gorbachev, and the Dalai Lama. This photo phenomenon began when Chade-Meng just happened to notice a lot of official-looking cars and security people wandering around at Google, and surmised that there must be a famous visitor. The visitor turned out to be Jimmy Carter, and Chade-Meng had his first photo posted outside his office.

Interestingly, Meng's (and Google's) orientation toward compassion is not strictly perceived as an antidote to bullying, stress, burnout, or workplace violence. It is also perceived as an essential path toward creating a highly effective workforce, highly capable leaders, and a profitable business. In an April 2011 TEDtalk, Meng addressed these issues by talking about how compassion works at Google.

Google is a company born of idealism. It's a company that thrives on idealism. And maybe because of that, compassion is organic and widespread company-wide. In Google, expressions of corporate compassion almost always follow the same pattern. It's sort of a funny pattern. It starts with a small group of Googlers taking the initiative to do something. And they don't usually ask for permission; they just go ahead and do it, and other Googlers join in, and it just gets bigger and bigger. And sometimes it gets big enough to become official. So in other words, it almost always starts from the bottom up.[22]

Meng points to numerous examples of "organic social action" as instances of how compassion has actually become "fun" at Google. He also mentions what he believes to be the value of compassion for the profitability of the enterprise. First, citing author Jim Collins' *Good to Great* concept of the Level 5 Leader, Meng believes that compassion is the way to grow these leaders internally. These leaders, he continues,

in addition to being highly capable, possess two important qualities, and they are humility and ambition. These are leaders who are highly ambitious for the greater good. And because they're ambitious for a greater good, they feel no need to inflate their own egos. And they, according to the research, make the best business leaders.[23]

Compassion, says Meng, "also creates an inspiring workforce. Employees mutually inspire each other toward greater good. It creates a vibrant, energetic community where people admire and respect each other." And "this mutual inspiration promotes collaboration, initiative and creativity. It makes us a highly effective company."[24] Meng suggests that a company can "brew compassion" by (a) creating a culture of passionate concern for the greater good, (b) providing for a very high level of autonomy, and (c) by focusing on inner development and personal growth.

Fostering Compassion in the Workplace

This idea of focus was also expressed by CompassionLab's co-founder, Peter Frost, when he observed that compassion as a healing force in organizations served as a constant reminder of the power and importance of the Lab's research. In reflecting on that idea, he referred to a Cherokee proverb about the struggle each of us faces in staying focused on what matters. As the story goes,

> *He said to them, "A fight is going on inside me . . . it is a terrible fight and it is between two wolves. One wolf represents fear, anger, envy, sorrow, regret, greed, arrogance, self-pity, guilt, resentment, inferiority, lies, false pride, superiority, and ego. The other wolf stands for joy, peace, love, hope, sharing, serenity, humility, kindness, benevolence, friendship, empathy, generosity, truth, compassion, and faith. The same fight is going on inside you, and inside every other person, too." They thought about it for a minute and then one child asked his grandfather, "Which wolf will win?" The old Cherokee simply replied . . . "The one you feed."[25]*

The Lab contends that by

> *feeding the wolf of compassion, we can see the impact of small acts and begin to understand the extraordinary accomplishment of collective healing, as well as to think more deeply about how organizations build unique capabilities that bring out the best of the human condition.[26]*

Our contention is that ever-widening compassion for all life is the pathway to developing more conscious human beings. Organizations that aspire to facilitate that pathway recognize that we come to our workplaces as whole human beings, and that most of us will at times in our lives experience suffering and pain, or other anguish. A culture of care, where we are able to be open about our experience and receive nurturance in the process, can help us move on more quickly from these experiences and become more loyal and productive contributors to our organizations, communities, and societies.

Far too few organizations recognize that supporting their people to bring their private lives into the workplace—including their private pain and suffering—also invites them to bring their best and true selves into the workplace. Those with this recognition make sure that (a) managers and leaders themselves model compassion, (b) that there are processes and procedures in place that allow for responding to the needs of others, and (c) that codes of conduct include compassionate approaches to working through employee conflict and anger. These organizations consequently have employees with a stronger sense of responsibility for the well-being of others, who collaborate with other employees based on mutual care and concern, and who have increased sensitivity to the needs of customers and other stakeholders.

In addition to training and codes of ethics, leaders certainly play a role by modeling acts of compassion in their own relationships. Where an organization's leader models the open expression of certain feelings and shows concern for members' pain, others in the organization are much more likely to experience compassionate feelings as legitimate, and to share them openly with their colleagues. These leaders and organizations are rewarded with increased employee performance and productivity, along with reduced costs due to lost work time, stress, and other emotional issues. These costs are not insubstantial. A 2002 study by the Grief Recovery Institute estimated that firms lose more than 75 billion dollars annually from employees' grief-related incidents, a loss that is likely to be even greater a decade or more later.[27]

Readers can, right now, sign on to the Charter for Compassion, created by Karen Armstrong, a former Catholic nun and religious historian. Armstrong created the Charter when she won the 2008 TED Prize, which is awarded annually to one exceptional individual who receives $100,000 and the granting of "One Wish to Change the World." The charter was created through the voices of thousands of people all over the world, and then crafted by a gathering of multi-faith leaders. It reads, in part:

The principle of compassion lies at the heart of all religious, ethical, and spiritual traditions, calling us always to treat all others as we wish to be treated ourselves. Compassion impels us to work tirelessly to alleviate the suffering of our fellow creatures, to dethrone ourselves from the centre of our world and put another there, and to honour the inviolable sanctity of every single human being, treating everybody, without exception, with absolute justice, equity, and respect.[28]

Learn more about the Charter, sign on with your support, and find out how it is being used in organizations, schools, and communities all over the world at www.charterforcompassion.org.

Feeding the "wolf of compassion" in our own lives, and finding and creating workspaces where this practice is a way of life, may be essential work for all of us. His Holiness the Dalai Lama has written:

Once we have a firm practice of compassion our state of mind becomes stronger which leads to inner peace, giving rise to self-confidence, which reduces fear. This makes for constructive members of the community. Self-centredness on the other hand leads to distance, suspicion, mistrust and loneliness, with unhappiness as the result.[29]

Through compassion, we bring forth the possibility of peace, harmony, and justice that our deepest selves desire. The most profound call of these troubled times is the conversion of the pain of separation into an embrace of the entirety of the human family. Compassion is, to quote Nomfundo Walaza, "the catalyst to change the world."

*The best way to find yourself is to lose yourself
in the service of others.*[1]

— MAHATMA GANDHI

*I've learned that you shouldn't go through life with a
catcher's mitts on both hands. You need to be able to
throw something back.*[2]

— MAYA ANGELOU

TEN

GIVING BACK

The Story of the Tata Group

A more gracious host than Ravi Kant, Vice Chairman and former managing director of Tata Motors, you are most unlikely to meet. As we passed through the armed security at the door of Tata Motors Limited headquarters in Mumbai's Bombay House, stood in line with other vendors and visitors, offered our credentials, and followed our escort to Kant's executive suite, we wondered if we shouldn't be more intimidated than exhilarated by this interview opportunity. We quickly got over our qualms once Kant welcomed us into his office. We were immediately charmed and enthralled by this man, who is known as one of the more influential business leaders in Asia. Suave, unassuming, handsome, articulate and generous are just a few of the adjectives that come to mind to describe his persona. We couldn't wait to hear his story and the story of the company he helped to transform.

The Tata Group has business interests in energy, consumer products, chemicals, information technology, and materials, among others. At last report, Tata was made up of over 115 companies, operating in more than 80 countries. The better known companies include Tata Motors, Tata Steel, Tata Tea, Titan Industries, Tata Communications, and the luxurious Taj Hotels. These companies generate revenues of $83 billion annually, with a global workforce of nearly 450,000 people, 28 publicly listed companies, and an Indian shareholder base of 3.5 million. Tata Motors was founded in 1945 as a manufacturer of locomotives. The company moved into the commercial vehicle business in 1954, which became a highly successful and profitable business in India. After dominating that market, the company entered the passenger vehicle market in 1991, producing a number of models over the next several years, including the Indica, which became one of the best selling autos in the history of the Indian automobile industry.

A major economic downturn in the mid- to late-1990s took a significant toll on Tata Motors, shrinking the market for commercial vehicles at the same time that major investments had been made in passenger cars. Facing a considerable financial loss in the early part of this century, the company undertook a dramatic transformation through which it drastically reduced costs, strengthened its position in India, and took extraordinary steps to focus on a vastly increased global presence.

Ravi Kant became Managing Director of Tata Motors in 2005. Along with Tata Group President Ratan Tata, the great-grandson of founder Jamsedji Tata, Kant presided over a period of exponential growth and transformation. During this period the company acquired South Korea's Daewoo truck manufacturing business; became the controlling stockholder in Spain's Aragonese Hispano Carrocera, one of the largest manufacturers of bus and coach cabins in Europe; and entered into a joint venture with Brazil's Marcopolo, producer of over half of the bus bodies made in Brazil and exporter to more than 60 countries. Then, in an extremely bold move recognized the world over, Tata acquired the British company, Jaguar Land Rover.

The degree of change that occurred during that period has received a great deal of international attention. Tata Motors, Ratan Tata, and Ravi Kant have each been frequent subjects of case studies and interviews by those who seek to understand how such significant and successful change has occurred. In one such interview with the *McKinsey Quarterly*, Mr. Kant spoke at length about his philosophy of leading a change of this magnitude.

I certainly learned that the wisest approach is not to give
orders but to sell new ideas internally. Generally, people with

greater experience, especially in a successful company, are
often resistant to change because they have been successful
doing things the way they have been used to, not realizing
that the context has changed. This process of selling new
ideas took longer, of course, but unless people are convinced
about what you are asking them to do, they are not going to
make it happen.[3]

Engaging young people to promote innovation is also a signature approach of Mr. Kant's, as he explains in an example of new product development.

As a means of accelerating change, we identified
individuals who would serve as examples to others. For
example, I asked one young person if he would take over
our new small-truck project. I had to sell the idea to him
and encourage him to take the risk. As things turned out,
the project became a phenomenal success and he did a
fantastic job. A lot of other young people now want to take
on this sort of challenge. Now people are saying that if you
respond to challenges and take risks, you can cut through
the hierarchy and rise up in the organization.[4]

This same young person of whom Mr. Kant spoke was subsequently assigned to lead the team that developed the now famous "people's car," the Tata Motors Nano. The Nano—known as the world's cheapest (around $2,400 US) road car—was the vision of Ratan Tata, who saw the potential for providing affordable transportation for families who either had no transportation at all, or who were currently traveling unsafely by bicycle or scooter in India's infamous traffic. While the car is currently experiencing some challenges in the marketplace, it has been hailed the world over as an innovative feat of design, cooperation, ingenuity, and determination. In 2008, London's *Financial Times* reported,

If ever there were a symbol of India's ambitions to become
a modern nation, it would surely be the Nano, the tiny car

*with the even tinier price-tag. A triumph of homegrown
engineering, the Nano encapsulates the dream of millions of
Indians groping for a shot at urban prosperity.*[5]

In completing his McKinsey interview, Mr. Kant chose to emphasize that, above all else, there is a "Tata way" of achieving success
"transparently, ethically, and meeting our corporate social responsibility. We want to make India proud."[6] When he speaks of the "Tata
way," he is speaking to an unparalleled commitment to giving back to
society—which is the very essence of the Tata identity, grounded in
its history and the beliefs of its founder, Jamsetji Tata. "Corporate responsibility is in our DNA," Mr. Kant told us, but it is hard to compare
the Tata business model and tradition of altruism to any commonly
known form of what has become generally known as corporate social
responsibility, or CSR.[7]

The company that Jamsetji Tata founded in 1868 was built on his
belief that "in a free enterprise, the community is not just another stakeholder in business but is, in fact, the very purpose of its existence."[8] This
principle has permeated every aspect of the enterprise for nearly a century and a half, and it has led to the Tata business model of "trusteeship."

Unique among family-run companies worldwide, family members
own only three percent of the company. The Tata Trusts own close
to two-thirds of Tata Sons, the holding company. The Tata trusts actually make up the largest development funding source in India, giving
many millions of dollars inside and outside the country to a multitude
of prioritized causes, including education, health, agriculture, science,
community development, human rights, culture, and the environment.
Through its initiatives, the trusts have established their fair share of
India's most significant institutions, including the Indian Institute of
Science, the Tata Institute of Fundamental Research, and the Tata Me-
morial Hospital. The hospital was initially commissioned by the Sir
Dorabji Tata Trust in 1941, and is now a premier cancer research and
treatment center in Mumbai.

The trusts have become increasingly strategic in recent years, actively identifying areas of need and leverage for their social invest-

ments. The Tata trusts seek out nonprofit agencies with the capacity for carrying out their goals, rather than simply making ongoing contributions to existing beneficiaries. The trusts' diverse initiatives in rural development include poverty reduction in tribal communities, drought proofing in desert regions, crop diversification, community-based microfinance, reduction in the incidence of farmer suicides, and alternative sustainable water supply systems.

Tata gives back with its money, but also through its knowledge, technology, and ingenuity. The Nano automobile, of course, is one example. A more recent innovation, as reported in *The Economist* (March 2011) and popularly called the "nano house," is being developed by Tata Steel around a similar recognition of the needs of India's most disadvantaged populations. The company is currently piloting a build-it-yourself, pre-fabricated flat pack house in thirty locations, working with local *panchayats* (councils) to secure feedback from potential users, and incorporating ideas into the product's final design. It is anticipated that the home kits, which can be assembled in about a week's time, will include all the necessary construction materials, for a price of about $700 US. Twelve Tata Consultancy Services, in collaboration with two other companies, developed the Swach, a cheap water filter, partially made out of rice husks. The same company, working with Tata Teleservices, developed an early warning system for fisherman after the 2004 Asian tsunami, as well as developing an instructional package that teaches adults to read in forty hours.[9]

Giving Back and Transformation

Many terms could be used for giving back, but perhaps the most common is altruism. Social scientists who study altruism define it as voluntary actions that address needs outside oneself, without the burden of self-serving expectations. A good deal of research appears to support the idea that giving back is good for human health and well-being, and that the spirit of altruism is worth developing in ourselves and others. Tara Parker-Pope, in a *New York Times* article titled, "In Month of Giving, a Healthy Reward," highlights some of those research findings.

> *An array of studies has documented this effect. In one, a 2002 Boston College study, researchers found that patients with chronic pain fared better when they counseled other pain patients, experiencing less depression, intense pain, and disability. Another* **study, at the** *Buck Institute for Age Research in Novato, Calif., also found a strong benefit to volunteerism, and after controlling for a number of variables, showed that elderly people who volunteered for more than four hours a week were 44% less likely to die during the study period. How giving can lead to mental and physical changes in health isn't entirely clear, although studies suggest that altruism may be an antidote to* **stress.** *A Miami study of patients with H.I.V. found that those with strong altruistic characteristics had lower levels of stress hormones.*
>
> *By contrast, being self-centered may be damaging to health. In one study of 150 heart patients, researchers found that people in the study that had more "self-references" (those who talked about themselves at length or used more first-person pronouns) had more severe heart disease and did worse on treadmill tests.*[10]

And like Ms. Walker (the subject of Parker-Pope's *New York Times* article), numerous people have reported feeling better after helping others. A 1988 *Psychology Today* article dubbed this effect the "helper's high." Analyzing two separate surveys of a total of 3,200 women who regularly volunteered, the article described a physical response from volunteering, similar to the results of vigorous exercise or meditation. The strongest effect was seen when the act of altruism involved direct contact with other people.[11]

In another review of the research, author Shu Pang writes in the *Dartmouth Undergraduate Journal of Science*:

Altruism promotes deeper positive social integration, distraction from self-preoccupation, enhanced meaning and purpose, a more active lifestyle, and the presence of positive emotions such as kindness that displace harmful negative emotional states. Thus, it is entirely possible to assert that altruism enhances mental and physical health. The argument for causality is further strengthened by the inarguable assertion that emotional states of unselfish love and kindness displace negative emotional states like anxiety, hatred and fear, which cause stress-related illness by debilitating immune function. In the face of danger, the negative emotional states are important, but oftentimes, the fight-flight response and its corresponding negative emotions stay turned on for a long time even after there is no longer danger. Positive emotions elicited by altruism, thus, can gain dominance over anxiety and fear, turning off the fight-flight response and thus turning off negation emotions that would have compromised the body's immune system.[12]

Research supports altruism's impact on practitioners in terms of reduced stress and anxiety, more effective pain and depression management, better immune responses and health outcomes, as well as life satisfaction and even longevity. Promoting such positive emotions and the kinds of altruistic behaviors that produce these kinds of outcomes are surely beneficial to the individuals, communities, and societies in which they occur.

From a moral development point of view, altruistic behaviors represent the most developed of Richard Barrett's "Seven Levels of Consciousness." In describing this level, which Barrett simply calls Service, he writes,

We arrive at this level of consciousness when the pursuit of making a difference becomes a way of life. At this level of consciousness we embark on a life of self-less service. We are fully at ease with uncertainty and can tap into the deepest sources of wisdom. We learn to operate with humility and compassion.[13]

Surely this is a level of consciousness worth facilitating in the transformative workplace. For organizations that make environmental and social responsibility an essential part of their culture, the rewards in the marketplace can be great. A study by Harvard's Robert Eccles and George Serafeim with Ioannis Ioannou of the London Business School has shown that what they call "high-sustainability firms"—organizations that are deeply committed not only to environmental issues but also to a broad range of CSR (corporate social responsibility) initiatives—"generate significantly higher profits and stock returns, suggesting that developing a corporate culture of sustainability may be a source of competitive advantage for a company in the long-run." In their comparative study of 90 "high-sustainability" and 90 "low-sustainability" firms, the researchers found that

> *a more engaged workforce, a more secure license to operate, a more loyal and satisfied customer base, better relationships with stakeholders, greater transparency, a more collaborative community, and a better ability to innovate may all be contributing factors to this potentially persistent superior performance in the long-term.*[14]

Giving Back in the Workplace

Syngenta India, the agricultural company discussed more fully in the chapter "Manifesting Intention," is another extraordinary Indian company well known for giving back. Prakash Apte, formerly president and managing director of Syngenta, has now "retired" to be the non-executive chairman of the company, as well as serving as director of the Syngenta Foundation. The Foundation has multiple projects through which they seek to improve food security by helping small farmers in developing countries increase their productivity through sustainable agriculture. None of these projects is more significant to Mr. Apte than the project serving Maharogi Sewa Samiti (MSS). MSS is a community in central India, founded in 1949 by Baba Amte to support persons with leprosy. Over the years, it has become home to some 6,000 people who, with the Syngenta Foundation's help, are now able to produce enough vegetables to help sustain their livelihoods beyond the subsistence level.

MSS has had success in improving yields through demonstration projects, training and education, irrigation techniques, and crop planning, which has led to projects in other nearby locations. The Foundation, in cooperation with MSS, has also established the Anandwan Institute for Transfer of Agriculture Technology (AITA). The Institute, which opened in 2010, offers vocational and professional training in agricultural science as well as technology and business, and expects to add courses for rural youth, school drop-outs, and young professionals in the area. These and other Syngenta projects address not only poverty and sustainable livelihoods, but help to address the looming and enormous global issue of food and water security.

Of course, organizations with a strong orientation toward giving exist all over the world, employing a plethora of approaches to their giving as well as engaging their multiple stakeholders in the process. Some, such as the Tata and Syngenta organizations, are large global organizations that give in the true spirit of altruism, without expectation of return to themselves. To others, such as Tom's Shoes in the US, giving has been adopted as a highly successful business model. According to Tom's founder Blake Mycoskie, "Giving is what fuels us. Giving is our future. It's the core of our business and it's time we celebrate it."[15] The idea behind the company (although Blake refers to it as a movement, rather than a company) is a simple one: "One for One." When you purchase a pair of shoes from TOMS, a pair of shoes is also given to a child in need. The "movement" started in 2006 when Blake visited Argentina and learned the degree to which going without shoes impacts human health and well-being. Since then, over 1,000,000 people have been the recipients of footwear. In 2010, a trip to Nepal was the beginning of the second TOMS product based on the One for One model. There, Blake learned that there are 165,000,000 people in the world with impaired eyesight, and that 80% of cases of blindness in the developing world are preventable. Working with a partner, the Seva Foundation, TOMS launched its eyewear venture, through which customers' purchases help to restore sight through interventions including eye exams, cataract surgeries, and medications.

In another initiative designed to engage customers in giving back, Howard Schultz, Chairman and CEO of Starbucks, announced in 2011 that the company would partner with Community Development Financial Institutions (CDFI's) in a project called Create Jobs for USA. The idea came out of a group of Starbucks employees invited by the CEO to participate in a brainstorming pizza party at his home at which Schultz said, "Let's try to take a big swing at job creation that will be unprecedented and unorthodox."[16] The initiative invited customers to donate $5 at Starbucks stores, the entirety of which was channeled by the Starbucks Foundation to the CDFI's, and was used for lending to small businesses. Partners Banana Republic, Google Offers, Citi, MasterCard, and other companies also joined the effort, which raised more than $15.2 million in donations. CDFIs turned those funds into $105 million in financing for businesses to create or retain more than 5,000 jobs over the life of the initiative.

Fostering Giving in the Workplace

Organizational giving back, or altruism, is not only good for beneficiaries and the moral development of their employees. It is increasingly seen as being good for, if not an imperative for, business success. The popular book *Good for Business: The Rise of the Conscious Corporation* claims to be a primer for organizations attempting to embrace an enhanced social role for themselves and other stakeholders, including consumers. Co-authors Andrew Benett, Cavas Gobhai, Ann O'Reilly, and Greg Welch point to four "cornerstones of a conscious corporation:"

> **Have a purpose beyond profit.** *According to the authors, those companies that align themselves with a social role or cause will not only benefit those helped by the cause, but will enhance their corporate brand. More than simply stating a*

position, companies should clearly define their social mission and objectives, and carry them out by partnering with charitable organizations. Support can include a donation of a portion of its annual profits, corporate volunteerism, and ways for customers to share in helping the cause.

Treat people well. *Businesses must not be driven by laws of compliance or threat of exposure, but instead should be proactive in choosing to do what's in the best interest of the customer. And in an era where the ratio of CEO pay to that of the average worker is 364:1 (up from 10:1 just two decades ago), many corporations have a long way to go in respecting employees' interests and needs. Greater consideration for vendors, community members, board members, and even competitors is critical in forming a more conscientious corporate profile.*

Champion sustainability. *Most large corporations have grown past the point of debating environmental sustainability and now actively seek ways to make it happen. Many are also finding cost savings through greater energy efficiency and less waste. As with socially responsible programs, businesses need to communicate what they are doing in the environmental arena—and why. By educating consumers, businesses will find greater buy-in and program success.*

Respect consumers' power. *Conscious corporations are those that enter into a two-way conversation with their markets, acknowledging the more powerful role today's consumer plays in defining and promoting the brand. This may involve greater use of website interaction, social media, and blogs, especially in industries that are dogged by customer-service complaints. Even in the area of social responsibility, corporations can invite customers to weigh-in on preferences for charitable causes.*[17]

Organizations that aspire to create conditions that allow their people to develop a life of service, and to foster a culture of giving back, have dozens of options for achieving that goal. None, however, is more powerful than making service to others the purpose of the enterprise. Few are likely to exemplify service at a level of the Tata Group, given their century and a half of experience, but all can take steps in that direction. Program examples and business models are abundant in the business literature, including the emerging research and publications related to the concept of the "conscious" business.

Two organizations, the Pay It Forward Foundation and the Random Acts of Kindness Foundation, make it easy for individuals, teams, and divisions within organizations—and for schools, churches, and service organizations within communities—to promote a culture of giving back. Pay It Forward was popularized when Catherine Ryan Hyde published a book by that title that later became a film. The book and film urged people to do three good deeds for others in response to good deeds done for them, with the intention of starting a global movement of altruism. The Foundation's relatively new president, Charley Johnson, has received a great deal of attention because he left a lucrative family business to build momentum and coalesce the myriad Pay It Forward related initiatives around the world. When he introduced a program of providing free bracelets to those who would use them to promote the concept, the idea quickly caught on. Over a million bracelets have now been paid forward in well over one hundred countries around the world. While far short of Johnson's vision of engaging the world's 7 billion people, the work the foundation is doing is shifting minds through the simple act of giving back.

The term "random acts of kindness" is attributed to Anne Herbert, who is said to have once written, "Practice random acts of kindness and senseless acts of beauty" on a place mat in a restaurant. The Random Acts of Kindness Foundation, founded in 1995, is a resource for schools, service organizations, and communities, offering "activity ideas, lesson plans, project plans, teacher guides, project planning guides, publicity guides, and workplace resources." Their website is www.actsofkindness.org. The Foundation is the United States delegate to the World Kindness Movement (www.worldkindness.org), an organization that grew out of Japan's Small Kindness Movement, and now brings together representatives from similar organizations around the world. The organization's mission is "to inspire individuals towards greater kindness and to connect nations to create a kinder world."

Whatever the approach, evidence suggests that giving back in transformative workplaces generates better health and immune responses, lowers stress and anxiety (with an increased ease of response to uncertainty), and produces more positive emotion and life satisfaction as well as more humility and compassion for employees. For organizations that create those opportunities the payoffs can be great in terms of higher profits and stock market performance, customer loyalty and satisfaction, better relationships with stakeholders, and a greatly enhanced reputation in the marketplace. These investments pay off and also contribute to creating a world that works for everyone.

*Today we are faced with a challenge that calls
for a shift in our thinking, so that humanity stops
threatening its life-support system. We are called to
assist the Earth to heal her wounds and in the
process heal our own—indeed, to embrace the whole
creation in all its diversity, beauty, and wonder.[1]*

— WANGARI MAATHAI

*We are caught in an inescapable network of
mutuality, tied in a single garment of destiny.
Whatever affects one directly, affects all indirectly.
This is the interrelated structure of all reality.
You can never be what you ought to be until I
become what I ought to be.[2]*

— MARTIN LUTHER KING, JR.

ELEVEN

EMBRACING THE WHOLE

The Story of the GreenHouse Project

When we greeted Mabule Mokhine at our guest house in Johannesburg, South Africa, we had no idea that our interview would turn out to be one of the most inspiring and enlightening of our entire journey. We knew of Mabule's work in environmental sustainability and community organizing in urban Johannesburg from our friends at the Berkana Institute. But we were not prepared for the opportunity to tap into the depth of his wisdom, his humanity, his loving heart, and a worldview that can truly be said to embrace the whole of the universe.

Mabule came naturally to his current role as Acting Executive Director of the GreenHouse Project. He grew up spending most every day of his early years gardening in his backyard in Soweto, a job expected of most young people at the time. The garden was a place where he could work and reflect, and his experience led to a deep and lifelong connection to the earth. Often, once his chores were finished, he would gather with friends. Their conversations sometimes turned to what they might do to change living conditions in their township. Those early experiences and conversations have been the foundation for Mabule's lifelong work on a local, national, and global scale: to change the living conditions of the world's impoverished people.

As a young man, after studying the sciences at the University of Cape Town, Mabule began his community work by coaching youth soccer teams and tutoring students in mathematics. Over time, his passion for community and deep connection to the earth led him to

- work with the Community Zero Waste Programme;
- facilitate sustainable development learning experiences;
- work with the environmental and leadership development programs of Earthlife Africa and Common Purpose;
- service as a convener for the Berkana Exchange, a global network of leadership learning centers; and
- offer presentations at the Waste Conference in Berkeley (San Francisco), and the 2nd Summit on Sustainable Development in South Africa.

Mabule's work with the GreenHouse Project began in 2000, as a part of his role at Earthlife Africa. The project, initiated by Earth-life Africa and the City of Johannesburg, is located in Joubert Park, adjacent to one of the most impoverished areas of the city. Joubert Park was established in 1891 as a greenspace where Johannesburg's white inhabitants could take part in a variety of leisure activities. Over the years, as park facilities developed, residents could enjoy a fish pond, military band concerts on Sunday afternoons, performances in an open air theater built in the 1960's, a life-sized chessboard, and outdoor art exhibits. At Christmas time the park became a fairy tale land, with lighted trees, piped carols, and family activities. The ponds and vegetation of the Victorian Hothouse could be enjoyed year round, and the Johannesburg Art Gallery, opened in 1915 and expanded in the 1940s, housed world class art.[3] Black residents were of course excluded from these activities, though they were a part of the city's economy, primarily as workers in the mines.

Fast forward to the end of apartheid, and Johannesburg experienced a period of massive "white flight," while blacks, now free to live where they wanted, increasingly dominated the inner city. Because of mass poverty and unemployment, however, inner city neighborhoods became dilapidated and crime-ridden. The neighborhoods around Joubert Park became the most dangerous in Johannesburg. Fortunately, with the advent of public and private initiatives in recent years, these areas in the inner city are beginning to show signs of rejuvenation.

This is the context in which the GreenHouse Project (GHP) was established. As we walked through Joubert Park with Mabule, he explained that the GHP essentially does two things: demonstration and outreach. GHP is designed, he says, "to inspire people to what sustainable living is. Through demonstration a person can see how else things can be done. Outreach is about what relationships we can begin to build so that you can actually live your inspiration."[4] The GHP provides small community gardening plots and offers workshops for residents, including pre-schoolers, in permaculture techniques and healthy nutrition.

Project volunteers go out into the neighborhoods, collecting materials that are then sorted at a recycling center started by a workers' cooperative in 2006. Its recycling program helps people to see the impact that each individual has on earth's well-being. To Mabule, some of the great breakdowns we are seeing in society are "between people and people, people and the things we use, and people to the earth."

We use things only once or twice, and then they go in the dump. There is a disconnect between using something and then suddenly, having no relationship with it, or to what happens to it when it is thrown away. The connection between man and earth should be a given, but if it is not apparent to an average person, and if an average person is in the majority, that says a lot about the state of how we live life and what we need to be doing.[5]

The project's offices, constructed by community members through a Learn and Build program, are in a repurposed structure made of straw bales and other renewable resources. Materials from the old shed were recycled and repurposed as well, becoming both art and utilitarian items, including a solar cooking stove and a rainwater capture system. A current project will convert Joubert Park's old Victorian Conservatory, using similar experimental construction techniques. The GHP's mode of operating comes from a belief that ordinary things make change.

It's not the complex things that will bring the change that
people are looking for; it's the most basic things. If that is true,
then I can start doing that change in my own space with
myself. If I can project this possibility on every single living
human being, then there is the change.[6]

While Mabule's work is inspirational, a far more interesting story
was the one he told us about the roots of his own inspiration. We
were privileged to explore the deep questions of life's meaning with
him, and he began to describe what the African traditions of ubuntu
mean in his life and in his work. To Mabule, ubuntu is not a concept
or a theory or a religion, it is simply being. Ubuntu is so deeply who
he is, that it is just breathing in and breathing out, putting one foot in
front of the other, and walking the earth as a human being. Ubuntu,
Mabule tells us

is the state of connectedness with the self and the Self in its
totality, the earth, other people. It is the oneness of the self with
other selves. It is difficult to explain in the English language.
When you are with people who are very centered in the self
that is connected with other selves, everything is different.
The way they talk, how they relate to the other person and
other things in life, it is different. To them, being in that
state, time takes a different meaning altogether. If you go into
traditional knowledge systems, how you build your house,
the energy that goes into building it, the relationships that
you bring into building your house, what your house stands
for, it is all an expression of ubuntu, of a state of being.
Your standing with everyone in the community and their
standing in relation to you is taken for every member of the
community—that is ubuntu. It is a state of consciousness that
becomes subtle to our senses because of the way we live.[7]

Mabule's description of ubuntu is consistent with the writings of
Archbishop Desmond Tutu, who believes that ubuntu is "the essence
of being human."[8] "Ubuntu," Tutu writes,

is very difficult to render into a Western language. It speaks of the very essence of being human. When we want to give high praise to someone we say, 'Yu, u nobunto.' 'Hey so-and-so has ubuntu.' Then you are generous, you are hospitable, you are friendly and caring and compassionate. You share what you have. It is to say, 'My humanity is inextricably bound up in yours. We belong in a bundle of life.'[9]

Writer Sonal Panse notes that ubuntu

speaks of the fact that my humanity is caught up and is inextricably bound up in yours. I am human because I belong. It speaks about wholeness, it speaks about compassion. A person with Ubuntu is welcoming, hospitable, warm and generous, willing to share. Such people are open and available to others, willing to be vulnerable, affirming of others, do not feel threatened that others are able and good, for they have a proper self-assurance that comes from knowing that they belong in a greater whole. They know that they are diminished when others are humiliated, diminished when others are oppressed, diminished when others are treated as if they were less than who they are. The quality of Ubuntu gives people resilience, enabling them to survive and emerge still human despite all efforts to dehumanize them.[10]

This worldview is the foundation of Mabule Mokhine's life, as well as his dream for the future. "My dream," he says, "is to live in an Earth and Human Conscious society where homesteads grow their own food, harvest rainwater, treat and reuse grey water, generate energy from sustainable sources, and trade surplus resources equitably among themselves and with other neighbourhoods."[11]

Embracing the Whole and Transformation

A worldview is simply the story we tell ourselves about who we are, where we came from, where we're going, and what it all means.

These stories are the lenses through which we perceive everything around us, the perspectives through which we make decisions about our lives, the biases through which we decide who to love, who to hate, what path to take, and who to leave behind. They are eminently useful as they serve to make sense of our world. Without them we would probably be afraid to get out of bed in the morning.

However, it is quite difficult to change these stories once our own identities become bound up in them. This is true for individuals as well as for families, clans, organizations, cultures, and societies. We make up the stories that inform our individual and collective actions and then we may quite literally hold on to them for dear life. This, many would say, is the problem with our current stories. Violent conflicts at all levels are carried out in the name of worldviews that divide us rather than connect us, and make us want to kill each other to preserve them. In the long run, vast numbers of people are living out a worldview that not only disconnects us from each other, but from all of nature and the greater cosmos of which we are a part.

One writer has described the current dominant world view as one

> *dominated by the story called scientific materialism, where nature is believed to be made up of "dead" stuff, of lifeless atoms and molecules. Nature has no consciousness, no feelings, no intrinsic value, meaning, or purpose. And so we relate to nature without sufficient respect for its inherent sacredness. We plunder and rape and exploit it, and the consequences are not at all pretty. We face looming crises in ecology, in social systems, and in our personal lives as we struggle to make sense and meaning out of a world made up of cold, mindless, meaningless stuff. In such a world, all life—including human life and consciousness—is just a fluke, an accident. This is an alarming story, and it has drastic consequences.[12]*

The need for a new story more appropriate to our times is being called for by many scientists, spiritual leaders, writers, and advocacy organizations. One of those voices, the late Thomas Berry, has eloquently spoken and written about this call for over four decades. In 1978, for example, he published "New Story" as a part of a series of booklets he wrote based on the ideas of French philosopher, Teilhard de Chardin. Our first encounter with the piece was a revision published in Berry's book, *Dream of the Earth*.

> *It's all a question of story. We are in trouble just now because we do not have a good story. We are in between stories. The old story, the account of how the world came to be and how we fit into it, is no longer effective. Yet we have not learned the new story. Our traditional story of the universe sustained us for a long period of time. It shaped our emotional attitudes, provided us with life purposes, and energized action. It consecrated suffering and integrated knowledge. We awoke in the morning and knew where we were. We could answer the questions of our children. We could identify crime, punish transgressors. Everything was taken care of because the story was there. It did not necessarily make people good, nor did it take away the pains and stupidities of life or make for unfailing warmth in human association. It did provide a context in which life could function in a meaningful manner.[13]*

We had the privilege of meeting Thomas Berry, who, among other things, co-wrote *The Universe Story: From the Primordial Flaring Forth to the Ecozoic Era – A Celebration of the Unfolding of the Cosmos.* When we invited him to take part in a conference we were planning in 1993, he reciprocated with an invitation to visit him at his home at the Riverdale Center of Religious Research, which he founded in 1970. There we experienced his graciousness, his twinkling sense of humor, and an intelligence and wisdom beyond any we have encountered before or since.

Thomas Berry grew up in the hills of North Carolina, where his enchantment with the natural world led him on a life's journey of dedicated learning and writing. Over his lifetime, he became a Passionist priest, a cultural historian, a student of and professor of Asian religions, the author of over a dozen books, an advisor to the Clinton White House on environmental issues, and a self-described "ecologian." Berry is best known for *The Universe Story*, in which he and co-author Brian Swimme laid out the history and evolution of the earth, the universe, and humanity, and called for a transition from what they termed the earth-destroying Technozoic era of the present time to a visionary, co-creative, and earth-enhancing Ecozoic era.

In "Twelve Understandings Concerning the Ecozoic Era," written later in his life, Berry summarized his beliefs about the current situation and what is needed to bring about that shift. "The effects of human activity on Earth have become so pervasive and invasive," he wrote, "that the survival and health of the Earth community now rest on decisions being made, and actions being taken, by humans," and that there is a need "to move from the current technozoic period where Earth is seen as resource for the benefit of humans, to an Ecozoic Era where the well-being of the entire Earth community is the primary concern."

> *The epic task or "Great Work" of our time is to bring into being*
> *the Ecozoic Era. It is a task in which everyone is involved*
> *and from which no one is exempt, and it will require change*
> *in every aspect of human society. On it the fate of the Earth*
> *depends, and in it lies the hope of the future.*[14]

In his final book, *The Great Work: Our Way Into the Future*, Berry explicitly lays out what he believes to be the work of our time not only for individuals, but for corporations and the fields of education, religion, politics, and the law.

Berry also embraced the Earth Charter as "a comprehensive set of values and principles for the realization of the Ecozoic Era."[15] Discussions about creating such a charter were underway as early as 1987 with the aspiration of developing a universal set of guiding principles for sustainable development. Momentum built for such an initiative when, in 1994, Maurice Strong and Mikhail Gorbachev set in motion a process of drafting a charter that drew upon hundreds of existing international documents. After numerous iterations with the involvement of diverse contributors, a formal document came together in March, 2000. The Earth Charter has since been endorsed by thousands of organizations and stands as

> *a declaration of fundamental ethical principles for building*
> *a just, sustainable, and peaceful global society in the 21st*
> *century. It seeks to inspire in all people a new sense of global*
> *interdependence and shared responsibility for the well-being*
> *of the whole human family, the greater community of life, and*
> *future generations. It is a vision of hope and a call to action.*[16]

While a universal worldview that embraces the whole is not yet a reality, increasing numbers of people world-wide are understanding that we are, in fact, all one, and that our future depends on the decisions we make and the actions we take individually and collectively. Adult development researcher Susanne Cook-Greuter describes the perspective of those individuals.

> *The metaphor of climbing a mountain can serve as an*
> *illustration of what it means to gain an increasingly higher*
> *vantage point. At each turn of the path up the mountain I can*
> *see more of the territory I have already traversed. I can see the*
> *multiple turns and reversals in the path. I can see further into*
> *and across the valley. The closer I get to the summit, the easier*
> *it becomes to see behind to the shadow side and uncover*
> *formerly hidden aspects of the territory. Finally at the top, I*
> *can see beyond my particular mountain to other ranges and*
> *further horizons. The more I can see, the wiser, more timely,*
> *more systematic and informed my actions and decisions*
> *are likely to be because more of the relevant information,*
> *connections and dynamic relationships become visible.*[17]

Managers, leaders, and others in the workplace who observe and act from that perspective have a capacity for

> *more integrated and complex thinking, doing and feeling.*
> *They have a broader, more flexible and more imaginative*

perspective on the whole organization and its multiple contexts. They tend to cultivate relationships with many stakeholders, see promising connections and opportunities in novel places, and deal with problems in adaptive and proactive ways.[18]

Unfortunately, Cook-Greuter and others claim that as yet, only a very small percentage of people function from that perspective.

Embracing Wholeness in the Workplace

If highly evolved leaders are few and far between, it only makes sense that workplaces making wholeness a central theme for the development of their organizations and their people are also few and far between. However, the story of the transformation of Ray Anderson and Interface, the highly successful company he founded, may be an exception to the rule. Interface is one of the largest manufacturers of modular carpet in the world, and was founded by the late Ray Anderson in 1973. Initially the company's focus was on producing carpet tiles that could be replaced when worn out. The organization took a massive turn, however, when Anderson read Paul Hawken's book, *The Ecology of Commerce.* "Within ten pages," Anderson said,

I felt a spear in the chest. It was an epiphanal experience. Hawken makes the point that the species of earth are in steep decline and the biggest problem is the institution of business. There's only one institution that can turn things around, and that's the one that's doing the biggest damage—business and industry. As the founder, chairman and the CEO of my company (at that time), I "got it," right in the chest.[19]

Paul Hawken spoke to what happened next in the eulogy he delivered at the August 2011 funeral of Anderson:

We don't know exactly what happened to Ray in 1994. Yes, he read a book. But something remarkable was already there within his being that came to life. What we do know is that

from that point seventeen years ago, Ray could see. He saw
benevolence and beauty, the tightly knit longleaf pine forests,
the undulant riverine corridors of the Chattahoochee, the
tantalizing pure light of life reflected on bracts and fronds,
the drifting silvery spider silk that takes tiny passengers to new
forests. Once your eyes open to the magnificence of creation,
you cannot unsee.

He did not see nature as an abstraction to be worshiped
but as the matrix of reformation, the source of goodness, the
architecture of our spirit, the template of a future delineated
by people who know that business has no purpose lest it serve
and honor all of life, that our lives rely upon the kindness of
strangers and the damp forest floor and spirited grasses and
on you, his family, friends and fiercest admirers who loved
this man. He loved us all.[20]

Since 1996, Interface has reduced fossil fuel consumption by 60
percent and total energy use by 44 percent, curbed greenhouse gases
by 82 percent, reduced water use by 73 percent, and decreased waste
going to landfills by 67 percent. Meanwhile, revenue has grown 66
percent and earnings have zoomed. Since 2003, Interface has made
83 million square yards of carpet with zero environmental impact
linked to its production. The commitment of the people to the vision
of what is possible for Interface is also astounding. One story told by
Anderson speaks to the impact of that commitment on the design of
Interface products.

Our product designer asked his design team to go into the
forest, and spend a day and figure out nature's design
principles. How would nature design a floor covering? And
they spent a day and it finally dawned on them that you look
at the forest floor and there are no two things alike. No two
sticks, no two stones, no two leaves, no two anything alike. So
you got this sort of chaotic mix of diversity and you can pick
up a rock here and drop it there and you can't tell you've
changed a thing. Pick up a limb here and drop it there and

you can't tell you changed a thing. They came back to the studio and designed carpet tiles where the design in the face of the carpet tile, no two tiles were alike. We introduced that product—we called it Entropy, for obvious reasons: disorder. And in a year and a half it became the bestselling product in our line, faster than any other product ever has.[21]

Another story speaks to the degree to which that same level of commitment is instilled in Interface employees. When a female executive visited Interface to learn about the company's achievements, she expressed grave doubts to Anderson.

"I don't believe this stuff," she said, so Anderson let her loose. Soon, she began to quiz a fork lift driver.

"Ma'am, I come here every day to save the Earth," the driver said.

Anderson said, "She about collapsed."

The driver then explained how changes on the factory floor have reduced company costs and cut fuel consumption. Then he cut the conversation short because the emissions from his forklift were creating waste.

"She was a totally changed person," Anderson said. "It was love on the factory floor."[22]

Anderson was rightfully proud of the degree to which his values and vision became inculcated into the entire organization and contributed to the development of its people:

The psychologist Abraham Maslow had it right when he said that people want more than subsistence, or even development and advancement. They also want to be identified with a higher purpose. Interface's environmental commitment and more recently our reinvigorated citizenship, or social equity commitment, especially to education and the communities in which we operate, have positively affected both hiring and retention, and productivity as well. Better people are applying, and the best people are staying and working with purpose. The financial value of that is perhaps incalculable, too, but all of us in business know that in the long run people, and only people, make the difference in any company's success or failure. After eight years of nurture, sustainability is in the very DNA of Interface as well as in our mission statement. Our core values support sustainability. Our people are galvanized by this shared higher purpose. You can't beat that for bringing people together! When Fortune magazine names a smallish, billion dollar Georgia-based manufacturer one of the 100 best companies in America to work for, two years in a row, something is going on![23]

Upon his passing, Anderson left his company and the world with a vision of what is possible. In expressing his equation for future success, he said he imagined

more happiness with less stuff. That would reframe civilization itself and our whole system of economics if not for our species then perhaps for the one that succeeds us; the sustainable species, living on a finite earth, ethically, ecologically, and happily in balance with nature and all her natural systems for a thousand generations or ten thousand generations, that is to say, into the indefinite future.[24]

Another organization well-known for its expansive and inclusive worldview is Patagonia, the supplier of hardware and apparel for outdoor enthusiasts. Patagonia was founded by Yvon Chouinard, whose passion for rock-climbing as a young man was the impetus for creating the company. His first product, a hardened steel climbing piton—which he forged by himself and sold out of the back of his car in the late 1950s—became so successful that he formed his first company, Chouinard Equipment, Ltd. When the pitons became known as an environmental hazard, he switched gears and began to produce alternative aluminum chocks. By the early 1970s Chouinard had introduced a line of outdoor apparel and formed Patagonia with his wife, Malinda.

The 1970s were also the years when Patagonia began to take on a role in environmental issues and challenges, leading to a commitment of one percent of sales to such causes. In those early years, the company also became known for its employee benefits—including a cafeteria offering healthy foods, an on-site child care center, flexible working hours, and job sharing. Each year the company takes on a national education campaign for a selected environmental concern, as well as offering training and tools for environmental activists. The company is on a continual path to making its materials, structures, manufacturing, and distribution methods more responsible and sustainable.

A notable example of shifts made at the company is the transition from using conventionally grown cotton to organically-raised cotton in Patagonia apparel. In 1992, a group of executives visited a large cotton farm in California, and were astounded to learn the degree to which conventional practices were a major threat to the environment in terms of water consumption and chemical usage. The facts of the matter are, indeed, astonishing. Reports claim that "25 percent of the world's pesticides are used in cotton growing; 20,000 deaths annually are attributed to unintentional chemical poisoning; 8.1 tons of topsoil per acre are lost annually."[25] Over 700 gallons of water are needed to produce the cotton needed to make a single t-shirt! The costs associated with Patagonia's shift to organic material nearly took the company under, but given the company values, it almost had no choice. The experience of one supplier to the facts of conventional methods led him to say, "I came as a representative of business; I left a citizen of the earth."[20] It is this kind of shift of mind that is responsible for the choices the company makes, and the leadership it has come to exert among its peers.

Another of Patagonia's initiatives, the "Don't Buy This Jacket" campaign, has drawn criticism from those who see it as a hypocritical marketing ploy, rather than a sincere intention to encourage citizens to consume less. The campaign began in the lead-up to the holiday shopping season in 2011 with a full-page *New York Times* advertisement, which read, in part,

*Because Patagonia wants to be in business for a good long
time—and leave a world inhabitable for our kids—we want
to do the opposite of every other business today. We ask you to
buy less and to reflect before you spend a dime on this jacket
or anything else.*[26]

Then, in 2013, the company produced "Worn Wear," a 27-minute
video featuring the stories of people who have been using or wearing
a Patagonia product for many years.[23] In the film, Chouinard explains
its rationale. "We can't be a society that is based on consuming and
discarding endlessly. What we are trying to do is to make clothes that
can be handed down, that can last forever."[27] A Worn Wear website
now invites Patagonia fans to submit stories about their long-lasting
and beloved apparel.

In a May 2013 letter to employees announcing the company's
next steps, Chouinard wrote that Patagonia was morphing itself into
a new holding company called Patagonia Works, for the purpose of
"using business to help solve the environmental crisis." The holding
company will expand its interests in food, water, energy, and waste,
along with clothing, and use a $20 million fund to help like-minded,
responsible start-up companies bring about positive benefit to the
environment. "Others might see Patagonia Works and $20 Million &
Change as revolutionary business ventures,"[28] he wrote.

*We think both are just next logical steps to doing business
more responsibly. Economic growth for the past two centuries
has been tied to an ever-spiraling carbon bonfire. Business—
and human—success in the next 100 years will have to come
from working with nature rather than using it up. That is
a necessity, not a luxury as it's seen now in most business
quarters. We invite and encourage all companies to start to
work with us in that direction.*[29]

In its written history, the company has been open about its own
need to stay continually aware of and responsive to its impact on
the planet.

*During the past thirty years, we've made many mistakes
but we've never lost our way for very long. Although we
first intended Patagonia as a way to free ourselves from the
limitations of the original climbing business, precisely those
limitations have kept us on our toes and helped us thrive. We
still pursue climbing and surfing, activities that entail risk,
require soul, and invite reflection. We favor informal travels
with friends—doing what we love to do—to the camera-
covered event. We can't bring ourselves to knowingly make
a mediocre product. And we cannot avert our eyes from the
harm done, by all of us, to our one and only home.*[30]

Fostering Wholeness in the Workplace

The Interface story and the Patagonia story represent how a shift in worldview and an embrace of the whole can make a difference. For Ray Anderson, it was reading Paul Hawken's book, and for the stakeholders of Patagonia, it was seeing for themselves the destruction for which their own enterprise was responsible. Neither company focuses on sustainability in their business as a marketing ploy, or because it's a trendy topic. Neither has taken steps toward increased responsibility—from design, sourcing, manufacture, and distribution—simply to reduce cost and increase growth and profits, even though that has been the result in both cases. Neither Ray Anderson nor Yvon Chouinard became spokespersons for the earth's well-being to draw attention to themselves or their businesses. They think and act from a transformed consciousness of who they are, and how what they do matters to the planet.

Fortunately, other leaders are creating workplaces where employees and other stakeholders are developing more expansive and inclusive worldviews. Among them are adherents to what is becoming a "conscious business" movement, which appears to have been started by advocates of corporate social responsibility. A conscious business is said to be concerned with its "impact on a human's inner and outer world as well as animal and environmental well-being, both short-term and long-term effects of its actions or inaction," and which "chooses to be of benefit to the world and to function with awareness."[31] Their leaders are said to

> *inspire, transform, and bring out the best in those near*
> *them; understand that their role is to serve the purpose*
> *of the organization and to support the people within the*
> *organization; have an ongoing ability to energize, engage,*
> *and influence other people to find affirmative ways to restore*
> *dedication to organizational commitments and vision;*
> *connect with others by demonstrating empathy, honesty, and*
> *sensitivity to diverse viewpoints of others; show compassion*
> *and respect, listen attentively, elicit concerns and calm fears,*
> *answer questions honestly, involve employees at all levels in*
> *the organization's decision-making process; and purposely*
> *cultivate and nurture a culture of consciousness that is built*
> *around compassion, trust, care, and elevation of humanity.*[32]

In the nonprofit and social entrepreneurship world, there are thousands upon thousands of organizations that are founded on principles that embrace the whole of life and strive to offer products, services, or advocacy aimed at creating a more sustainable world for all. It is likely that most of these organizations would agree with Mabule Mokhine's sentiments when he said, "For me, I feel I am walking the edge between what is and is no more, and what should and is yet to be."[33] That is the edge that most of us are walking as we try to make our way from a worldview, a set of beliefs and assumptions, and a way of being in the world that are no longer working.

The challenges in making this shift are great. One case in point is the 2013 decision by the government of Ecuador to lift its ban on oil drilling in a part of the Yasuni National Park, which is home to the world's greatest diversity of plant and animal species, tribes of indigenous people who hunt and forage on the land just as their ancestors did, and enormous oil reserves. The ban on drilling was previously accepted when the United Nations forged an alliance of nations that were willing to pledge $3.6 billion to declare the area as an "intangible zone," where drilling would not be allowed. When only $13 million came forward, Ecuador's President Rafael Correa put out bids for drilling in the area, which many fear will go to Chinese oil companies. China loaned Ecuador over $7 billion to help take care of its debt and development projects when the country became an untenable global financial risk, after it defaulted in 2008 and 2009 on billions of dollars in what the government termed "illegitimate" debt.

Indigenous and environmental groups protesting the opening of more space for drilling in Yasuni have been muzzled or decertified. One such long-established group, Fundación Pachamama, had its headquarters raided and closed down, and the government dissolved the organization.[34] With a 27 percent poverty rate and no access to capital other than China and exploitation of its oil reserves, one could generously say that Ecuador is between the veritable rock and a hard place. It should be noted that Ecuador has, for years, been in litigation to force Chevron to pay billions of dollars to clean up oil contamination caused by Texaco, before they purchased in the company in 2001.

This still unfolding story, one of many that could be told around the world, points to an almost unimaginably complex global economic system based on a worldview that separates us from each other and the natural world. As Thich Naht Hanh writes in his book, *The World We Have*,

> We have constructed a system we can't control. It imposes
> itself on us, and we become its slaves and victims. We have
> created a society in which the rich become richer and the
> poor become poorer, and in which we are so caught up in our
> own immediate problems that we cannot afford to be aware
> of what is going on with the rest of the human family or our
> planet Earth. In my mind I see a group of chickens in a cage
> disputing over a few seeds of grain, unaware that in a few
> hours they will all be killed.[35]

Clearly, what is needed is a transformed system based on a dramatically shifted worldview, a universally accepted new story of who we are and what our role is in the larger scheme of things. One of the most beautiful writings of Thomas Berry makes this claim better than we ever could. In writing about his beloved Hudson River Valley, he wrote

> Tell me a story. How often we said that as children. Tell
> me a story. Story illumined the world for us in childhood.
> Even now we might make the request: tell me a story. Tell
> me the story of the river and the valley and the streams and
> woodlands and wetlands, of the shellfish and finfish. Tell
> me a story. A story of where we are and how we got here
> and the characters and roles that we play. Tell me a story,
> a story that will be my story as well as the story of everyone
> and everything about me, the story that brings us together in
> a valley community, a story that brings together the human
> community with every living being in the valley, a story that
> brings us together under the arc of the great blue sky in the
> day and the starry heavens at night, a story that will drench
> us with rain and dry us in the wind, a story told by humans
> to one another that will also be the story that the wood
> thrush sings in the thicket, the story that the river recites in
> its downward journey, the story that Storm King Mountain
> images forth in the fullness of its grandeur.[36]

There is no more important work to be done than for each of us to participate in shaping and sharing a story that embraces the whole of life. Nobelist Wangari Maathai spoke the urgency of this work in her acceptance speech:

> In the course of history, there comes a time when humanity
> is called to shift to a new level of consciousness, to reach a
> higher moral ground. A time when we have to shed our fear
> and give hope to each other. That time is now.[37]

If there is to be peace in the world,
There must be peace in the nations.
If there is to be peace in the nations,
There must be peace in the cities.
If there is to be peace in the cities,
There must be peace between neighbors.
If there is to be peace between neighbors,
There must be peace in the home.
If there is to be peace in the home,
There must be peace in the heart.[1]

— LAO TZU (570 - 490 B.C.)

Before directing the lightning in the sky, we must first
harness the storms in our own hearts.[2]

— MOTTO OF THE RASUR FOUNDATION INTERNATIONAL

TWELVE

BEING PEACE

The Story of the Rasur Foundation International

The story of how Rita Marie Johnson became the founder of the Rasur Foundation International, an organization that has become a significant influence in the global peace movement, is one that began when she was only 10 years old, growing up in rural Missouri. Rita Marie's first inkling that she was destined to do peace work occurred while she and her brother were waiting on their farmhouse porch to begin the annual Fourth of July fireworks. Growing impatient and deciding to go for a walk down the road, Rita Marie remembers coming upon an extraordinary Missouri sunset, and being immediately filled with a sense of peaceful calm. During her first encounter with what she now refers to as being "guided into her life," she clearly heard her inner voice say, "You will work for peace." She remembers thinking, "I couldn't imagine what it could possibly mean," but she also recollects a sense of deep reassurance that the meaning would become clear.[3]

When we attended Rita Marie's *BePeace™* course at the University for Peace in Costa Rica she shared her initiation story, as well as the story of a life's work that has led to the world's first national infrastructure for creating peace. After completing her education in the United States and working in many positions serving a variety of needy populations, Rita Marie learned that Costa Rica was the only country in the world without a standing army. She decided that her next move was to relocate to Costa Rica and learn from them, and to find out how she might help that country in its quest for peace.

Upon moving to Costa Rica, Rita Marie found a like-minded mentor in Robert Muller, the UN's Assistant Secretary-General for over forty years, and one of the founders of Costa Rica's University for Peace (UPeace). During her tenure at the University from 1999 to 2002, Muller introduced Rita Marie to an old and prophetic Costa Rican poem called *Rasur*. The poem, written by Roberto Brenes Mesén in 1946, is summarized as the story of

> *a master teacher, Rasur, who mysteriously appears one day*
> *and silently woos the children of the village, Quizur, deep into*
> *a mountain. There he awakens the wisdom of the children*
> *so that they realize the knowledge within their hearts and*
> *they experience the love that heals all wounds. They share*
> *this newfound awareness with their parents and, in this way,*
> *Quizur becomes a tiny culture of creativity and peace.*[4]

Inspired by the book's prophesy that Costa Rica would become a model of peace in the world, Rita Marie established the Rasur Foundation to help bring peace education to the country and the world.

While at UPeace, Rita Marie wrote a book, *The Return of Rasur: The Story That Holds the Answer to Education in our Time*, and produced a musical called Rasur. The musical was performed in the largest theatre in Costa Rica, and proclaimed by the country's president, himself a Nobel Peace Prize winner, to be "a cultural event of national interest."[5] During this period Rita Marie continued to develop her own practice of living peacefully. She continued to learn more about disciplines and methodologies for inner calm and peaceful communication that might inform her work. Finally, she had what she describes as an "aha!" moment, when she discovered a link between HeartMath and Non-Violent Communication. The integration of these two methodologies became the *BePeace™ course*. The aim of the course is to provide practitioners with the skills

- to "feel peace," defined as the ability to remain peaceful under stress (an emotional skill);
- to "speak peace," defined as the ability to communicate empathically and honestly (a social skill); and
- to "teach peace," as one refines the practice through experience and training.[6]

The Rasur Foundation International founded the Academy for Peace on a campus that Rita Marie named Quizur near Costa Rica's capital city of San Jose, and it became the site of teacher and practitioner training in the BePeace™ methodology. Hundreds of teachers were trained in the methodology, an initiative that impacted many thousands of children. During this period Costa Rica passed a law requiring peace education in all of the country's public schools.

UPeace continues to offer the course to its own students and others on an annual basis. The university describes the power of the course as arising from

the synergy of combining coherence with connection,
which allows individuals to resolve issues efficiently and
peacefully, and expects practicing participants to be able to:
  - Release stress, worry, anger, and depression.
  - Open up and rely on your intuition.
  - Create deep self-confidence.
  - Resolve inner & interpersonal conflicts efficiently.
  - Become calm and clear when facing conflicts.
  - Connect with your feelings and needs.
  - Communicate honestly and empathically.

These benefits, according to UPeace, "lead to enriched relationships and the ability to contribute continuously to creating a more peaceful world."[7]

Rita Marie's most notable accomplishment to date has been her influence in passing the 2009 legislation that created Costa Rica's Ministry of Peace, making it the third country in the world to have such a ministry (the others are Nepal and the Solomon Islands). Beginning in 2006, Rita Marie and the foundation initiated the proposal for the new ministry, which drew enthusiastic support from President Óscar Arias Sánchez, a 1987 recipient of the Nobel Peace Prize. Three years of effort led to the passage of the bill in 2009, and gained recognition for Rita Marie and her team. In making its own announcement of the bill's passage, Canada's campaign to establish a similar ministry wrote: "Congratulations are due to Rita Marie Johnson and her team at the Rasur Foundation, the principal NGO voice for a Minister of Peace, who worked for 3 years on this project."[8] Just after the Ministry was established, Costa Rica hosted the Global Alliance Summit for Ministries and Departments of Peace at Quizur, a gathering of 200 people from 41 countries, facilitated by Rita Marie's foundation.

To complete what Rita Marie refers to as a national infrastructure for peace, her foundation also formed an alliance of nonprofit organizations to create a national plan for peace promotion, which is now facilitated by the government as a full partner. With teachings in the schools, a grassroots movement of NGO's, and the Ministry for Peace now well established, Rita Marie characterizes Costa Rica's model as "bottom-up, inside-out, top-down, and all-around."[9] Rita Marie continues to support the work in Costa Rica and spread her teachings to other places in the world, including the implementation of BePeace™ methodologies in a dozen U.S. schools.

Being Peace and Transformation

In a letter written in recognition of the Global Alliance Summit for Ministries and the Departments of Peace event in Costa Rica, the Dalai Lama spoke to the need for peace in the individual hearts of all human beings.

> *Peace is not something which exists independently of us, any more than war does. Those who are responsible for creating and keeping the peace are members of our own human family, the society that we as individuals participate in and help to create. Peace in the world thus depends on there being*

*peace in the hearts of individuals. Peace based merely on
political considerations or prompted by other compulsions
will only be temporary and superficial.*[10]

Peace in individual hearts is what the Dalai Lama and other
Buddhist teachers term "equanimity." Equanimity is referred to as
"the crown and culmination of the four sublime states," the others being love, compassion, and sympathetic joy.[11] As one teacher
describes it, "Equanimity is essentially an umbrella for our most
coveted human virtues: integrity, honesty, empathy, authenticity,
patience, compassion, etc."[12] It is a way of being in the world and
a developmental challenge that includes and transcends the others
we have written about in this book. It is a state of consciousness
that most of us are unlikely to achieve in our lifetimes, although we
may experience moments of its presence for small or fleeting peri-
ods of time. One group of researchers wrote in a recent article that
while "equanimity captures potentially the most important psychological element in the improvement of well-being," it is a "mental
state or trait that is not easily achieved and typically requires some
form of practice."[13]

Buddhists also refer to love, compassion, sympathetic joy, and
equanimity as "the four immeasurables." The emerging field of contemplative science is, in recent years, attempting to better understand
this state of consciousness, to better define it, and even measure it
objectively. The researchers mentioned above, for example, suggest
that equanimity is an even-minded state which is

*(i) a mental attitude of openness, even-mindedness, and
acceptance that one purposefully cultivates (e.g., during
formal meditation practice and/or throughout daily
activities), and (ii) an enduring state or trait that is the end
result of this form of training.*[14]

Through long training, they suggest, equanimity becomes an ef-
fortless way of being in the world. It is not simply practicing peace or
taking peaceful actions, it is "being peace."

These researchers refer to a clear distinction that Buddhist schol-ars make between mindfulness—a way of being that we discussed in the Practicing Inner Reflection chapter—and equanimity. Mindfulness, they write, "emphasizes the ability to remain consciously aware of what is happening in the field of experience, while equanimity allows awareness to be even and unbiased by facilitating an attitude of non-attachment and non-resistance." To explain that distinction they use the following useful metaphor from the classical Buddhist tradition.

> Loving-kindness (metta) is likened to the sentiment felt by a mother toward a newborn infant (May she be well! May he thrive!); compassion (karuna) is the feeling extended to a sick child (May she be free from pain and suffering!); sympathetic joy (mudita) is how a mother feels toward a grown boy who leaves home to marry (Though it may be painful for me, I feel joy for him!); and equanimity is how a mother might feel on hearing about her grown child's business dealings—she is attentive and caring about his welfare (not disengaged or indifferent), yet has no emotional entanglement to the content of the news she hears. (Nanamoli 1991, p. 314).[15]

The researchers also emphasize that equanimity is "the essential foundation of psychoanalytic theory," because this discipline holds that "all forms of emotions should be held in awareness with an attitude of acceptance in order to be healthy."[16] These definitions and distinctions, they believe, are important in that so much of the literature on well-being and human flourishing aims at "maximiz-ing pleasure and sustaining happiness while avoiding or eliminating pain and ameliorating the effects of emotional discomfort." Alterna-tively, they write,

> It may be that overall well-being is better served by learning to cultivate equanimity, both as an effective state for responding skillfully to whatever is arising in the present moment, and as a healthy trait that can be strengthened over time and integrated into one's character.[17]

The Dalai Lama has been instrumental in supporting and con-tributing to research that aims to help create a more peaceful and just world. One such case in point is his long relationship with the University of Wisconsin's Richard Davidson, who serves as the found-ing chair of the Center for Investigating Healthy Minds. Much of Da-vidson's research is based on a meeting at the request of the Dalai Lama in 1992, in which the two explored the potential contribution that science could make to learning about and advancing the positive effects of meditative practice. Since that time, Richardson and his staff have studied the brains of numerous Tibetan monks, as well as highly experienced and novice meditators. The work of the center has ex-panded to include work with preschool children in Madison, as well as with soldiers suffering from PTSD.

Davidson is confident that the results of the Center's research will have far-reaching impact, from eliminating bullying to reducing obesity rates. "We have really big ambitions for this work," he says. "It's not just to conduct mundane scientific research but it's really to transform the world."[18] Like so many others, he believes that peace in the larger world will begin with the inner peace of individuals. "I think that any kind of change has to begin with ourselves, and I think most people would agree that we're in a friggin' mess right now in the world," he says.

> *And the mess has been created by us. It's a product of
> greed, it's a product of lack of compassion, it's a product of
> not being able to understand our interdependence among
> ourselves and among the physical resources on the planet.
> And in order to promote more positive change I think that we
> need to each embody it ourselves first.*[19]

While few may embody the kind of inner peace that could trans-form the world, Rita Marie Johnson has expressed her faith in that potential. "In all of my experience of teaching peace," she says,

> *I have found that every human being has a heart's desire to
> be able to be a better person, to be a more peaceful person.*

*I believe that peace is inevitable. It is within us. It is our
essence. It is who we are. We have what it takes to achieve
peace on earth. We can find our way home.*[20]

Being Peace in the Workplace

Given that so few individuals have the capacity for "being peace,"
it stands to reason that few workplaces embrace that way of being
as part of their larger purpose. One organization that does just that,
however, is the Kyocera Corporation. Founded by Kazuo Inamori in
1959, when he was just 27 years old, this global corporation now has
over 30,000 employees world-wide, producing a wide variety of products from cell phones to cameras. From the beginning, Inamori says,
he felt strongly that "elevating my own mind and polishing my own
heart were absolutely necessary if I were to continue to successfully
develop the business."[21]

The early commitment Inamori made in his own life is reflected in
the goals of the company, and made explicit in its motto, management
rationale, and management philosophy.

Corporate Motto
"Respect the Divine and Love People"
*Preserve the spirit to work fairly and honorably,
respecting people, our work, our company, and our global
community.*

Management Rationale
*To provide opportunities for the material and intellectual
growth of all our employees, and through our joint efforts,
contribute to the advancement of society and humankind.*

Management Philosophy
*To coexist harmoniously with nature and society.
Harmonious coexistence is the underlying foundation of
all our business activities as we work to create a world of
abundance and peace.*

These ideas are also codified in this excerpt from the Kyocera Employee's Action Guideline Pocketbook.

> *'What is the right thing to do as a human being?' is the criterion for making decisions.*
>
> *A company is a collective entity made up of the consciousness of all employees who work there. Each employee holds certain thoughts as he or she undertakes their work. The way of thinking and attitudes of all employees combine to become the corporate culture and climate, ultimately crystallizing in corporate performance.*
>
> *Employees are asked to ascertain clearly the direction in which the company is heading, and the company goals. Based on that awareness, employees should attain a correct understanding of their role. Then, devote themselves on a daily basis to attaining a sense of responsibility, good faith, diligence, justice, fairness and other aspects of wonderful human nature, as explained in the Kyocera Philosophy. As individual employees grow, Kyocera, the sum total of individual growth, remains a company that is increasingly trusted and respected by society and customers.*[22]

Inamora's commitment to these ideas is derived from his belief that "the human race is facing a turning-point in history. In politics, business and other areas of society, the old order no longer seems to function well. A new framework and way of thinking are being sought." This new way of thinking, he writes, is "a philosophy that enables all living things on earth to survive and thrive—the spirit of 'Living Together.'" Most important for businesses fulfilling their public responsibilities, he concludes, "is building mutually supportive relationships in order for society—including businesses—to continue their existence. It is vital that business management is based on the spirit of Living Together for mutual development to occur."[23]

Inamora's reach has extended well beyond Kyocera. In 1983, in response to a request from just six young business owners who wanted to learn from him, he began a teaching process that would eventually become the global school called Seiwajyuku that now has 70 branches in Japan and 16 branches in other countries.[24] In a year-end study session in 2013, Inamora told the institution's Japanese students, "However affluent you become, you will never be able to gain a sense of fulfillment, as long as you have unchecked desire. Whether you can feel happiness or not depends on your own inner being." [25]

Kazuo Inamora retired from Kyocera in 1996 to become an ordained Buddhist monk at age 65. This development, however, did not mean that he withdrew from spreading his influence around the world. In 2006, at age 74, he published the best-selling book *A Compass to Fulfillment: Passion and Spirituality in Life and Business*, followed six years later by *Amoeba Management: The Dynamic Management System for Rapid Market Response*, a book that describes Kyocera's approach to management by dividing the company into small units called amoebas that can "uphold the policy of the company as a whole." In 2006, the Inamori International Center for Ethics and Excellence was established at Case Western Reserve University in Cleveland, Ohio for the purpose of fostering ethical leadership around the world. The Center offers an annual Inamori Ethics Prize whose ethical behaviors have "greatly improved the condition of humankind." The 2013 prize was awarded to Yvon Chouinard, the founder of Patagonia, Inc.[26]

At age 77, when Japan Airlines was entering bankruptcy protection, Inamori was tapped to become its CEO. He accepted that role, without pay, on the condition that sharing "the idea that the company's goal is to make all employees happy is a prerequisite, before sharing any other ideas."[27] He told the press that "my simple philosophy is to make all the staff happy," he says. "It has been my golden rule since I founded Kyocera when I was 27."[28] In just under three years, Inamori led the company through a complete restructuring and its relisting on the Tokyo Stock Exchange. It can be assumed that Inamori's work in the world is not finished. He once told an interviewer when asked about his future goals, "As long as I live, I would like to continue to contribute to the material and spiritual happiness of humanity and society."[29]

Of course, Kazuo Inamori is not the only CEO whose aspirations include becoming more conscious themselves, and encouraging that development in their employees and other stakeholders. One such leader is William Ford, Executive Chairman of the Ford Motor Company, who told an audience at the 2013 Wisdom 2.0 conference that his own long spiritual practice is the underpinning of his leadership philosophy and decision-making. Ford has been known to take many personal and professional risks in his career, including his advocacy for greater environmental standards for the industry, his personal engagement with employees and families who suffered deeply from the company's Rouge Plant explosion in 1999, his willingness to put up everything to ensure the company's health during the recent economic crisis, and his current concerns about "global gridlock," caused in large part by the number of vehicles on the road around the world.[30]

Another leader speaking at the Wisdom 2.0 Conference, Mark Bertolini, CEO of the Aetna Insurance Company, told the story of his own personal transformation. In 2001, his son was diagnosed with an incurable cancer. Bertolini left his job and literally spent almost a year in a hospital room caring for his son, as well as donating his kidney. During his son's recovery time, Bertolini broke his neck in a near-fatal skiing accident with his daughter. He currently suffers from continual neuropathic pain, which he deals with not through drugs, but through a combination of acupuncture, cranial-sacral therapy, yoga, and meditation, approaches not generally funded by health insurance providers. These experiences have led him on a search for medical evidence that would support access to these alternative approaches. "We really need to redefine health," he says,

as keeping people healthier so they're more productive. If they're more productive, they're more economically viable. If they are economically viable, they are happier. And when they are happier, particularly in groups, we have better communities, we have less uncivil dialogue among each other, and we develop, love and nurture our children, and grow our communities, and make the planet a better place.[31]

Bertolini maintains a highly disciplined daily personal practice, because

> *I know I'm heading into a chaotic world where I'm going*
> *to hear a lot of good and bad things, and I'm going to be*
> *challenged about my own worth, and unless I can bring*
> *myself to that environment in a steady and mindful way and*
> *to be present in the moment every opportunity I get, then I*
> *can't help the people around me and lead them.*[32]

That's equanimity!

Fostering Inner Peace in the Workplace

As more and more research comes forth with evidence that inner peace has a significant impact on health, and as more and more leaders come forth and speak to the role of peace and equanimity in their personal and professional success, it is likely that more and more managers and leaders will promote this state of well-being in the workplace. As we noted in the Practicing Inner Reflection chapter, meditation, yoga, and other offerings are now fairly common in all kinds of enterprises. The question we need to ask, however, is how these practices might move beyond individual well-being to impact the larger world. As Pema Chodrin has written

> *For many, spiritual practice represents a way to relax and*
> *a way to access peace of mind. We want to feel more calm,*
> *more focused; and with our frantic and stressful lives, who*
> *can blame us? Nevertheless, we have a responsibility to think*
> *bigger than that these days. If spiritual practice is relaxing,*
> *if it gives us some peace of mind, that's great—but is this*
> *personal satisfaction helping us to address what's happening*
> *in the world? The main question is, are we living in a way*
> *that adds further aggression and self-centeredness to the mix,*
> *or are we adding some much-needed sanity?*[33]

One movement toward achieving greater global sanity is called "peace through commerce." One of its leading advocates, Timothy Fort of George Washington University, speaks to the urgency of creating global conditions of peace. He writes:

> *Given what we have seen in the world, given terrorism, changing borders, a proliferation of weapons of all kinds of different levels of destruction, given ethnic warfare and given the ecological damage wrought by war, how can we not try to think through how we might create conditions of peace— politically, religiously, and economically?*[34]

In considering the possibilities, Fort asks,

> *How do individual businesses treat their own employees? How do they treat the citizens of countries in which they work? Are they culturally sensitive or are they imperialistically domineering? Are they ecological stewards or do they dump toxic waste in the rivers used by disfavored ethnic groups for their drinking water? Do they consort with corrupt officials? What do they do about encouraging voice in the workplace or in protecting human rights or gender equity? How do they impact religious beliefs?*[35]

Peace through commerce stems from the same roots as the "conscious capitalism" movement, and while the two approaches are different, they have similar aspirations for the role that businesses can play in bringing about peace from the individual to the global sphere. The philosophy of Timothy Fort's organization is that "peace is not simply the absence of war and conflict; it is also a virtue, a higher order state of mind and prosperity, a disposition for benevolence and justice."[36] His scholarship and approach focus on three levels of business virtues or ethics, which he calls hard trust, real trust, and good trust.

> *Hard trust comes from a company's respect for the law, the threat of lawsuits, and boycotts. Real trust is embodied by*

corporations that have internalized standards of integrity,
transparency, and human decency into the corporate DNA,
and "do the right thing" at every opportunity and every level.
Good trust, meanwhile, goes beyond "doing the right thing" to
aspiring to be a force for positive change in the world. [37]

Norway's Business for Peace Foundation has adopted Fort's concept of Good Trust as the basis for its annual Oslo Business for Peace Award, which is given to individuals based on their ethical and responsible decision making. Awardees are selected by a committee of Nobel Prize winners in Peace and Economics.[38]

Timothy Fort is optimistic about ethical business practices as a way for businesses to contribute to peace through commerce. "The good news," he writes,

is that significant work has already been done to set out
what businesses should do from legal, managerial, and
spiritual perspectives. The additional good news is that
the recommendations are not that controversial. Instead,
the practices are pretty well accepted. By more mindfully,
comprehensively, and seriously pursuing them, ethical
business behavior could have an unexpected payoff: a kind of
commerce where corporations are instruments of peace.[39]

Let us hope that his optimism is grounded in realism, and that the workplace can become the context in which we can all bring peace into our own lives and into our families, communities, and societies.

As human beings, our greatness lies not so much in being able to remake the world—that is the myth of the atomic age—as in being able to remake ourselves.[1]

—MOHANDAS GANDHI

You've got to find what you love and that is as true for work as it is for lovers. Your work is going to fill a large part of your life and the only way to be truly satisfied is to do what you believe is great work. And the only way to do great work is to love what you do. If you haven't found it yet, keep looking and don't settle. As with all matters of the heart, you'll know when you've found it.[2]

—STEVE JOBS

CONCLUSION

MAKING WORK THAT TRANSFORMS

Choosing Transformation

The question we address in this book is, "How might the places we work—in addition to being places where we accomplish the goals and purposes of the enterprise—also be places where we can become who we are meant to be as human beings?" Workplaces that fulfill this purpose in our lives create a context in which we can grow and develop to our highest potential as fully aware and conscious participants in the evolution of life on our planet.

Not everyone, however, has the privilege of working for an organization like Patagonia or Interface or Oleana, or for leaders like Ravi Kant, Alex Khajavi, or Prakash Apte. Few people have had the opportunity to head up organizations like the Desmond Tutu Peace Center, Creative Handicrafts, or the Rasur Foundation International. Many people are in jobs that stifle their creativity, crush their spirit, or even make them physically or emotionally ill. Steve Jobs has admonished us to be persistent in finding "great work" that we love, but many would view this as a fantasy far from their current reality. And yet many people do believe that each of us, as Rumi said long ago, "has been made for some particular work, and the desire for that work has been put in every heart."[3] We also believe, as Thomas Berry has written, that each of us has a role to play in what he called The Great Work of shifting from a system that is destroying the planet, to one that treasures all of life.

Lao Tzu is believed to have said that, "The journey of a thousand miles begins with one step."[4] In this case, the journey of making work that transforms begins with a personal choice for transformation. Believing that you have a unique role to play in the larger scheme of things, and then committing yourself to a path of development, is not an easy choice to make. A lot of things can get in the way, including busyness, the complexities of life, and even messages from the past (or present) that make you question your worthiness. This choice can even be painful, if what is preventing your improvement involves surfacing realities that you would just as soon keep hidden. The first step may simply be a commitment to yourself that your own growth and development matters: You matter. Your life matters. There are things to be done in the world, and if you don't do them, they won't get done.

What you choose to do next will be a function of your personal circumstances and your assessment of where you are along your own development path. There are many ways to make that assessment, but one way is to look back on the chapters in this book to see if any of them have particular resonance for you. Do you have a sense that you need to take more time for inner reflection and attend to your own well-being? Is the way you're looking at the world right now working for you? Do the ideas of giving back, embodying compassion or being peace evoke some interest or energy? Do you have a desire for more autonomy or meaning in your work?

Another consideration regarding the idea of making work that transforms is where you are in relationship to your workplace. If you work for an organization that supports you in your development, you are most fortunate. If not, one obvious choice is to leave and find a workplace that fits your personal development goals, as well as your skills and talents. Another is to stay where you are and find ways to make the work you do more transformative. If you have an entrepreneurial bent, you may find that now is the time to start that venture you always dreamed of. If you are in a management or leadership position from which you can influence how your workplace supports the personal and professional development of the people, you can do a lot to make both the workplace (and the world) a better place. If the focus of your work is your home and family, you could not possibly be in a better place from which to influence your own transformation, and the transformation of your family members.

One other consideration in choosing transformation may seem obvious, but it is probably worth a reminder: engaging in a process of personal growth and development is not possible without some kind of reflective practice. That practice could be meditation, yoga, prayer, gardening, walking, communing with nature, or any other activity that helps you to be aware of the present moment. The time spent focused on simply being, rather than thinking and doing, not only creates the space for inner peace and growth in consciousness, but contributes to overall health and well-being.

While this is neither a self-help book nor a career search guidebook, the next few sections of this chapter may offer some inspiration about making the work you do more transformative—that is, making where you work a place where you and those you work with can become more and more of who you are meant to be in the world.

Making Your Own Work Transformative

If you are like most people, you spend most of your waking moments in some kind of work. It can certainly be challenging to act on a commitment to transformation without making the use of your workplace as the context for your personal growth and development. It is usually relatively easy to develop new ways of *doing* things in the workplace, but it is more challenging to develop new ways of *being* at work.

One approach to making your own work more consistent with who you are—or who you want to be in the world—is called job crafting, which one group of researchers define as "active changes that employees make to their jobs to better suit their own motives, strengths and passions, resulting in more engaging and fulfilling work."[5] These researchers study what they term "unanswered callings," or occupations that people would be engaged in if they could do anything at all. Their research has turned up a number of ways that people craft their current work or leisure time to make them more consistent with an authentic sense of calling. These include:

- Task emphasizing: highlighting or dedicating more time, energy and attention to aspects of the work they really want to be doing.
- Job expanding: adding tasks or assignments that incorporate aspects of an unanswered calling.
- Role reframing: altering one's perception of the work's meaning or broadening the social role of the work.
- Leisure or hobby crafting: engaging in activities that are related to the "unanswered calling."[6]

Researchers conclude that "individuals with a calling orientation are more likely to find their work meaningful and will modify their duties and develop relationships to make it more so. They are found to be more satisfied in general with their work and their lives."[7] Research that we cited in an earlier chapter (Chapter 7: Engaging in Meaningful Work) takes that conclusion a step further. Michael Steger and his colleagues have found that people who feel that their lives and experiences have meaning report feeling "more happy, more satisfied with their lives, less depressed and anxious, and more satisfied with their jobs." Moreover, those who "feel like they've found an occupational path infused with a sense of higher purpose and spiritual calling report more well-being and more investment in their career development."[8]

Another way of thinking about making one's work more transformative is Mihaly Csikszentmihalyi's concept of "flow." Flow, according to Csikszentmihalyi, occurs "when our physical or mental capacities are stretched to their limits in pursuit of a worthwhile goal."[9] Most of us will have experienced this kind of flow more than once, when we feel so totally and completely engaged in what we are doing that we actually lose track of time and what is occurring around us. Csikszentmihalyi cites eight factors that contribute to the flow experience, each of which offers clues about how one might make work more transformative.

First, flow is likely to occur when one confronts a challenging task that requires skill. Here, there must be a balance between the demands of the activity and one's ability to meet those demands. If the activity is too easy, boredom will result; if it is too hard, it will cause anxiety.

The second element is the merging of action and awareness, in which one is so absorbed in the task at hand that the activity becomes spontaneous, and one ceases to be aware of oneself as standing separate from it.

In the third and fourth elements, optimal experience is more likely to occur when one's task has clear goals and provides immediate feedback.

Fifth is a high degree of concentration, which limits the dissipation of energy caused by extraneous concerns.

The sixth element is called the paradox of control: one feels a sense of control without actively trying to be in control. More precisely, it might be said that one ceases to worry about losing control.

In the seventh, preoccupation with the self disappears.

The final element is an altered sense of time. Hours may seem like minutes, or conversely, one may experience a sense of what sports psychologists call "elongated time," in which things seem to move in slow motion.[10]

One can imagine trying to create greater challenges in the workplace, developing new skills in order to be able to take on more difficult work, setting clear goals, asking for feedback, and seeking the kind of autonomy that leads to a sense of being in control without trying. Bringing these changes into one's work may be challenging in itself, but well worth the effort. "The happiness that follows flow," claims Csikszentmihalyi, "is of our own making, and it leads to increasing complexity and growth in consciousness."[11] With expansive consciousness, we can act from a place of knowing, he continues, such that

each of us is responsible for one particular point in space and time in which our body and mind forms a link within

the total network of existence. We can focus consciousness on
the tasks of everyday life in the knowledge that when we act
in the fullness of the flow experience, we are also building a
bridge to the future of the universe.[12]

Making these kinds of changes takes more than commitment. It also takes courage. It may include having to speak up or take a stand about personal needs and desires, and may carry with it some risk. According to the *Oxford Dictionary*, the word courage comes from the French *cor*, or heart, and its synonyms include bravery, pluck, valor, fearlessness, intrepidity, nerve, daring, audacity, boldness, and grit. One person who exhibited all of those attributes is the South African writer/journalist, Heidi Holland. Ms. Holland passed away in 2012, but in her lifetime, she was in many ways the epitome of taking risks and lifting her voice on behalf of her beliefs. Her story holds significant lessons for anyone whose challenges involve courage and tenacity.

Heidi's courage showed up not in asking an organization's leaders for a larger or more challenging role, but in challenging the powerful in two countries undergoing their own transformative change. In her regular newspaper columns and her definitive history of the ANC, *100 Years of Struggle: Mandela's ANC*, she boldly took on South Africa's leaders for what they were failing to bring about for their people. She is most famous, however, for her interactions with Zimbabwe's Robert Mugabe and the book she wrote about those experiences, *Dinner with Mugabe: The Untold Story of a Freedom Fighter Who Became a Tyrant*. It took Heidi two years to set up her well-known face-to-face interview with Mugabe, who, at the time, was generally viewed, she recalls, "as the biggest monster on earth."[13] When it was finally arranged, Mugabe then kept her waiting in a hotel room for two weeks before he was ready to grant her an audience. In preparation for the interview, Heidi asked a psychologist friend,

How can I hang in there? I don't want to toady to him and I
don't want him to tell me what he wants me to know. On the
other hand, I don't want to have a fight with him. I know that

if I ask him anything that touches his sensitivities, he'll just get rid of me.[14]

The psychologist suggested that she prepare a number of unexpected questions that might throw Mugabe off. When Heidi saw Mugabe becoming annoyed during the interview, she followed the suggestion and asked him, "Have you ever been deeply in love?" The question defused the situation, and Heidi had an historic and unprecedented 2.5 hour interview with the fearsome Mugabe.[15]

During our interview with Heidi at her guest house in Johannesburg, she told us that she considered her face-to-face interview with Mugabe to be her "best example of tenacity, an ability or determination to just hang on, knowing that you'll eventually get it. I think I have that in a shovel load. I think that's one of my defining qualities."[16] At the same time, Heidi also understood how difficult it can be to speak out against injustices, especially when people have long been put down or demoralized. Speaking of the current situation in South Africa, she noted,

There are quite a lot of constraints here about speaking truth to power, not least the fact that people's hearts are heavy still from the oppression that they suffered under Apartheid for half a century. It doesn't get better overnight. People have internalized Apartheid, people have memories. People were told for years and years that they weren't good enough, that they were inferior. And, sometimes you are wise to hold your tongue a little bit, to pick your battles.[17]

Upon her passing, one reporter who had interviewed Heidi expressed his admiration for her "years of morally courageous journalism in southern Africa, often at times when such efforts could have had dangerous personal consequences."[18] Others used words such as sheer drive, wit, charm, a light touch, great style, warmth, a bright spark, vivacious, humane, perceptive, tenacious, tireless, and tough-minded. People like Heidi—who are challenging what is to bring forth something better in their organizations, their communities and their societies—exist everywhere. It is worth learning about their stories and following their example when those qualities are required. Howard Zinn, the outspoken American historian, author, and activist once wrote of these people,

> *The power of a bold idea uttered publicly in defiance of dominant opinion cannot be easily measured. Those special people who speak out in such a way as to shake up not only the self-assurance of their enemies, but the complacency of their friends, are precious catalysts for change.*[19]

Making Your Own Transformative Work

For many people, entrepreneurship is the answer to finding work that nurtures their development and feeds their soul's calling. While some entrepreneurs are motivated by economic considerations, or taking on the mantle of a family enterprise, many more are driven by social responsibility or a wish to serve others. Many are driven by an inherent creative impulse or a desire to take their own innovations or inventions to market. Some are unable to find satisfaction through working for others, and are seeking more autonomy and independence in their work life. Others become entrepreneurs through necessity, when they become unemployed and must make use of their skills and talents in other ways. Many are driven, in the words of philanthropists Charles Bronfman and Jeffrey Solomon, authors of *The Art of Doing Good*, "to go for it and take a chance on change because they cannot bear to leave the world the way it is."[20]

Some people simply appear to have been born to create their own organizations. They have a sense of destiny about the work they have been chosen to do. The organizations or initiatives they create are a way to enact their life's stories in their work in the world. In Chapter 12: Being Peace, we told the story of one of those individuals, Rita Marie Johnson, founder of the Rasur Foundation International. One might say that when she heard the words, "You will work for peace" as a very young child, her life's work as a peacemaker was chosen for her.

When we visited Rita Marie Johnson, she encouraged us to interview a young Costa Rican entrepreneur, José Miguel Aguilar Berrocal, founder of the Fundación Acción Joven (Foundation for Youth Action). When we met José in his offices in San Jose, we were not only charmed by his presence, but enthralled with the story of how his life experience led him to his work in the world. As José tells the story, he grew up a highly privileged child in the Guanacaste region of Costa Rica, known for its stunning mountains, dense forests, and broad sandy beaches. It was an idyllic setting for José, whose family wealth gave him plenty of time and resources to enjoy his childhood riding horses, swimming, surfing, fishing, and driving tractors on their farm. José was the oldest child in his family and excelled in school, while learning important values at home.

This lifestyle was interrupted when, due to an El Niño effect, the area received no rain for two years and the family's fortunes changed dramatically. José was sent to live with his grandparents and to attend school in San Jose, where he found himself to be a very small and lonely fish in the sea of a huge high school in a tough neighborhood. He describes himself during this period as "invisible," a "real zero," and recalls that he became insecure, stressed, and unsure about how to fit in. Due to behavioral issues, he was expelled from high school, and enrolled in an alternative school for youth with similar problems. He expresses enormous gratitude to those who mentored him in this new setting, and also attributes a portion of the credit for turning his life around to the sport of surfing, where he excelled and began to gain new confidence in his skills and talents. What his youthful experiences also gave him was empathy for other young people and their struggles.

José's empathy and sense of personal responsibility, along with a graduation requirement at university, led him to his future work. Private universities in Costa Rica, like many others around the world, had a requirement that each graduate complete 150 hours of community service work (called TCU in Costa Rica). José noted that not only was it difficult to find TCU placements with any socially redeemable value, but that university students looked at the whole process as a useless requirement to be tolerated, at best. At the same time, he realized that there was a great deal to be done in communities, particularly with troubled youth, and that how the TCU requirement was being administered meant that an enormous resource for change was being wasted. Upon graduation, while working for a non-profit serving youth, he took on his first project that linked the needs of young people with university volunteers and available resources from the private sector.

This kind of linkage became the basis for Fundación Acción Joven, the non-profit that José founded in 2006. From its beginning working in just one high school, the foundation now works with dozens of universities to match students with TCU requirements in schools where they work with students and administrators, in order to identify projects that will improve conditions for at-risk youth and their communities. The foundation has received numerous prestigious awards, as well as recognition by the Costa Rican government as an "Organization of Public National Interest." José has been awarded an ASHOKA fellowship, designated as a National Peace Builder by the Ministry of Justice, and selected as a fellow of the Central American Leadership Initiative.

Clearly, José's foundation is making a difference in the lives of youth in Costa Rica, as they are finding a reason to stay in school by engaging in real work that benefits their schools and communities. Moreover, the participating schools are experiencing true transformation as they begin to make an impact on the world around them. To José, however, the most significant impact is the consciousness raising that is occurring among the universities' students. Most of them have lived lives with the kind of privilege José knew before his family's fortunes sent him into a life of loneliness and despair, and are encountering, for the first time, the social realities they will face as future leaders.

Choosing entrepreneurship is an opportunity not only to create a transformative workplace for yourself and others who engage with your enterprise, but also a way to potentially contribute to the transformation of the larger community, if not the world. In our travels, we interviewed two other entrepreneurs who are making that kind of impact. The first, Joe Mancini, along with his wife, Stephanie, founded the Working Centre in Kitchener, Ontario, Canada. At its founding in 1986, the organization was simply a help center focusing on assisting people who were looking for work. Today it is a self-organizing hotbed of entrepreneurial activity, where people who see needs in the community are matched with mentoring and resources to create projects to meet those needs. The Centre has purchased and renovated four buildings and five houses, and spawned over forty projects, each with a few paid staff and a bevy of volunteers. The projects include St. John's Kitchen, a community gathering space (and refuge for many) where over 100 volunteers prepare and serve 300 meals every day, making use of food that would otherwise be wasted in the community. Other initiatives include an income tax service, a second-hand furniture store, a thrift shop, a barter system, a bicycle repair, a recycling store, a psychiatric outreach project, and Hospitality House, which serves people with life-threatening illnesses who lack proper housing and care. The Centre operates its own Waterloo School for Community Development, teaching people the skills and concepts needed for local democracy.

In the neighboring community of Waterloo, we were fortunate to interview another entrepreneur with aspirations for transforming the larger society. Paul Born is President and co-founder of the Tamarack Institute for Community Engagement, an award-winning non-profit that focuses on citizen engagement, collaborative leadership and community innovation, and whose broad vision is to end poverty in Canada. The Institute's Vibrant Communities Canada project operates in over 100 communities in Canada. Each functions as a learning community, and uses a multi-sectoral approach in which leaders and citizens are engaged in developing comprehensive poverty reduction strategies. As Paul declared in 2013, "Our goal is [to] have aligned poverty reduction strategies in every city, every Province and territory and within the federal government so that we reduce poverty for one million Canadians within the next four years."[21]

Paul was no newcomer to entrepreneurship by the time he started Tamarack. He was born into a family of refugees from the Ukraine, who landed in a British Columbian Mennonite community, where he developed many of the values that drive his work to this day. His first entrepreneurial venture was a chicken hatching business that he started at age sixteen. In just one year, his venture had over eighty employees and moved more than 10,000 chickens per day. In his latest book, *Deepening Community: Finding Joy Together in Chaotic Times*, Paul reports that he developed his ability to bring dreams into reality through his long experience in gathering eggs in his family's business.

> *I performed a task every day from the age of six to eighteen, one with an unintended consequence (unintended by my parents, who gave me the task): learning to dream. For two or more hours a day, I collected eggs from the nearly twelve thousand chickens on our farm—I was assigned to gather 350 dozen eggs—walking down aisles of cages behind an egg wagon that was six feet long and about three feet high, as it lumbered along on its large balloon-like tires.*
>
> *As I threw my arms back and forth with the rhythm of a fly fisherman, picking up three eggs in each hand and laying them into cartons, my mind could be otherwise occupied. I learned to daydream in extreme detail. Not only did I come up with big, bold ideas, but also I used the time to break them into the micro details and processes that would see them come to reality (if only in my mind).[22]*

As Paul reflects on how this experience has informed his life's work, he concludes, "I grew up wanting to make a difference in the world, so this skill of mentally turning dreams into reality has proven to be useful."[23]

Leading and Managing the Transformative Workplace

Leaders and managers have, perhaps, the greatest opportunity to use their influence to create workplaces in which those they serve can become more and more of who they are meant to be in the world. Introduction of the concept of transformative leadership is attributed to well-known historian and Pulitzer Prize winning presidential biographer, James MacGregor Burns. Burns saw transformative leadership as a moral undertaking based on his belief that "people can be lifted into their better selves."[21]

Researcher and Professor of Management, Bernard M. Bass, further developed the work of Burns, developing what he defined as the four elements of transformational leadership:

1) ***Individualized Consideration.*** The degree to which the leader attends to each follower's needs, acts as a mentor or coach to the follower, and listens to the follower's concerns and needs. The leader gives empathy and support, keeps communication open, and places challenges before the followers. This also encompasses the need for respect and celebrates the individual contribution that each follower makes to the team. The followers have a will and aspiration for self-development, and have intrinsic motivation for their tasks.

2) ***Intellectual Stimulation.*** Such leaders encourage their followers to be innovative and creative. They encourage new ideas from their followers and never criticize them publicly for their mistakes. The leaders focus on the "what" in problems and do not focus on the blaming part of it. They have no hesitation in discarding an old practice set by them if it is found ineffective.

3) ***Inspirational Motivation.*** The degree to which the leader articulates a vision that is appealing and inspiring to followers. Leaders with inspirational motivation challenge followers to leave their comfort zones, communicate optimism about future goals, and provide meaning for the task at hand. Followers need to have a strong sense of purpose if they are to be motivated to act. Purpose and meaning provide the energy that drives a group forward. The visionary aspects of leadership are supported by communication skills that make the vision understandable, precise, powerful, and engaging. The followers are thus willing to invest more effort in their tasks, they are encouraged and optimistic about the future, and believe in their abilities.

4) ***Idealized Influence.*** The degree to which the leader acts as a role model for their followers. Transformational leaders must embody the values that the followers should be learning and mimicking

back to others. If the leader gives respect and encourages others to be better, those influenced will then go to others and repeat the positive behavior, passing on leadership qualities for other followers to learn. This will earn the leader more respect and admiration from the followers, putting the leader at a higher level of influence and importance. The foundation of transformational leadership is the promotion of consistent vision, mission, and a set of values to the members. Their vision is so compelling that they know what they want from every interaction. Transformational leaders guide followers by providing them with a sense of meaning and challenge. They work enthusiastically and optimistically to foster the spirit of teamwork and commitment.[25]

All of the dozens of leaders and managers we interviewed for this book are transformative leaders as defined by contemporary feminist researcher and professor, Dr. Rounaq Jahan, who wrote, "A transformative leader, simply defined, is a person who can guide, direct, and influence others to bring about a fundamental change, change not only of the external world, but also of internal processes."[26]

One particular leader, however, stands out in our minds for both his *doing* in the world and his *being* in the world. That leader is Dr. Tom Inui, who currently plays a number of roles at Indiana University School of Medicine, including (a) professor and director of research for the university's Center for Global Health Research, (b) research scientist in the Indiana University Center for Health Services and Outcomes Research, and the Regenstrief Institute Center for Health Services Research, and (c) director of the AMPATH Research Network, which focuses on improving the health of the Kenyan people. Tom's prior accomplishments are too vast to mention here, but they include teaching positions at Johns Hopkins University, the University of Washington, and Harvard Medical School, as well as numerous professional awards.

We first met Tom when he served as a senior scholar at the Fetzer Institute, where we acted as learning advisors for the Institute's Fellows and Scholars Program. The intention of the program was to engage emerging and established leaders in a long-term circle of transformation aimed at connecting the inner life of spirit with their outer action in the world. During that time, we developed deep affection and admiration for Tom as a humble, always humorous, and brilliant human and leader. What we have come to most admire about Tom over the years is his embodiment of a deeply internalized set of personal values, and his ability to use those values to influence transformation in individuals and large institutions in the medical field.

After serving on the Pew-Fetzer Task Force on Health Professions Education, and a brief stint as president of the Fetzer Institute, Tom was recruited by the Indiana University School of Medicine (IUSM) to lead a Relationship-Centered Care Initiative (RCCI), whose intention was to accomplish a large-scale organizational change and cultural shift. Upon accepting this call, Tom believed that if even one medical school/academic medical center could seriously undertake this kind of change process (organizational formation), document its journey, share perspectives with peer schools, and measure the impact of what it has done on the members of the academic community,"[27] it could galvanize a long-term cultural shift in the world of academic medicine.

The urgency of this shift was documented in Tom's prior research, which revealed a disturbing fact about students' experience of medical education. "As they move through their undergraduate medical education experience," he reported,

> our students also move from being open-minded to being
> fact-surfeited, from being intellectually curious to being
> increasingly focused on just that set of knowledge and skills
> that must be acquired to pass examinations, from being
> open-hearted and empathetic to being emotionally well-
> defended, from idealistic to cynical about medicine, medical
> practice, and the life of medicine.[28]

In his report, Tom highlighted some steps that might be taken to reverse this situation, including author and educator Parker Palmer's concept of individual *formation*. By formation, Palmer means "intensive personal reflection to gain self-knowledge, to clarify one's values and to develop an authentic personal ethos of service."[29]

In the RCCI initiative, Tom and his colleagues chose to take the formation concept to the scale of the institution, using a variety of approaches including David Cooperrider's Appreciative Inquiry methodology, and Complex Responsive Theory, based on the idea that social system change is a function of relationships and interactions between and among people and their environments.

They acted from the belief that "change occurs one person at a time, and from the inside out: from inside the personnel and culture of the organization and from inside the identities and values of each person in the organization."[30]

Outcomes of the RCCI are well documented, and include a dramatic shift in overall student satisfaction with their medical education. At IUMS, the Graduation Questionnaire administered by the Association of American Medical Schools had for many years indicated that overall student satisfaction with their experience was well below the national average. That trend shifted in 2004, the second year of the RCCI, and continued to rise year after year. The impact of the RCCI has now extended well beyond the confines of IUMS. Since the inception of immersion experiences for interdisciplinary teams from other medical schools, over twenty-five highly regarded institutions from around the country have been influenced and supported in leading their own transformative cultural change initiatives.

Through Tom's leadership, the experience has now extended to Kenya, where he directs the AMPATH Research Network. In that initiative, Tom has led the mission to generate and embrace a set of values that include:

- service with humility;
- a spirit of collaboration and partnership;
- integrity in relationships;
- mutual respect and mutual benefit in organizational partnerships;
- a focus on vulnerable populations; and
- efforts to eliminate health disparities.[31]

The RCCI and AMPATH initiatives, driven as they are by values, exemplify what James MacGregor Burns identified as the purpose of transforming leadership. "Deep and durable change, guided and measured by values," he wrote, "is the ultimate purpose of transforming leadership, and constitutes both its practical impact and its moral justification. And that is the power of values."[32]

A Final Word on Transformative Leadership

Readers may not have noticed that this book is dedicated to our late friend and mentor, Dr. Michael J. Cleary. Mike was responsible for many things in our lives, including the fact that we are a couple with six children and their mates, along with six amazing grandchildren. We each met Mike independently. Dave met him when he worked with Mike on a technical committee for the American Society for Quality Control. Carole met Mike when she reached out to him for help in serving Jackson, Michigan auto suppliers who were trying to meet the quality mandates of Ford, General Motors, and Chrysler during a dramatic downturn of business in the early 1980s. The three of us started working together to serve Jackson's threatened businesses, and later, with our friend and colleague Susan Leddick, created a national movement to help community colleges serve their own local employers. When people ask us how we met each other, we nearly always laugh and say, "Our partner, Mike Cleary, went to Japan for two weeks; we didn't know what to do without him, so we fell in love!"

In our dedication for this book, we called Mike an "exemplar." By this we mean that he was truly a model for all that we have talked about in this chapter. Mike made his work as a tenured faculty member transformative. He was an entrepreneur who founded an enterprise through which he and his employees were challenged to develop to their full potential. He was also a true transformative leader, in that he practiced the four elements identified by Bernard Bass: individualized consideration, intellectual stimulation, inspirational motivation, and idealized influence.

Mike graduated from Norwich University, served as a second lieutenant in the U.S. Army, earned a PhD at the University of Nebraska, and became a professor at Wright State University, where he taught management science for twenty-five years. In 1984, he founded PQ Systems, a Dayton-based global company that provides quality control software and training, including training materials that we jointly developed for the national community colleges project. The company, where Mike continued to serve as president until his recent passing, was in 2014 named among the top 25 Best Places to Work in Dayton. He was a member of the Miami Valley School Board of Trustees from 1990 to 2014, where his talented wife of fifty years, Barbara, serves as Chair of the English Department.

The accomplishments we have spoken about above are what *New York Times* columnist David Brooks would call "resume virtues," or those skills one brings to the marketplace. He distinguishes those virtues from "eulogy virtues," which are "deeper, who you are in your depth, what is the nature of your relationships, are you bold, loving, dependable, consistency."[33] In a TEDtalk, delivered in 2014, Brooks refers to *The Lonely Man of Faith*, a 1996 book written by the esteemed Rabbi Joseph B. Soloveitchik, in which he refers to the two sides of our natures, which he called Adam I and Adam II. Brooks describes Adam I as

> *the worldly, ambitious, external side of our nature. He wants to build, create, create companies, create innovation. Adam II is the humble side of our nature. Adam II wants not only to do good, but to be good, to live in a way internally that honors God, creation, and our possibilities. Adam I wants to conquer the world: Adam II wants to hear a calling and obey the world. Adam I savors accomplishment: Adam II savors internal consistency and strength. Adam I asks how things work: Adam II asks why we're here. Adam I's motto is success: Adam II's motto is love, redemption and return.*[34]

Rabbi Soloveitchik believed that these two sides of our nature were in a constant state of tension, and that it is our work to integrate them in the way we live our lives. This reasoning is why, in our dedication, we called Mike an "exemplar," for it is the integration of those two sides of human nature that Mike modeled for his wife; his sons

Sean, Tim, Matt, Dennis and their families; for the people of PQ Systems; and for all those who had the privilege of interacting with him in his professional and private life.

In the end, it is his wife Barbara's poem that, to us, best speaks to the Michael J. Cleary we knew and loved.

Tell me your life story
Drawing strangers into talk,
You listened.
Listening to the guest whose wife had dragged
    him to her school party,
Listened to the car wash guy, urging him
    back in school.
Visited the shoeshine stand to see how Clem's
    life was going.
Stopped by the little baker in town to check
    progress on building plans.
The old woman on the lake road could rattle on,
    A keen ear to soften her complaints
You knew the one selling fresh peas by the roadside,
    earth darkening her fingernails.
And the dry cleaner where you picked up shirts and
    paused to check on lives.
Finding the minutia of life endlessly fascinating,
    you connected.
Now, struck dumb in loss, we remember and know.
We know you saw in others the goodness of creation
Connected both in hardship and in joy.
We know you saw in us the face of God.
—BARBARA A. CLEARY, 2014

Mike Cleary, among so many others that we interviewed for this book, was a true transformative leader. These leaders are an inspiration to us, as we hope they will be to many others who seek to grow people, purpose, prosperity, and peace in and through their workplaces. There has never been a greater urgency for inspired leaders to step forth in the interest of transforming themselves, their organizations, their communities, and the greater society. The challenge is great and the task is forbidding, but each of us can choose to lead in our own way. As Mohandas Gandhi said, "As human beings, our greatness lies not so much in being able to remake the world—that is the myth of the atomic age—as in being able to remake ourselves."[35]

ENDNOTES

ACKNOWLEDGEMENTS

1. Freire, Paulo. *Pedagogy of the Oppressed*, 33. New York: Herder and Herder, 1970.
2. SAT World. "What is praxis?" Accessed February 25, 2012. http://www.satworld.cn/user1/doctorzhang/archives/2011/5161.html.
3. INTRODUCTION: Work that Transforms
4. Kofman, Fred. *Conscious Business: How to Build Value Through Values*, 279. Boulder, CO: Sounds True, 2006.
5. Barrett Values Centre. Accessed February 21, 2012. http://www.values-centre.com/uploads/2010-07-06/From%20Maslow%20to%20Barrett.pdf.
6. His Holiness the 14th Dalai Lama | The Office of His Holiness The Dalai Lama. "The Global Community." Accessed January 25, 2011. http://www.dalailama.com/messages/world-peace/the-global-community.

CHAPTER 1: Meeting Basic Needs

1. From the estate of Dr. Martin Luther King, Jr.
2. BrainyQuote. "He who would learn to fly one day must first learn to stand and walk and run and climb... - Friedrich Nietzsche at BrainyQuote." Accessed November 18, 2013. http://www.brainyquote.com/quotes/quotes/f/friedrichn159166.html.
3. Johny Joseph, interview by author, Mumbai, India, March 22, 2013.
4. Ibid
5. CNN Travel. "Creative Handicrafts: Underprivileged women found an 'ethicool' brand in Mumbai." Accessed February 12, 2012. http://www.cnngo.com/mumbai/shop/creative-handicrafts-underprivileged-women-found-ethicool-brand-mumbai-441168.
6. Johny Joseph, interview by author, Mumbai, India, March 22, 2013.
7. Ibid

8. Ibid

9. CNN Travel. "Creative Handicrafts: Underprivileged women found an 'ethicool' brand in Mumbai." Accessed February 12, 2012. http://www. cnngo.com/mumbai/shop/creative-handicrafts-underprivileged-women-found-ethicool-brand-mumbai-441168.

10. News Bureau | University of Illinois. "Researchers look for ingredients of happiness around the world." Accessed February 3, 2014. http:// news.illinois.edu/news/11/0629happiness_eddiener.html.

11. selfdeterminationtheory.org. "Theory." Accessed February 3, 2014. http://www.selfdeterminationtheory.org/theory.

12. Barrett Values Centre. Accessed February 21, 2014. http://www.values-centre.com/uploads/2010-07-06/From%20Maslow%20to%20Barrett.pdf.

13. "Facts and figures on poverty." Accessed November 14, 2013. http:// www.teamstoendpoverty.org/wq_pages/en/visages/chiffres.php.

14. "Work and Means of Subsistence." Accessed November 12, 2013. http:// www.teamstoendpoverty.org/wq_pages/en/visages/travail.php.

15. Ibid

16. Bornstein, D. (2011, November 03). Workers of the world, employed. *The New York Times*. Retrieved December 9, 2013 from http://opinion-ator.blogs.nytimes.com/2011/11/03/workers-of-the-world-employed/?nl= todaysheadlines&emc=thab1November 3, 2011, 9:30 pm&_r=0

17. Ibid

18. Arrien, Angeles. "Closure Part 2 – The Miracle Bridge." Chautauqua 2013. Last modified September 27, 2012. http://mountmadonnaschool. org/chautauqua/angeles-arrien-closure-part-2-the-miracle-bridge/.

CHAPTER 2: Challenging Assumptions

1. 101 Zen Stories. "101 Zen Stories." Accessed August 9, 2011. http:// www.101zenstories.com/index.php?story=toc.

2. Einstein (1948) " A Message to Intellectuals" Source: 'Albert Einstein' Green J. (Ed.), 2003 (p. 52)

3. Storer, Graeme. (2009, August). Challenging development practice through innovative approaches to leadership. Retrieved from http:// www.vbnk.org/uploads/VBNK approach to Leadership Development. pdf

4. Ibid

5. Ibid
6. Ibid
7. Ibid
8. Ibid
9. Mor Lean, interview by author, Phnom Penh, Cambodia, April 19, 2011.
10. Storer, Graeme. (2009, August). Challenging development practice through innovative approaches to leadership. Retrieved from http://www.vbnk.org/uploads/VBNK approach to Leadership Development. pdf
11. O'Sullivan, E. (2003) "Bringing a perspective of transformative learning to globalized consumption." *International Journal of Consumer Studies*, 27 (4), 326–330
12. Cranston, P. "Teaching for transformation." New Directions for Adult and Continuing Education no 93 (Spring 2002) p. 63-71
13. Ibid
14. Maryse Barak, interview by author, Cape Town, South Africa, April 1, 2011.
15. Deming, W. Edwards. Deming Four Day Video Seminar (1992) The W. Edwards Deming Institute. http://www.deming.org/resources/video. html.
16. 16. Clark, Nancy L., and William H. Worger. South Africa: The Rise and Fall of Apartheid, 48-
17. 52. Harlow, England: Pearson Longman, 2004.
18. 17. BrainyQuote. "We are what we think. All that we are arises with our thoughts. With our
19. thoughts, we... - Buddha at BrainyQuote." Accessed November 19, 2013. http://www.brainyquote.com/quotes/quotes/b/buddha101169.html.
20. Kegan, Robert, and Lisa Laskow Lahey. Immunity to Change: How to Overcome It and Unlock Potential in Yourself and Your Organization. Boston, Mass: Harvard Business Press, 2009.
21. BrainyQuote. "What a man believes may be ascertained, not from his creed, but from the assumptions on... - George Bernard Shaw at BrainyQuote." Accessed November 19, 2013. **http://www.brainyquote. com/quotes/quotes/g/georgebern397124.html.**
22. Kegan, Robert, and Lisa Laskow Lahey. Immunity to Change: How to Overcome It and Unlock Potential in Yourself and Your Organization.

Boston, Mass: Harvard Business Press, 2009.

23. Ibid

24. UXmatters : Insights and inspiration for the user experience commu-nity. "Dealing with Risky and Safe Assumptions :: UXmatters." Accessed November 19, 2013. **http://www.uxmatters.com/mt/archives/2010/04/dealing-with-risky-and-safe-assumptions.php**.

25. Abraham Lincoln Online -- Your Source for Lincoln News and Informa-tion. "Abraham Lincoln's Annual Message to Congress -- Concluding Remarks." Accessed December 4, 2013. http://www.abrahamlincolnon-line.org/lincoln/speeches/congress.htm.

CHAPTER 3: Attending to Well-Being

1. National Accounts of Well-being. "Bringing Real Wealth onto the Bal-ance Sheet." Last modified 2009. http://www.nationalaccountsofwellbe-ing.org/public-data/files/national-accounts-of-well-being-report.pdf.

2. New Economics Foundation. Accessed January 7, 2012. http://www.neweconomics.org/.

3. Ibid

4. Nic Marks, interview by author, San Jose, Costa Rica, January 18, 2011.

5. Nic Marks | Well-being researcher. "My inspirations | Nic Marks." Ac-cessed December 10, 2013. http://www.nicmarks.org/inspiration/.

6. National Accounts of Well-being. "Bringing Real Wealth onto the Bal-ance Sheet." Last modified 2009. http://www.nationalaccountsofwellbe-ing.org/public-data/files/national-accounts-of-well-being-report.pdf.

7. Happiness at Work. "Happiness at Work Survey." Accessed Octo-ber 28, 2013. https://app.happinessatworksurvey.com/.

8. Nic Marks, interview by author, San Jose, Costa Rica, January 18, 2011.

9. Ibid

10. BBC News. "Make people happier, says Cameron." Last modified May 22, 2006. http://news.bbc.co.uk/2/hi/uk_news/politics/5003314.stm.

11. Marks, interview.

12. Boniwell, Ilona. *Positive Psychology in a Nutshell: A Balanced Introduc-tion to the Science of Optimal Functioning*, 41. London: PWBC, 2006.

13. Williamson, Marianne. *A Return to Love: Reflections on the Principles of a Course in Miracles*, 190-191. New York, NY: HarperCollins, 1992.

14. Harvard Business Review. "Creating Sustainable Performance." Accessed October 23, 2013. http://hbr.org/2012/01/creating-sustainable-perfor-

mance/ar/1.

15. Ibid

16. Authentic Happiness | Authentic Happiness. "Learn more | Authentic Happiness." Accessed October 21, 2013. http://www.authentichappiness.sas.upenn.edu/newsletter.aspx?id=1533.

17. Harvard Business Review. "Building Resilience." Accessed October 21, 2013. http://hbr.org/2011/04/building-resilience/ar/1.

18. "The blue zones." *National Geographic*, n.d.

19. Welcome to the United Nations: It's Your World. "United Nations Official Document." Accessed October 8, 2014. http://www.un.org/en/ga/search/view_doc.asp?symbol=A/RES/65/309.

20. GNH Centre Bhutan. "About GNH." Accessed October 21, 2013. http://www.gnhbhutan.org/about/.

21. The New York Times - Breaking News, World News & Multimedia. "Index of Happiness? Bhutan's New Leader Prefers More Concrete Goals - NYTimes.com." Accessed October 20, 2013. http://www.nytimes.com/2013/10/05/world/asia/index-of-happiness-bhutans-new-leader-prefers-more-concrete-goals.html?_r=0.

22. Harvard Business Review. "What's the Hard Return on Employee Wellness Programs?" Accessed October 18, 2013. http://hbr.org/2010/12/whats-the-hard-return-on-employee-wellness-programs/.

23. Ibid

24. Bright Horizons Child Care | Preschool & Early Education Programs | Bright Horizons®. "School, Child Care & Daycare Careers: Employee Benefits at Bright Horizons | Bright Horizons®." Accessed November 7, 2013. http://www.brighthorizons.com/careers/work-benefits.

25. Ibid

26. Harvard Business Review. "What's the Hard Return on Employee Wellness Programs?" Accessed October 18, 2013. http://hbr.org/2010/12/whats-the-hard-return-on-employee-wellness-programs/.

27. Lövey, Imre, Manohar S. Nadkarni, and Eszter Erdélyi. *How Healthy Is Your Organization? The Leader's Guide to Curing Corporate Diseases and Promoting Joyful Cultures*. Westport, Conn: Praeger Publishers, 2007.

28. Harvard Business Review. "What's the Hard Return on Employee Wellness Programs?" Accessed October 18, 2013. http://hbr.org/2010/12/whats-the-hard-return-on-employee-wellness-programs/.

29. Ibid

30. Ibid

31. Dobyns, Lloyd, and Clare Crawford-Mason. *Quality or Else: The Revolution in World Business.* Boston: Houghton Mifflin, 1991.

32. Blue Letter Bible. "Ecclesiastes 8: The Preacher Solomon." Accessed March 23, 2013. http://www.blueletterbible.org/Bible.cfm?b=Ecc&c=8.

CHAPTER 4: Acting Autonomously

1. The Intelligent Optimist. "The Intelligent Optimist." Accessed May 9, 2013. http://odewire.com/50859/experiments-in-workplace-autonomy.html.

2. Workplace Democracy. "An interview with the authors of Freedom, Inc." Accessed May 12, 2012. http://workplacedemocracy.com/2009/10/13/an-interview-with-the-authors-of-freedom-inc/.

3. Accessed June 12, 2012. https://www.facebook.com/walk4wheels?ref=stream&directed_target_id=0.

4. Braaksma, Peter. *Nine Lives Making the Impossible Possible.* Oxford: New Internationalist, 2009.

5. The Chaeli Campaign. "Programmes | The Chaeli Campaign." Accessed May 13, 2013. http://chaelicampaign.co.za/programmes/.

6. Ibid

7. Zelda Mycroft, interview by author, Plumstead, South Africa, April 2011.

8. Ibid

9. Ibid

10. YouTube. "Hello Doctor EP 43 - Inspiration: The Chaeli Campaign." Accessed May 9, 2013. http://www.youtube.com/watch?v=QOdBtC4R7QQ&feature=related.

11. HEIRs - Happiness and Interpersonal Relations. Accessed June 1, 2013. http://www.happinesseconomics.net/ocs/index.php/heirs/markethappiness/paper/viewFile/286/184.

12. Ibid

13. Internet Encyclopedia of Philosophy. "Autonomy: Normative | Internet Encyclopedia of Philosophy." Accessed July 9, 2013. http://www.iep.utm.edu/aut-norm/.

14. McGill University. Accessed July 10, 2013. http://www.mcgill.ca/biomedicalethicsunit/sites/mcgill.ca.biomedicalethicsunit/files/LessonsAboutAutonomy.pdf.

15. The Intelligent Optimist. "The Intelligent Optimist." Accessed May 18, 2013. http://odewire.com/50859/experiments-in-workplace-autonomy.html.

16. HEIRs - Happiness and Interpersonal Relations. Accessed June 1, 2013. http://www.happinesseconomics.net/ocs/index.php/heirs/markethappiness/paper/viewFile/286/184.

17. IdeaMensch - Interviews with Entrepreneurs. "Julie Clow - Author of The Work Revolution." Accessed June 15, 2013. http://ideamensch.com/julie-clow/.

18. Ibid

19. Semler, Ricardo. *The Seven-Day Weekend: Changing the Way Work Works*. New York: Portfolio, 2004.

20. Ibid

21. *Management Innovation eXchange* (blog). "Retire-a-Little: Enabling More Fulfilled Working Lives." n.d. http://www.managementexchange.com/hack/retire-little-enabling-more-fulfilled-working-lives.

22. Harvard Business Review. "First, Let's Fire All the Managers." Accessed July 12, 2013. http://hbr.org/2011/12/first-lets-fire-all-the-managers/ar/1.

23. Ibid

24. Ibid

25. Ibid

26. Ibid

27. Occupational Health & Safety: keeping the workplace safe from hazards and in full compliance with laws and regulations -- Occupational Health & Safety. Accessed June 22, 2013. http://ohsonline.com/articles/2012/01/03/flexible-work-schedules-promote-better-health-study-says.aspx.

CHAPTER 5: Practicing Inner Reflection

1. "Listening Deeply for Peace." *Shambala Sun,* November, 2003.

2. Chang, Larry. *Wisdom for the Soul: Five Millennia of Prescriptions for Spiritual Healing*, 688. Washington, DC: Gnosophia Publishers, 2006.

3. SmartPlanet. "Indian spiritual university embarks on solar energy generation." Accessed December 4, 2012. http://www.smartplanet.com/blog/global-observer/indian-spiritual-university-embarks-on-solar-energy-generation/954.

4. De Carteret, Nikki, Christopher Drake, Gayatri Naraine, Jagdish Chander

Hassija, and Mohini Panjabi. *Visions of a Better World*. London: Brahma Kumaris World Spiritual University, 1993.

5. Sister Jayanti, interview by author, London, England, June 3, 2011.

6. Ibid

7. Spirit of Humanity Forum. "Aim." Accessed September 20, 2013. http://sohforum.org/aim/.

8. Oxford Muse. "Neville Hodgkinson | Oxford Muse." Accessed December 9, 2012. http://www.oxfordmuse.com/?q=node/146.

9. The Cycle of Time. "Neville Hodgkinson/The Sound of Silence/The Cycle of Time." Accessed December 9, 2012. http://www.cycleoftime.com/articles_view.php?codArtigo=44

10. Mezirow, Jack. *Learning As Transformation: Critical Perspectives on a Theory in Progress*. San Francisco: Jossey-Bass, 2000.

11. "Radical Pedagogy." Accessed November 29, 2012. http://www.radicalpedagogy.org/radicalpedagogy1/Volume_8__Issue_1.html.

12. "University of Massachusetts Medical School | UMass Medical School - Worcester." Accessed December 12, 2012. http://www.umassmed.edu/Content.aspx?id=41254&LinkIdentifier=id.

13. Ibid

14. Reuters. "Even when treated, depression costs employers." Accessed November 28, 2012. http://www.reuters.com/article/2010/02/09/us-depression-work-idUSTRE6183DO20100209.

15. Centers for Disease Control and Prevention. "CDC - Workplace Health - Implementation - Depression." Accessed December 16, 2012. http://www.cdc.gov/workplacehealthpromotion/implementation/topics/depression.html.

16. Practice in the Workplace. The Center for Contemplative Mind in Society. Retrieved October 25, 2013 from http://www.contemplativemind.org/practices/work.html

17. The Chart - CNN.com Blogs. "Mindfulness as good as antidepressant drugs, study says – The Chart - CNN.com Blogs." Accessed December 9, 2012. http://thechart.blogs.cnn.com/2010/12/06/mindfulness-as-good-as-antidepressant-drugs-study-says/.

18. Psychology Today: Health, Help, Happiness + Find a Therapist. "What Good Is Positivity? | Psychology Today." Accessed December 14, 2012. http://www.psychologytoday.com/blog/positivity/200903/what-good-is-positivity.

19. Fredrickson, Barbara L., Michael A. Cohn, Kimberly A. Coffey, Jolynn Pek, and Sandra M. Finkel. "Open Hearts Build Lives: Positive Emotions, Induced Through Loving-Kindness Meditation, Build Consequential Personal Resources." *Journal of Personality and Social Psychology* 95(5) (2008): 1045-62. doi:10.1037/a0013262.

20. CVL Home. "Spirituality in Business." Accessed November 29, 2012. http://www.visionarylead.org/articles/spbus.htm.

21. Carroll, Michael. *The Mindful Leader: Ten Principles for Bringing Out the Best in Ourselves and Others.* Boston: Trumpeter, 2007.

22. Leaders Portfolio. "Leaders Portfolio » Jeffrey S. Abramson - Partner, The Tower Companies." Accessed January 10, 2013. http://leadersportfolio. com/archives/1778.

23. "MHN Interview with Jeffrey S. Abramson: Vedic Architecture Changes Way People Feel, Work | Multi-Housing News Online." Accessed January 10, 2012. http://www.multihousingnews.com/news/mhn-interview-with-jeffrey-s-abramson-vedic-architecture-can-change-the-way-people-feel-and-work-2/1004020377.html.

24. "Beyond Building Green: Transcendental Meditation at Work." *YouTube.* n.d. http://www.youtube.com/watch?v=qzrVoqLSCGY&list=PL3D2931F C4D9F927B.

25. Ibid

26. *Transcendental Meditation® Blog* (blog). "D.C. philanthropist brings meditation to at-risk populations | Transcendental Meditation® Blog." n.d.

27. http://www.tm.org/blog/people/philanthropist-brings-meditation-to-at-risk-populations/.

28. 27. Neville Hodgkinson, interview with author, Oxford, England, June 3, 2011.

29. 28. Ibid

30. 29. *Meditation Techniques for Beginners* (blog). n.d. http://www.just-a-minute.org/.

31. 30. Jayanti, interview.

32. 31. Newton, James D. *Uncommon Friends: Life with Thomas Edison, Henry Ford, Harvey Firestone, Alexis Carrel & Charles Lindbergh.* San Diego, Calif: Harcourt Brace Jovanovich, 1987.

CHAPTER 6: Appreciating Beauty

1. BrainyQuote. "Everybody needs beauty as well as bread, places to play in and pray in, where nature may... - John Muir at BrainyQuote." Accessed September 12, 2012. http://www.brainyquote.com/quotes/quotes/j/johnmuir104245.html.

2. Fox, Matthew. *The Reinvention of Work: A New Vision of Livelihood for Our Time.* [San Francisco, Calif.]: HarperSanFrancisco, 1994.

3. Stockil, T. (2012, June 13). Artful development: How artforms can address business issues. Retrieved from http://www.aandbscotland.org.uk/documents/2012-06-13-10-36-11-96-Artful Development.pdf

4. Signe Aarhus and Kolbjorn Valestrand, interview with author, Espeland, Norway, June 15, 2011.

5. Kolbjorn Valestrand, interview with author, Espeland, Norway, June 15, 2011.

6. Norwegian American Weekly. "Fabric of a company: Oleana weaves a new corporate model." Accessed September 15, 2012. http://blog.norway.com/2010/04/22/fabric-of-a-company-oleana-weaves-a-new-corporate-model/.

7. Swedish news in English | Sweden news | Nordstjernan. Accessed September 19, 2012. http://www.nordstjernan.com/news/nordic/1919/.

8. Ibid

9. Ibid

10. Valestrand, interview.

11. Ibid

12. Signe Aarhus, interview with author, Espeland, Norway, June 15, 2011.

13. Oleana. Accessed September 20, 2012. http://www.oleana.no/Content.aspx?cc=12&lang=2.

14. Norwegian American Weekly. "Fabric of a company: Oleana weaves a new corporate model." Accessed September 15, 2012. http://blog.norway.com/2010/04/22/fabric-of-a-company-oleana-weaves-a-new-corporate-model/.

15. Swedish news in English | Sweden news | Nordstjernan. Accessed September 19, 2012. http://www.nordstjernan.com/news/nordic/1919/.

16. Stanford Encyclopedia of Philosophy. "Beauty (Stanford Encyclopedia of Philosophy)." Accessed September 18, 2012. http://plato.stanford.edu/entries/beauty/.

17. BrainyQuote. Accessed September 20, 2012. http://www.brainyquote.com/quotes/quotes/v/voltaire109642.html.

18. "Denis Dutton: A Darwinian theory of beauty | Talk Video | TED. com." *TED: Ideas worth spreading.* n.d. http://www.ted.com/talks/denis_dutton_a_darwinian_theory_of_beauty.html.

19. The Mouse Trap. "Maslow's eight basic needs and the eight stage developmental model." Accessed October 3, 2012. http://the-mouse-trap.com/2007/12/14/maslows-eight-basic-needs-and-the-eight-stage-devlopmental-model/.

20. *The Happiness Institute* (blog). "The Happiness Institute:: Happiness and Appreciation." n.d. http://www.thehappinessinstitute.com/blog/article.aspx?c=3&a=28&pcPage=110.

21. "Beauty and Spirit (Ken Wilber) on Vimeo." *Vimeo.* n.d. http://vimeo.com/12189377.

22. IRNIE / FrontPage. "A re-evaluation of the "big three" Accessed October 9, 2012. http://irnie.pbworks.com/w/page/8119768/bronwen.

23. Ackoff, Russell. Accessed October 9, 2012. http://www.acasa.upenn.edu/leadership.pdf.

24. Boyle, M. ""Solving business problems through the creative power of the arts: catalyzing change at Unilever"." *Journal of Business Strategy* Vol. 26, no. 5 (2005): 14-21. http://trainingartistsforinnovation.eu/wp-content/uploads/2011/11/Interview-JameHill-Unilever.pdf.

25. Ibid

26. Ibid

27. Ibid

28. Fetell, I. "aesthetics of joy » Blog Archive » Joyful sidewalks, joyful cities." aesthetics of joy. Accessed October 25, 2012. http://aestheticsofjoy.com/2011/05/joyful-sidewalks-joyful-cities/.

29. Ibid

30. Ibid

31. Ibid

32. Stockil, T. (2012, June 13). Artful development: How artforms can address business issues. Retrieved from http://www.aandbscotland.org.uk/documents/2012-06-13-10-36-11-96-Artful Development.pdf

33. Washington Post. "Pearls Before Breakfast: Can one of the nation's great musicians cut through the fog of a D.C. rush hour? Let's find out. - The Washington Post." Accessed October 25, 2012. http://www.washingtonpost.com/wp-dyn/content/article/2007/04/04/AR2007040401721.html.

34. Ibid

35. Ibid

CHAPTER 7: Engaging in Meaningful Work

1. Terkel, Studs. *Working; People Talk About What They Do All Day and How They Feel About What They Do.* New York: Pantheon Books, 1974.

2. Dostoyevsky, Fyodor, and H. Sutherland Edwards. *The house of the dead.* London: Dent, 1962.

3. *www.thebeachtimes.com,* n.d.

4. Alex Khajavi, interview by author, San Jose, Costa Rica, February 2, 2011.

5. Driscoll, L. "The importance of ecotourism as a development and conservation tool in the osa peninsula, costa rica." Center for Responsible Travel. Last modified April, 2011. http://www.responsibletravel.org/resources/documents/reports/Tinker_Final_Report_MASTER.pdf.

6. Slater, S. Greenster Magazine. Last modified June 25, 2009. https://www.greenster.com/magazine/natureair-worlds-first-carbon-neutral-airline/.

7. Khajavi, interview.

8. Ibid

9. Robert Kopper, interview by author, San Jose, Costa Rica, February 2, 2011

10. Marshall, C. "BBC NEWS | Americas | Costa Rica bids to go carbon neutral." BBC News - Home. Last modified August, 2008. http://news.bbc.co.uk/2/hi/americas/7508107.stm.

11. Beuchner, Frederick. Values.com. www.values.com/inspirational-quote-authors/1038-Frederick-Buechner.

12. Steger, Michael F. "Meaningful work: what makes work meaningful?" Psychology Today. Last modified June 9, 2009. http://www.psychologytoday.com/blog/the-meaning-in-life/200906/meaningful-work.

13. Steger, Michael F. "Meaningful Living." Laboratory for the Study of Meaning and Quality of Life. Accessed December 15, 2013. http://www.michaelfsteger.com/?page_id=113.

14. Ibid

15. Stever, Michael F., and B. Dik. "Work as Meaning: Individual and Organizational Benefits of Engaging in Meaningful Work." In *Oxford Handbook of Positive Psychology and Work.* Oxford: Oxford University Press, 2009.

16. NurrieStearns, M. "Matthew Fox, Beyond a Job: Doing The Great Work."

personaltransformation.com. Accessed December 12, 2012. http://www.
personaltransformation.com/matthew_fox.html.

17. Ibid
18. Ibid
19. Barrett, Richard. "From Maslow to Barrett: Overview of the Origins of the Seven Levels of Consciousness Model." Barrett Values Centre. Accessed February 9, 2012. http://www.valuescentre.com/uploads/2010-07-06/From%20Maslow%20to%20Barrett.pdf.
20. Pooja Warier, interview with author, Mumbai, India, April 2, 2011.
21. Under The Mango Tree. "Under The Mango Tree » Our Story." Accessed December 29, 2012. http://utmt.in/our-story/.
22. Parish, Billy, and Dev Aujla. *Making Good: Finding Meaning, Money, and Community in a Changing World*. [Emmaus, Pa.]: Rodale, 2012.
23. Wheatley, Margaret J., and Deborah Frieze. *Walk Out Walk On A Learning Journey into Communities Daring to Live the Future Now*. San Francisco: Berrett-Koehler Publishers, 2011.
24. Sisodia, Rajendra, David B. Wolfe, and Jagdish N. Sheth. *Firms of Endearment: How World-Class Companies Profit from Passion and Purpose*. Upper Saddle River: Wharton School Pub, 2007.
25. "The Three Stone Masons." n.d. Accessed December 29, 2012. www.bankofideas.com.au/Stories/fables.html.

CHAPTER 8: Manifesting Intention

1. The Brihadaranyaka Upanishad IV.4.5
2. Ralph Waldo Emerson. BrainyQuote.com, Xplore Inc, 2014. http://www.brainyquote.com/quotes/quotes/r/ralphwaldo383633.html, accessed March 11, 2012.
3. Prakash Apte, interview with author, Mumbai, India, April 14, 2011.
4. Ibid
5. Yahoo! Groups. "Gitatalk." Accessed May 11, 2012. https://groups.yahoo.com/neo/groups/gita-talk/conversations/topics/3666.
6. Ibid
7. The Indian School of Business. First International Conference on Igniting the Genius Within. October 23-26, 2008. http://www.isb.edu/clic/GeniusConference/Presentations.htm
8. Tomasello, Michael, Malinda Carpenter, Josep Call, Tanya Behne, and Henrike Moll. "Understanding and sharing intentions: The origins of

cultural cognition." *Behavioral and Brain Sciences* 28 (2005): 675-735. doi:10.1017/S0140525X05000129.

9.   Internet Encyclopedia of Philosophy. "Collective Intentionality." Accessed March 15, 2012. http://www.iep.utm.edu/coll-int/.

10.   Tomasello, Michael, Malinda Carpenter, Josep Call, Tanya Behne, and Henrike Moll. "Understanding and sharing intentions: The origins of cultural cognition." *Behavioral and Brain Sciences* 28 (2005): 675-735. doi:10.1017/S0140525X05000129.

11.   Ibid

12.   Nahmias, Eddie. "Is Neuroscience the Death of Free Will?" *The New York Times* (blog). November, 2011. http://opinionator.blogs.nytimes.com/2011/11/13/is-neuroscience-the-death-of-free-will/.

13.   Ibid

14.   Ibid

15.   O'Connor, Timothy. "Freedom with a Human Face." Indiana University. Accessed October 11, 2013. http://www.indiana.edu/~scotus/files/Freedom_Hum_Face.pdf.

16.   Stillman, Tyler F., Roy F. Baumeister, Kathleen D. Vohs, Nathaniel M. Lambert, Frank D. Fincham, and Lauren E. Brewer. "Personal Philosophy and Personnel Achievement: Belief in Free Will Predicts Better Job Performance." *Social Psychological and Personality Science* (2010): doi:10.1177/1948550609351600.

17.   Huston, Tracy. *Inside-Out: Stories and Methods for Generating Collective Will to Create the Future We Want.* Cambridge, Mass: Society for Organizational Learning, 2007.

18.   NPR. "Resistance Training For Your 'Willpower' Muscles." Last modified September 18, 2011. http://www.npr.org/2011/09/18/140516974/resistance-training-for-your-willpower-muscles.

19.   NPR. "Excerpt: Willpower: Rediscovering The Greatest Human Strength." Last modified September 18, 2011. http://www.npr.org/books/titles/140516995/willpower-rediscovering-the-greatest-human-strength?tab=excerpt#excerpt.

20.   Ibid

21.   Ibid

22.   All the conducting masterclasses. "Orchestra Done right New Brandenburg project by Orpheus Chamber Orchestra." Last modified May 6, 2011. http://conductingmasterclass.wordpress.com/2011/05/06/orches-

tra-done-right-new-brandenburg-project-by-orpheus-chamber-orchestra/.

23. Kofman, Fred. *Conscious Business: How to Build Value Through Values,* 208. Boulder, CO: Sounds True, 2006.

24. Gehman, Geoff. "Photographer makes sweet music with Orpheus - Morning Call." The Morning Call. Last modified March 29, 2009. http://articles.mcall.com/2009-03-29/features/4339863_1_orpheus-musicians-satirical-portrait.

25. Grella, George. "Musicality." *The Big City* (blog). May 10, 2010. http://thebigcityblog.com/musicality/.

26. Jacobs Center for Neighborhood Innovation | San Diego. "Revitalize Together." Accessed October 1, 2013. http://www.jacobscenter.org/.

27. Jacobs Center for Neighborhood Innovation. "2010 Social and Economic Impact Report." Last modified 2010. http://issuu.com/jacobscenter/docs/seir2010.

28. Ibid

29. Stanford Social Innovation Review: Informing and Inspiring Leaders of Social Change. "The People's IPO." Last modified 2007. http://www.ssireview.org/articles/entry/the_peoples_ipo.

30. Wheatley, Margaret J. *Turning to One Another Simple Conversations to Restore Hope to the Future.* San Francisco: Berrett-Koehler, 2009.

31. Policy Link. "Market Creek Plaza: Toward Resident Ownership of Neighborhood Change." Last modified 2005. http://www.policylink.org/find-resources/library/market-creek-plaza-toward-resident-ownership-of-neighborhood-change.

32. Ibid

CHAPTER 9: Embodying Compassion

1. Toynbee, Arnold, and Daisaku Ikeda. *Choose Life: A Dialogue.* London: I.B. Tauris, 2007.

2. His Holiness the 14th Dalai Lama | The Office of His Holiness The Dalai Lama. "The Medicine of Altruism | The Office of His Holiness The Dalai Lama." Accessed January 5, 2013. http://dalailama.com/messages/world-peace/the-medicine-of-altruism.

3. Personal communication. April 1, 2011.

4. Benvie, Janet. "AT-TUWANI: More than 100 villagers attend nonviolence workshop." Christian Peacemaker Teams. Last modified February 9, 2007. www.cpt.org/cptnet/2007/02/09/tuwani-more-100-villagers-attend-

nonviolence-workshop.

5. Nomfundo Walaza, interview with author, Cape Town, South Africa, April 1, 2011.

6. Ibid

7. Ibid

8. Barasch, Marc. *The Compassionate Life Walking the Path of Kindness*, 2nd ed., 13. San Francisco, CA: Berrett-Koehler, 2009.

9. The Episcopal Diocese of Western North Carolina. Accessed October 2, 2011. http://www.diocesewnc.org/uploads/File/weekly%20reflection%203-12-08.pdf.

10. The Desmond Tutu Peace Center. Accessed October 5, 2011. http://www.tutu.org/home

11. International Association for Child and Adolescent Psychiatry and Allied Professions (IACAPAP) Accessed October 9, 2013. http://www.iacapap2014.co.za

12. Nomfundo Walaza, interview with author, Cape Town, South Africa, April 1, 2011.

13. Brien, Tarryn. "Tutu's superwoman: preserving peace." INSP News Service. Last modified October 4, 2010. http://www.streetnewsservice.org/news/2010/october/feed-252/tutu%E2%80%99s-superwoman-preserving-peace-.aspx.

14. Lilius, Jacoba, Monica Worline, Jane E. Dutton, Jason Kanov, and Sally Maitlis. CompassionLab. Last modified March 8, 2011. Accessed November 12, 2012. http://www.compassionlab.com/docs/abscompassionfinal.pdf.

15. Ibid

16. Lewis, Helen. UBC News. Last modified March 7, 2002. Accessed February 10, 2011.

17. http://www.publicaffairs.ubc.ca/ubcreports/2002/02mar07/compassion.html.

18. Ibid

19. Geddes, Deanna, and Lisa T. Stickney. "The trouble with sanctions: Organizational responses to deviant anger displays at work." Human Relations. Last modified February 28, 2011. http://hum.sagepub.com/content/64/2/201.

20. Temple University. "Compassion, not sanctions, is best response to workplace anger." ScienceDaily. www.sciencedaily.com/releas-

es/2011/04/110414131853.htm (accessed October 15, 2011).

21. Ibid

22. Ibid

23. "Chade-Meng Tan: Everyday compassion at Google | Talk Video | TED.com." *TED: Ideas worth spreading.* April, 2011. http://www.ted.com/talks/chade_meng_tan_everyday_compassion_at_google.html.

24. Ibid

25. Ibid

26. *CompassionLab* | (blog). "Feeding the wolf of compassion | CompassionLab." January 2, 2013. http://www.thecompassionlab.com/2013/01/02/feeding-the-wolf-of-compassion/.

27. Ibid

28. Zaslow, Jeffrey. Putting a price tag on grief. Wall Street Journal. November 20, 2002; D1,D12.

29. Charter for Compassion. "Sign and Share the Charter for Compassion Charter for Compassion." Accessed May 9, 2011. https://charterforcompassion.org/the-charter.

30. "His Holiness the Dalai Lama." Facebook. Last modified October 21, 2013. https://www.facebook.com/DalaiLama/posts/10151710537002616.

CHAPTER 10: Giving Back

1. Mahatma Gandhi. BrainyQuote.com, Xplore Inc, 2014. http://www.brainyquote.com/quotes/quotes/m/mahatmagan150725.html, accessed October 9, 2013.

2. Maya Angelou. BrainyQuote.com, Xplore Inc, 2014. http://www.brainyquote.com/quotes/quotes/m/mayaangelo389346.html, accessed October 12, 2013.

3. Kumra, Gautam. "Leading change: An interview with the managing director of Tata Motors | McKinsey & Company." Insights & Publications | McKinsey & Company. Last modified January, 2007. http://www.mckinseyquarterly.com/Organization/Change_Management/Leading_change_An_interview_with_the_managing_director_of_Tata_Motors_1908.

4. Ibid

5. Pilling, David. Financial Times. Last modified September 24, 2008. Accessed October 15, 2013. http://www.ft.com/intl/cms/s/0/e68ab572-8a3e-11dd-a76a-0000779fd18c.html#axzz2hFrQ41bU.

6. Kumra, Gautam. "Leading change: An interview with the managing director of Tata Motors | McKinsey & Company." Insights & Publications | McKinsey & Company. Last modified January, 2007. http://www.mckinseyquarterly.com/Organization/Change_Management/Leading_change_An_interview_with_the_managing_director_of_Tata_Motors_1908.

7. Ravi Kant, interview with author, Mumbai, India, April 12, 2011.

8. Tata Power. Accessed October 9, 2013. http://www.tatapower.com/sustainability/policies.aspx.

9. The Economist. Accessed October 9, 2013. Last modified March 3, 2011. http://www.economist.com/node/18285497.

10. Parker-Pope, Tara. The New York Times. Last modified November 30, 2009. Accessed October 10, 2013. http://www.nytimes.com/2009/12/01/health/01well.html.

11. Luks, Allan. "Doing Good: Helper's High." *Psychology Today 22, no. 10, 34-42*, 1988.

12. DUJS Online. "Is Altruism Good for the Altruistic Giver?" Last modified May 22, 2009. Accessed October 15, 2013. http://dujs.dartmouth.edu/spring-2009/is-altruism-good-for-the-altruistic-giver.

13. Barrett, Richard. From Maslow to Barrett: Overview of the Origins of the Seven Levels of Consciousness Model. Accessed October 17, 2013. http://www.valuescentre.com/uploads/2010-07-06/From%20Maslow%20to%20Barrett.pdf.

14. Eccles, Robert G., Ioannis Ioannou, and George Serafeim. "The Impact of Corporate Sustainability on Organizational Processes and Performance." Harvard Business School. Last modified November 23, 2011. Accessed October 10, 2013. http://www.hbs.edu/research/pdf/12-035.pdf.

15. Tom's. Last modified 2011. Accessed October 8, 2013. http://images.toms.com/media/content/images/giving-report/TOMS_Giving-Report_2011.pdf.

16. Nocera, Joe. "We Can All Become Job Creators." The New York Times. Last modified October 17, 2011. Accessed October 4, 2013. http://www.nytimes.com/2011/10/18/opinion/nocera-we-can-all-become-job-creators.html?_r=1&nl=todaysheadlines&adxnnl=1&emc=tha212&adxnnlx=1318943157-p4STZ/eUxgQtA6e1CGi44A.

17. Benett, Andrew, Cavas Gobhai, and Ann O'Reilly. "Four Cornerstones

of the Conscious Corporation." In *Good for Business: The Rise of the Conscious Corporation*, 39-60. New York, NY: Palgrave Macmillan Trade, 2009.

CHAPTER 11: Embracing the Whole

1. Nobelprize.org. "Wangari Maathai Nobel Lecture." Last modified December 10, 2004. http://www.nobelprize.org/nobel_prizes/peace/laureates/2004/maathai-lecture-text.html.
2. Luther King, Martin. "Letter from Birmingham jail." Last modified April 16, 1963. https://kinginstitute.stanford.edu/king-papers/documents/letter-birmingham-jail.
3. "Joubert Park." In *Wikipedia*. n.d. Accessed January 10, 2014. http://en.wikipedia.org/wiki/Joubert_Park.
4. Mabule Mokhine, interview by author, Johannesburg, South Africa, April 6, 2011.
5. Ibid
6. Ibid
7. Ibid
8. Tutu, Desmond. *No Future Without Forgiveness*, 34-35. New York: Doubleday, 1999.
9. Ibid
10. Panse, S. "Ubuntu - African Philosophy." Buzzle. Last modified July, 2006. http://www.buzzle.com/editorials/7-22-2006-103206.asp.
11. FutureFit. "FUTUREFIT - Johannesburg Block 1." Accessed February 21, 2014. http://www.futurefit.co.za/joburg1.aspx.
12. De Quincey, Christian. "Nature Has a Mind of Its Own." *Tikkun Magazine 25(6): 45*, November/December, 2010.
13. Berry, Thomas. *The Dream of the Earth*, 123. San Francisco: Sierra Club Books, 1988.
14. Berry, Thomas. "Twelve Understandings Concerning the Ecozoic Era." Home. Accessed February 22, 2014. http://www.ecozoicstudies.org/index.php?option=com_content&view=article&id=22:twelve-understandings-concerning-the-ecozoic-era&catid=11:statements&Itemid=0.
15. Ibid
16. Sustainable Development – Earth Charter Initiative. "What is the Earth Charter?" Accessed February 4, 2014. http://www.earthcharterinaction.

org/content/pages/What-is-the-Earth-Charter%3F.html.

17. Cook-Greuter, Susanne. "Making the Case for a Developmental Perspective." Industrial and Commercial Training, Vol. 36 No. 7. Last modified 2004. http://www.cook-greuter.com/Making%20the%20case%20for%20 a%20devel.%20persp.pdf.

18. Ibid

19. Green Technology Magazine. "Restoring the Planet, One Carpet Tile at a Time." Last modified 2006. http://www.green-technology.org/green_ technology_magazine/ray_anderson.htm.

20. Hawken, Paul. ""Reimagining the World Was a Responsibility"." *GreenBiz* (blog). August 11, 2011. http://www.greenbiz.com/ blog/2011/08/11/reimagining-world-was-responsibility.

21. Makower, J. "Ray of Hope: A Conversation with Ray Anderson." *GreenBiz* (blog). October 1, 2004. http://www.greenbiz.com/ blog/2004/10/01/ray-hope-conversation-ray-anderson?page=0,1.

22. Kanellos, M. "Ray Anderson: 1934-2011." Green Technology. Last modified August 8, 2011. http://www.greentechmedia.com/articles/read/ray-anderson-1934-2011/.

23. Anderson, Ray. "A Better Way." Ray Anderson Foundation. Last modified June 4, 2003. http://www.raycandersonfoundation.org/pdfs/ rayslife/08-13-03-A-Better-Way.pdf.

24. Ibid

25. Laszlo, Christopher. *The Sustainable Company How to Create Lasting Value Through Social and Environmental Performance*, 62-63. Washington, DC: Island Press, 2003.

26. *The Cleanest Line* (blog). "The Cleanest Line: Don't Buy This Jacket, Black Friday and the New York Times." November, 2011. http://www. thecleanestline.com/2011/11/dont-buy-this-jacket-black-friday-and-the-new-york-times.html.

27. "Worn Wear: a Film About the Stories We Wear | Presented by Patagonia." *YouTube*. November, 2013. http://www.youtube.com/ watch?v=z20CjCim8DM.

28. Chouinard, Yvon. "Patagonia launches "$20 million & change" and Patagonia works-a holding company for the environment." Patagonia. Last modified May, 2013. http://www.patagoniaworks.com/docs/Letter.pdf.

29. Ibid

30. Patagonia Outdoor Clothing & Gear. "Patagonia's History - A Company

Created by Climber Yvon Chouinard and his commitment to the Environment." Accessed January 10, 2014. http://www.patagonia.com/us/patagonia.go?assetid=3351.

31. McEllin, Steve. "The Business of Consciousness." *The Examiner*, August 12, 2013.

32. Ibid

33. Mokhine, Mabule. The Berkana Institute Annual Report. Last modified 2010. http://berkana.org/wp-content/uploads/2011/09/2010_Annual_Report.pdf.

34. The Pachamama Alliance. ""We Stand in Solidarity with Fundación Pachamama in Ecuador"." Last modified December, 2013. http://www.pachamama.org/news/we-stand-in-solidarity-with-fundacion-pachamama-in-ecuador.

35. Confino, Jo. "Beyond environment: falling back in love with Mother Earth." The Guardian. Last modified February 20, 2012. http://www.theguardian.com/sustainable-business/zen-thich-naht-hanh-buddhidm-business-values.

36. Berry, Thomas. *The Dream of the Earth*. San Francisco: Sierra Club Books, 1988.

37. Maathai, Wangari. "Wangari Maathai - Nobel Lecture." Nobelprize.org. Last modified December 10, 2004. http://www.nobelprize.org/nobel_prizes/peace/laureates/2004/maathai-lecture-text.html.

CHAPTER 12: Being Peace

1. Attributed to Lao-Tze

2. Rasur Foundation International. "Our Story." Accessed January 18, 2014. www.rasurinternational.org/our-story.html.

3. Rita Marie Johnson, interview with author, San Jose, Costa Rica, January 21, 2011.

4. Academy for Peace Costa Rica. "The Return of Rasur." Accessed January 15, 2014. http://academyforpeacecr.org/documents/Return-of-Rasur-book-description.pdf.

5. Academy for Peace Costa Rica. "About Rita Marie Johnson, Director." Accessed July 10, 2012. http://academyforpeacecr.org/about_director.html.

6. Academy for Peace Costa Rica. "The Practice of BePeace." Accessed July 10, 2012. http://academyforpeacecr.org/bepeace.html.

7. UPeace Global Education Leadership. "Winter Course Offerings." Accessed April 10, 2012. http://www.globaleducationleadership.org/upeace/upeace-winter-institute/winter-course-offerings/#UPE6058.

8. Department of Peace Costa Rica. "COSTA RICA DECLARES A MINISTER OF PEACE." Last modified August 20, 2009. http://www.departmentof-peace.ca/2009/08/costa-rica-declares-a-minister-of-peace/.

9. Johnson, interview.

10. Shutts, Susie. "Costa Rica Creates Department of Peace." YES! Magazine. Last modified September 22, 2009. http://www.yesmagazine.org/peace-justice/costa-rica-creates-department-of-peace.

11. BuddhaNet - Worldwide Buddhist Information and Education Network. "Sublime States: Equanimity (upekkha)." Accessed January 19, 2014. http://www.buddhanet.net/ss06.htm.

12. BuddhaNet. "The Four Immeasurables." Accessed January 19, 2014. http://www.buddhanet.net/e-learning/buddhism/bs-s15.htm.

13. Gaëlle Desbordes, Tim Gard, Elizabeth A. Hoge, Britta K. Hölzel, Catherine Kerr, Sara W. Lazar, Andrew Olendzki, David R. Vago. 'Moving Beyond Mindfulness: Defining Equanimity as an Outcome Measure in Meditation and Contemplative Research.' Mindfulness. January 2014.

14. Ibid

15. Ibid

16. Ibid

17. Ibid

18. Ginsberg-Schutz, Maggie. "The World Wide Web." Madison Magazine. Last modified May, 2013. http://www.madisonmagazine.com/Madison-Magazine/May-2013/The-World-Wide-Web/index.php?cparticle=4&siarticle=3#artanc.

19. Ibid

20. Rutsch, Edwin. "Rita Marie Johnson on Empathy." Vimeo. May 26, 2010. http://vimeo.com/13054452.

21. The New Sun. "An Interview with Dr. Kazuo Inamori." Last modified 2002. http://www.newsun.com/inamori.html.

22. KYOCERA GROUP GLOBAL SITE. "Management Based on the Kyocera Philosophy | Management Philosophy." Accessed January 24, 2013. http://global.kyocera.com/ecology/base.html.

23. KYOCERA GROUP GLOBAL SITE. "Corporate Motto / Management Rationale." Accessed January 27, 2014. http://global.kyocera.com/ecology/

rationale.html.

24. Seiwajyuku - USA -. "A Brief History." Last modified January, 2012. http://www.seiwajyuku.org/ch/?page_id=1131.

25. KYOCERA GROUP GLOBAL SITE. "Seiwajyuku Year-end Study Sessions with Dr. Inamori held." Last modified December 26, 2013. http://global. kyocera.com/inamori/news/news60.html.

26. Case Western Reserve University. "Inamori Ethics Prize." Accessed January 27, 2014. http://case.edu/events/inamori/index.html.

27. Maxwell, Kenneth. "'Mikoshi' Management: How Kazuo Inamori Lifted Japan Airlines - Japan Real Time." *Wall Street Journal* (blog). July 30, 2012. http://blogs.wsj.com/japanrealtime/2012/07/30/mikoshi-manage-ment-how-kazuo-inamori-lifted-japan-airlines/.

28. Ibid

29. Oi, Mariko. "Beer with boss Kazuo Inamori helps Japan Airlines revival." *BBC News* (blog). November 15, 2012. http://www.bbc.co.uk/news/business-20293487.

30. "Wisdom 2 Bill Ford, Jack Kornfield." *YouTube*. February, 2013. http://www.youtube.com/watch?v=9W0Wy8-06t4.

31. "The Power of Mindfulness in the Workplace - Why This Matters: Mark Bertolini, Soren Gordhamer." *YouTube*. October 2, 2013. http://www.youtube.com/watch?v=rBjmH-JIJzQ.

32. Ibid

33. Chödrön, Pema. *Taking the Leap: Freeing Ourselves from Old Habits and Fears,* 2. Boston, Mass: Shambhala Publications, Inc, 2009.

34. Fort, Timothy L. *Business, Integrity, and Peace: Beyond Geopolitical and Disciplinary Boundaries*, 4. Cambridge: Cambridge University Press, 2007.

35. Fort, Timothy L. "The Peace Through Commerce Wrinkle." Last modified 2006. http://www.peacethroughcommerce.org/searchresults.asp?cat=237.

36. Fort, Timothy L. "The Matrix of Peace." Accessed January 30, 2014. https://www.peacethroughcommerce.org/SearchResults.asp?Cat=239.

37. Strong, Michael. "Waging Peace through Commerce." Policy Innovations. Last modified March 12, 2008. http://www.policyinnovations.org/ideas/commentary/data/000043.

38. Business for Peace Foundation |. "The Power of being Businessworthy – Marrying performance with higher purpose." Accessed Janu-

ary 27, 2013. http://businessforpeace.no/.

39. Fort, Timothy L. *Business, Integrity, and Peace: Beyond Geopolitical and Disciplinary Boundaries*, 4. Cambridge: Cambridge University Press, 2007.

CONCLUSION: Making Work Transformative

1. Mahatma Gandhi. BrainyQuote.com, Xplore Inc, 2014. http://www. brainyquote.com/quotes/quotes/m/mahatmagan163698.html, accessed November 10, 2014.

2. Stanford News. "Text of Steve Jobs' Commencement address (2005)." Last modified June 14, 2005. http://news.stanford.edu/news/2005/june15/jobs-061505.html.

3. Rumi. BrainyQuote.com, Xplore Inc, 2014. http://www.brainyquote. com/quotes/quotes/r/rumi133528.html, accessed January 10, 2014.

4. Lao Tzu. BrainyQuote.com, Xplore Inc, 2014. http://www.brainyquote. com/quotes/quotes/l/laotzu137141.html, accessed January 10, 2014.

5. Berg, Justin M., Adam M. Grant, and Victoria Johnson. "When Callings Are Calling: Crafting Work and Leisure in Pursuit of Unanswered Occupational Callings." *Organization Science* (2010): 973-994. doi:10.1287/orsc.1090.0497.

6. Ibid

7. Wrzesniewski, Amy, Clark McCauley, Paul Rozin, and Barry Schwartz. "Jobs, Careers, and Callings: People's Relations to Their Work." *Journal of Research in Personality* (1997): 21-33. doi:10.1006/jrpe.1997.2162.

8. Steger, Michael F. "Meaningful Living." Laboratory for the Study of Meaning and Quality of Life. Accessed March 14, 2014. http://www. michaelfsteger.com/?page_id=113.

9. Cooper, Andrew. "The Man Who Found the Flow." Lion's Roar. Last modified September 1, 1998. http://www.lionsroar.com/the-man-who-found-the-flow/.

10. Csikszentmihalyi., Mihaly. "Finding Flow." Psychology Today. Last modified July 1, 1997. http://www.psychologytoday.com/articles/199707/finding-flow.

11. Cooper, Andrew. "The Man Who Found the Flow." Lion's Roar. Last modified September 1, 1998. http://www.lionsroar.com/the-man-who-found-the-flow/.

12. Csikszentmihalyi, Mihaly. "Finding Flow." Psychology Today. Last modified July 1, 1997. http://www.psychologytoday.com/articles/199707/

finding-flow.

13. Heidi Holland, interview with author, Johannesburg, South Africa, April 2011.

14. Ibid

15. Ibid

16. Ibid

17. Ibid

18. Spector, J Brooks. "RIP Heidi Holland, author on African revolutions." The Star. Last modified August 15, 2012. http://www.iol.co.za/the-star/ rip-heidi-holland-author-on-african-revolutions-1.1362807#.UvkdIftf8ig.

19. Zinn, Howard. *You Can't Be Neutral on a Moving Train: A Personal History of Our Times*, 33. Boston: Beacon Press, 1994.

20. Bronfman, Charles, and Jeffrey Solomon. *The Art of Doing Good: Where Passion Meets Action,* viii. San Francisco: Jossey-Bass, 2012.

21. Tamarack Institute for Community Engagement - Community Development Across Canada. "Our Impact by the Numbers." Last modified February, 2013. http://tamarackcommunity.ca/annual_report.html.

22. Born, Paul. *Deepening Community: Finding Joy Together in Chaotic Times,* 135-136. San Francisco: Berrett-Koehler, 2014.

23. Ibid

24. James MacGregor Burns. BrainyQuote.com, Xplore Inc, 2014. http:// www.brainyquote.com/quotes/quotes/j/jamesmacgr166517.html, accessed November 10, 2014.

25. Bass, Bernard M, and Ronald Riggio. *Transformational Leadership: Industrial, Military, and Educational Impact*, 2nd ed., 6-7. Mahwah, N.J.: Lawrence Erlbaum Associates, 2005.

26. Jahan, Rounaq. "Transformative Leadership in the 21st Century." Home page of CAPWIP, the Center for Asia Pacific Women in Politics. Accessed May 10, 2014. http://www.capwip.org/resources/womparl-conf2000/downloads/jahan1.pdf.

27. Suchman, Anthony L., David J. Sluyter, and Penelope R. Williamson. *Leading Change in Healthcare: Transforming Organizations Using Complexity, Positive Psychology, and Relationship-Centered Care,* 268. London: Radcliffe Pub, 2011.

28. Inui, Tom. "A Flag in the Wind." Boston University Medical Campus | Boston University. Last modified February, 2003. http://www.bumc. bu.edu/mec/files/2010/06/AAMC_Inui_2003.pdf.

29. Ibid

30. Suchman, Anthony L., David J. Sluyter, and Penelope R. Williamson. *Leading Change in Healthcare: Transforming Organizations Using Complexity, Positive Psychology, and Relationship-Centered Care,* 266. London: Radcliffe Pub, 2011.

31. Tom Inui, interview with author, Indianapolis, Indiana, July 23, 2011.

32. Burns, James MacGregor. *Transforming Leadership: A New Pursuit of Happiness,* 213. New York: Atlantic Monthly Press, 2003.

33. Brooks, David. "Should you live for your résumé ... or your eulogy?" *TED: Ideas worth spreading.* March, 2014. http://www.ted.com/talks/david_brooks_should_you_live_for_your_resume_or_your_eulogy?language=en.

34. Ibid

35. Mahatma Gandhi. BrainyQuote.com, Xplore Inc, 2014. http://www.brainyquote.com/quotes/quotes/m/mahatmagan163698.html, accessed November 10, 2014.

CPSIA information can be obtained at www.ICGtesting.com
Printed in the USA
LVOW08s0409171215

466771LV00005B/5/P